The Press and the Ford Presidency

The Press and the Ford Presidency

Mark J. Rozell

Ann Arbor

THE UNIVERSITY OF MICHIGAN PRESS

Copyright © by the University of Michigan 1992
All rights reserved
Published in the United States of America by
The University of Michigan Press
Manufactured in the United States of America

1995   1994   1993   1992   4   3   2   1

A CIP catalogue record for this book is available from the British Library.

Library of Congress Cataloging-in-Publication Data

Rozell, Mark J.
    The press and the Ford presidency / Mark J. Rozell.
       p.   cm.
    Includes bibliographical references and index.
    ISBN 0-472-10350-4 (alk. paper)
    1. Ford, Gerald R., 1913–   .   2. United States—Politics and
government—1974–1977.   3. Press and politics—United States.
E866.R69   1992
973.925′092—dc20   92-8700
                                                               CIP

For my parents

Preface and Acknowledgments

This study is the second of a number of books that I plan to write on modern presidential journalism. It follows the research agenda that I initiated with *The Press and the Carter Presidency* (1989). My goal is to develop an understanding of how leading journalists report and assess modern presidential leadership and performance by examining the press treatment of individual presidents.

Journalists play a central role in the development of a presidential image. To be sure, a president and his public and press relations staffers devote much effort to creating and sustaining a positive image. This study makes it clear that a president and his image crafters generally cannot script their own press coverage and expect journalists dutifully to follow the White House plan. Journalists consider themselves independent agents and they bring a degree of skepticism to their coverage of political leaders. Nonetheless, a president and his image crafters can succeed at times at getting the press to accept White House definitions of issues and the president's leadership efforts, to soften its criticism of the administration, and to portray the chief executive's activities in a favorable manner.

A major difficulty for some presidents in developing a positive image is that modern journalists have conceptions of leadership that color their evaluations of presidential activities. The most prominent journalistic conception of leadership is based on idealistic perceptions of the "great" activist presidents. According to this view, a "successful" president is one who articulates an activist agenda, builds public and elite support for his programs, and quickly moves the administration's agenda through Congress. Presidents who do not conform to this definition of leadership, whatever the circumstances, fare poorly in press evaluations.

The press coverage of Gerald R. Ford's presidency illustrates the leadership biases that journalists bring to their evaluations of modern presidents. An analysis of Ford's press coverage also teaches much about the nature of post-Watergate press-presidency relations. Ford had the unenviable task of following the nation's first president to resign in disgrace, and, therefore, he had to live up to very high expectations of ethical standards, cooperating with the press and political opponents, and establishing a new style of leadership. Still reeling from the deceptions of the Richard Nixon White House, journalists exhibited a great deal of skepticism and even cynicism toward political leadership when Ford came into office. The first post-Watergate president to lead in this environment, Ford established important precedents for the conduct of modern press-presidency relations. The Ford years thus represent a crucial transitional phase in the relationship between journalists and presidents.

A number of organizations and individuals made this project possible. A grant from the Gerald R. Ford Foundation enabled me to spend time researching White House documents at the Ford Presidential Library in Ann Arbor, Michigan. An American Political Science Association research grant defrayed expenses incurred while working on this study. A Mary Washington College faculty development award provided a much needed course reduction. The Alice P. Jepson Fellowship supplemented my salary during the time that I worked on this project.

I benefited from the opportunity to interview members of the Ford White House involved in press relations. These individuals generously gave their time to answer my queries about the Ford years: John G. Carlson, President Gerald R. Ford, William Greener, Robert T. Hartmann, John W. Hushen, Ronald H. Nessen, J. William Roberts, Larry Speakes, Jerald F. terHorst, Louis M. Thompson, Jr., Gerald Warren, Margita White.

David Horrocks, the supervisory archivist at the Gerald R. Ford Library, and members of his staff helped to steer me in the right direction many times while I examined White House documents.

The two reviewers of this study, Holli Semetko (University of Michigan) and Raymond Tatalovich (Loyola University of Chicago), were most thorough and constructively critical in their comments on earlier versions of the manuscript. Colin Day and Deborah Evans of the University of Michigan Press have been supportive of this project and most helpful in the development of the manuscript.

I appreciate the generosity of professional colleagues who shared both their insights on the press-presidency relationship and materials from their research projects. In particular, I thank John Anthony Maltese (University of Georgia), who shared with me some interview materials and draft chapters of his book on the White House Office of Communications, and Charles O. Jones (University of Wisconsin–Madison), who provided helpful suggestions on my work.

Departmental secretary Dora Minor typed this manuscript from its first draft all the way through the final revisions. She also typed the transcripts of my interviews. Several political science department aides assisted with the typing and proofreading tasks: Sherril O'Brien, Paige Turney, Lisa Rourke, Raelenne Jensen, and Linda-Joy Noronha. Senior secretary Judy Singleton also proofread the manuscript.

I am most fortunate to work among professional colleagues in the department of political science and international affairs at Mary Washington College who are both supportive of my scholarly pursuits and good examples of scholars within and without the classroom: Lewis P. Fickett, Jr., Victor A. Fingerhut, John M. Kramer, Richard J. Krickus, and Karen Parsons. My students at Mary Washington College, particularly those in my Political Journalism and Presidency seminars, provide a stimulating environment in which to discuss and debate ideas about presidents and the press.

My wife, Lynda M. Rozell, who read and commented on the manuscript, is my best critic and wholly supportive of my work, always patient and understanding of what is important to me. This book is dedicated to my parents. It is just a small expression of gratitude for their love and support.

Contents

CHAPTER 1

Introduction

Gerald R. Ford became President of the United States under the most unusual circumstances in U.S. history. Chosen by President Richard M. Nixon in October 1973 to replace Spiro T. Agnew as the vice president, Ford assumed the presidency on August 9, 1974, after Nixon resigned in disgrace. Ford, the man of Congress who had represented Michigan's fifth Congressional District for twenty-five years, had never sought national public office. He had one ambition beyond faithfully representing his constituents and being House Minority Leader: to become the Speaker of the House. By the early 1970s Ford realized that, as a Republican member in a legislative chamber likely to be dominated by the Democrats for years, he could never fulfill his dream. He thought seriously about retiring from public life in 1976 after completing a final two-year term in the House.

Fate delivered Ford a different future. As the Watergate scandal slowly unfolded throughout 1973, and the vice president, Spiro "Ted" Agnew, could not successfully withstand legal inquiries into a kickback scheme he had participated in as a governor of Maryland, President Nixon searched for a replacement for the nation's second highest public officer.

The questions of how and why Nixon came to select Ford to replace Agnew have not been definitively answered. One popular explanation is that Nixon chose Ford as an "insurance policy" against impeachment.[1] In explaining his motivation for choosing Ford, Nixon allegedly said contemptuously to Nelson Rockefeller, while pointing to the president's Oval Office chair, "Can you imagine Jerry Ford sitting in this chair?"[2] According to this view, Nixon could not believe that Congress would impeach him if that meant Ford would become president. Nixon aide H. R. Haldeman wrote that, without Watergate, John Connally would have been chosen to replace Agnew.[3]

Another explanation is that Nixon wanted to choose someone widely trusted and respected on Capitol Hill, first, to ensure confirmation and, sec-

1. See, for example, John Dean, *Blind Ambition: The White House Years* (New York: Simon and Schuster, 1976), 339.

2. Robert T. Hartmann, *Palace Politics: An Inside Account of the Ford Years* (New York: McGraw Hill, 1980), 117.

3. H. R. Haldeman, *The Ends of Power* (New York: New York Times Books, 1978), 323.

ond, to enable the White House to develop a better relationship with the legislature. Ford fit that bill perfectly. Ford liked to say that he had many political opponents on Capitol Hill but no enemies. Clearly, he enjoyed the personal admiration and respect of his colleagues, regardless of partisan affiliation. And Ford, a long-time friend of Nixon, had been an unflinching supporter of the president—both of Nixon's policies and Watergate defense.

Whatever Nixon's motivations, the Ford selection took most of the country by surprise. Politicians and political observers alike expected perhaps John Connally, Nelson Rockefeller, or some other nationally prominent Republican to be Nixon's choice. Certainly, few thought of the unassuming, generally not well known House Minority Leader, Gerald R. Ford.

The manner in which Ford entered the national spotlight profoundly influenced the development of his public and press image. Because Ford did not come to the national scene as a well-known commodity, observers formed impressions of him practically overnight. Journalists, especially, had to confront the task of describing and analyzing Nixon's vice presidential choice for the nation without any advance warning or preparation.

Journalists initially presented an unflattering portrait of Nixon's new vice president. Because the press already had anointed other Republicans to the status of "nationally prominent" or "presidential" material, journalists immediately characterized Ford as "undistinguished" and a "second-level party man." The press formed an early judgment of Ford as not "presidential."

When Nixon resigned the presidency, Ford assumed that office with a great deal of public and press fanfare that could clearly be explained by a widespread delight to be rid of Nixon. Hence, Ford opened his presidency amid most favorable press coverage. As Ford recalled: "In the first month of my Presidency, I had received the kind of press coverage that every politician loves but almost never gets."[4]

That favorable press coverage did not reflect any favorable perception of a Ford agenda or of substantive policy achievements. It did not reflect any wholesale journalistic change of heart from the earlier assessments of Nixon's second vice president. Instead, journalists appeared pleased to have a president who could be believed and who also did not harbor any deep suspicions of the press or political opponents. And Ford symbolically showed that he planned to conduct an "open" administration—to be available to the press, to answer journalists' questions, to let candor rule, and to conduct a presidency of the people.

Ford's favorable press coverage came crashing down after the unexpected pardon of Richard M. Nixon, a controversial decision that substan-

---

4. Gerald R. Ford, *A Time to Heal* (Norwalk, Conn.: Easton Press, 1987), 178.

tially helped to set the tone for Ford's press coverage throughout his brief term in office. In his first month in office, Ford had made great strides in moving beyond the cynicism and paranoia that characterized White House–press relations during the Nixon years. With the Nixon pardon, dropped on the U.S. public one Sunday morning, as Deputy Press Secretary John W. Hushen said, "like Pearl Harbor,"[5] Ford would have to work even harder at restoring trust in public leaders and institutions. This task was made all the more difficult by the fact that, according to Gladys Lang and Kurt Lang, "the nation was, both before and after the pardon, in a strongly punitive mood. . . . This stands in marked contrast to the usual readiness of the American public to minimize political wrongdoing, to forget transgressions, and to forgive their perpetrators."[6]

Throughout Ford's term in office, the White House had considerable difficulty effecting a positive presidential press image. Indeed, there are serious limitations on what a White House can do to effect a press image. No White House can completely script or determine its own news coverage. But a White House can influence press coverage and the administration's image, and doing so is a necessary part of presidential leadership.

Ford's national press image certainly did not help him to get a grip on the awesome duties of his office. A president constantly portrayed as a "bumbler," an intellectual lightweight lacking a leadership vision, will experience great difficulty trying to build public and congressional support for his decisions. And Ford did experience such difficulties. True, leading journalists liked Ford and eventually came back to lauding his integrity—even though they never agreed with the pardon of Nixon—but they did not perceive him as capable enough to exercise presidential powers.

In part, Ford's leadership image fared poorly in the national press because journalists expected him to aspire to an idealistic notion of presidential leadership—one that requires the chief executive to articulate a vision for the future characterized by far-reaching, innovative policies to alleviate public problems. A president who practices fiscal austerity and tries to steer a cautious policy course is not credited by the press with visionary leadership and is not perceived as "big enough" for the presidency.

Among political journalists, therefore, there are *general expectations of presidential leadership* applied to all modern chief executives. Leaders are expected to display specific characteristics and to behave in a certain fashion. There is a great deal of imagery associated with a president's ability to present

---

5. Author interview with John W. Hushen, Washington, D.C., May 14, 1990.

6. Gladys Engel Lang and Kurt Lang, *The Battle for Public Opinion: The President, the Press, and the Polls During Watergate* (New York: Columbia University Press, 1983), 226.

himself as a "leader." The president must project an aura of being in command of his duties, and he must be able to move other political leaders and the people to follow his "vision" or plans.

Journalists, in their evaluative tasks, also apply a set of *specific expectations of the president*. In this case, journalists harbored certain notions of what Gerald R. Ford should and could do as President of the United States. According to the press, Ford had to (1) unite the country after the bitter Watergate and Vietnam debacles, and (2) work constructively with Congress to get the country "moving again." Journalists perceived Ford as trustworthy and as a conciliatory person who knew his way around Capitol Hill. Hence, Ford could restore faith in government and he could draw on his vast experience to "lead" Congress.

The purpose of this study is to identify and assess the national journalistic evaluations of the Ford presidency. To that end, I shall identify the major themes in journalists' assessments of Ford's presidency. I analyze how journalists come to their assessments and how they apply basic notions of presidential leadership to their reviews of an incumbent's performance in office. My focus is on the journalists themselves. How do they define and analyze presidential leadership? What are their evaluative criteria? How do they frame their judgments of presidential success and failure? How do they define "success" and "failure"?

Evaluating the presidency is a difficult task, especially for journalists who must work with short deadlines and information constraints. Scholars have the luxury of an academic environment in which to ponder such matters as presidential leadership. And scholars are expected to produce and identify definitions and measures of leadership. Journalists, too, have definitions and measures of leadership. Their definitions and measures are implicit in their writings but never made clear to their readers. When journalists determine that a president is "failing" the task of leadership, readers generally do not understand the bases for that judgment.

This study makes clear some of the basic, underlying notions of presidential leadership in modern political journalism. Based on a comprehensive review of journalistic commentary on one presidency, journalists' implicit leadership criteria are identified and analyzed. This study also builds upon my earlier work on the national press treatment of Jimmy Carter's presidency.[7] Although each work deals with a different president, I found important similarities in the press assessments of Ford and Carter.

Ford's press relations are most noteworthy because Gerald R. Ford became president immediately after Nixon's resignation from office, at a time

---

7. Mark J. Rozell, *The Press and the Carter Presidency* (Boulder, Colo.: Westview Press, 1989).

when the press-presidency relationship experienced great difficulties. Many of the traditional notions of the press-presidency relationship came under attack in the wake of Watergate. Journalists began to treat public leaders with greater suspicion than ever before. Richard M. Pious writes that "the legacy of Watergate is wolfpack journalism."[8] Indeed, many scholars—and leading journalists as well—have confirmed that Vietnam and Watergate resulted in a press highly suspicious of official leadership and most aggressive in its coverage of the presidency.[9] The Ford White House had to operate in this environment of press cynicism and learn how to deal with a much changed, but not clearly defined, press-presidency relationship.

What transpired in the press-presidency relationship during Ford's term very much helped to set the tone for future press-presidency relations. Clearly, many of the events of the Carter and Reagan administrations, and now the Bush administration, are an outgrowth of the development of press-presidency relations during the Ford years. Journalists set some new standards for how they covered the presidency in the Ford administration. The Ford White House adopted press strategies borrowed and adapted by subsequent White Houses. Ford's press people made strategic errors that later administrations recognized and learned from. Most important, the Ford years helped to set the tone for post-Watergate press-presidency relations.

Method of Analysis

My analysis of the press assessments of Ford's administration is derived from a comprehensive review of national print media sources from October 1973 through January 1977. I begin the chronological narrative with Nixon's appointment of Ford to the vice presidency, because the early press judgment of Nixon's choice profoundly influenced the press's later evaluations of President Ford.

The selection of national print media sources is adopted from Stephen Hess's description of the news organization hierarchy in *The Washington*

8. Richard M. Pious, *The American Presidency* (New York: Basic Books, 1979), 417.

9. See Lang and Lang, *Battle*, 258–61; William L. Rivers, *The Other Government: Power and the Washington Media* (New York: Universe Books, 1982), 19; Robert M. Entman, "The Imperial Media," in *Analyzing the Presidency*, 2d ed., ed. Robert E. DiClerico (Guilford, Conn.: Dushkin Publishing, 1990), 156; Michael Baruch Grossman and Martha Joynt Kumar, *Portraying the President: The White House and the News Media* (Baltimore: Johns Hopkins University Press, 1981), 299–301; David Broder, *Behind the Front Page: A Candid Look at How the News Is Made* (New York: Simon and Schuster, 1987), 167; James Deakin, *Straight Stuff: The Reporters, the White House, the Truth* (New York: William Morrow, 1984), 295; Sam Donaldson, *Hold On, Mr. President!* (New York: Ballantine Books, 1987), 68–69; Haynes Johnson, *In the Absence of Power* (New York: Viking Press, 1980), 170; Tom Wicker, *On Press* (New York: Viking Press, 1978), 61.

Reporters.[10] According to Hess, there is a "solar system of Washington news gathering." This system includes "the sun," or the "political government," and the various planets, the Washington news organizations. These news organizations form "an inner ring, a ring of middle distance, and an outermost ring."

The inner ring comprises the most influential news organizations. These organizations are most important to the political government because "through them it learns what the country is learning about what it is doing." The inner ring organizations include: Associated Press, United Press International, American Broadcasting Company, National Broadcasting Company, Columbia Broadcasting System, *Newsweek*, *U.S. News and World Report*, *Time*, *New York Times*, *Washington Post*, and the *Wall Street Journal*.[11] In another study, Hess showed that press officers, in recognition of the inner ring's influence, give preferential treatment to the most prominent news media.[12]

This study focuses on those inner ring sources that comprise the nucleus of Washington journalism—the print media. Hess notes that Washington news has a rhythm set by the major national news dailies (*New York Times*, *Wall Street Journal*, and *Washington Post*). This news "travels a circuitous route back into the political government and out again to the rest of the country via the electronic media."[13] Print journalism thus becomes the focal point of national opinion development, and journalists become the molders of public perceptions of presidential leadership and performance. Television networks have a "secondary impact" on the political government. And the wire services do not emphasize interpretive reporting and news analysis as much as the major print media sources.

Therefore, this study is based on the news analyses, commentaries, and editorials on the Ford presidency contained in three national news dailies (*New York Times*, *Wall Street Journal*, *Washington Post*) and the three national news weeklies (*Newsweek*, *Time*, *U.S. News and World Report*).

---

10. Stephen Hess, *The Washington Reporters* (Washington, D.C.: Brookings Institution, 1981).

11. Hess, *Washington Reporters*, 24, n. 24. Hess also included the now defunct *Washington Star* in his list of inner ring organizations. I excluded the *Star* from this study because a seventh print media source would yield little, if any, substantive information beyond what I found in the other six inner ring sources. I also wanted to achieve continuity with my earlier study of Carter's press relations to facilitate more reliable comparative analysis. Finally, a *Wall Street Journal* survey cited by Hess reveals the three news dailies most frequently read by high-level federal officials to be the *Washington Post* (90 percent), *Wall Street Journal* (62 percent), and *New York Times* (45 percent).

12. Stephen Hess, *The Government/Press Connection* (Washington, D.C.: Brookings Institution, 1984), 100.

13. Hess, *Washington Reporters*, 96.

In collecting data for this study I read every news article, news analysis, editorial, and opposite-editorial page column (by the regularly featured syndicated columnists) during the time period covered. From these news articles, news analyses, editorials, and opinion columns, I transcribed all of the judgmental press comments about Ford's performance in office. I then organized these commentaries both chronologically and thematically—chronologically to give insight into the development of press perceptions of the president over time, and thematically to provide an understanding of the leading portrayals of the president and the underlying values of presidential leadership among prominent journalists. From that organization I constructed a chronological narrative of the major press assessments of Ford's performance. The use of a chronology conveys how certain journalistic assessments developed and became reinforced, molding the Ford press profile. The chronology also makes clear how certain themes in the press reviews persisted once a basic presidential image had been framed. What also becomes clear is the great difficulty White House press officers experience when they confront and try to change the negative elements of a president's basic press image. Regarding press coverage of elections, Stanley Kelley writes: "The press gets there first with the most publicity, and the first impressions of elections tend to endure."[14] Regarding press coverage of the presidency, this study shows that Kelley's insight could also read: The press gets there first with the most publicity, and the first impressions of *presidents* tend to endure. Very germane to this study is George C. Edwards's assessment that journalists "frame the news in themes" as a way to "simplify complex events" and then reinforce these themes through constant repetition. Thus, images or stereotypes are created that people perceive as "reality."[15] Indeed, numerous studies confirm the crucial role that the media play in establishing what Richard Neustadt calls "a dominant tone, a central tendency, in Washington appraisals of a President."[16] Samuel Kernell writes that "prominent journalists serve as important opinion leaders in establishing a president's reputation."[17] William L. Rivers reports that Washington's leading journalists have been elevated "to a kind of academy of national sages and prognosticators."[18] Grossman and Kumar add that Washington influentials and constituents "take their assessment of the President" from the media.

---

14. Stanley Kelley, *Interpreting Elections* (Princeton: Princeton University Press, 1983), 166.

15. George C. Edwards, *The Public Presidency: The Pursuit of Popular Support* (New York: St. Martin's Press, 1983), 159, 166.

16. Richard Neustadt, *Presidential Power and the Modern Presidents: The Politics of Leadership from Roosevelt to Reagan* (New York: Free Press, 1990), 53.

17. Samuel Kernell, *Going Public: New Strategies of Presidential Leadership* (Washington, D.C.: Congressional Quarterly Press, 1986), 53.

18. Rivers, *The Other Government*, 9.

Reality as refracted through the lens of the news media is for most people their only glimpse of what is going on at the White House. It provides them with a basis to judge the person who occupies the Oval Office and suggests the activities that may be needed to secure an individual or a general interest.[19]

Leading studies of the mass media and political communications establish the important link between journalistic opinion and public perceptions of political leaders and institutions.[20] The key point is made by George C. Edwards.

It is the press that provides citizens with most of what they know about the chief executive, his policies, and their consequences. . . . The press is thus the principal intermediary between the president and the public, and relations with the press are an important aspect of the president's efforts to lead public opinion. If the press portrays the president in a favorable light, he will have fewer obstacles in obtaining public support. If, on the other hand, the press is hostile toward his administration, the president's task will be more difficult.[21]

I employ a qualitative content analysis approach instead of any of the quantitative content analysis techniques more commonly used in political science. Strictly speaking, I am not presenting a content analysis of newspaper coverage of the president. This study, instead, examines journalistic opinion of the president's leadership. Other studies of press coverage of politics, including my own,[22] employ accepted quantitative techniques to

---

19. Grossman and Kumar, *Portraying*, 299.

20. See Douglass Cater, *The Fourth Branch of Government* (Boston: Houghton Mifflin, 1959); Bernard C. Cohen, *The Press and Foreign Policy* (Princeton: Princeton University Press, 1963); Doris A. Graber, *Mass Media and American Politics*, 3d ed. (Washington, D.C.: Congressional Quarterly Press, 1990); Graber, *Processing the News: How People Tame the Information Tide* (New York: Longman, 1984); Jon A. Krosnick and Donald R. Kinder, "Altering the Foundations of Support for the President through Priming," *American Political Science Review* 84, no. 2 (June, 1990): 497–512; Kurt Lang and Gladys Lang, "The Mass Media and Voting," in *American Voting Behavior*, ed. Eugene Burdick and Arthur J. Brodbeck (Glencoe, Ill.: Free Press, 1959): 217–35; Maxwell E. McCombs and Donald L. Shaw, "The Agenda-Setting Function of the Press," in *Media Power in Politics*, 2d ed., ed. Doris A. Graber (Washington, D.C.: Congressional Quarterly Press, 1984): 73–82; Arthur H. Miller, Edie N. Goldenberg, and Lutz Ebring, "Type-Set Politics: The Impact of Newspapers on Public Confidence," *American Political Science Review*, 73, no. 1 (March, 1979): 67–84; David L. Paletz and Robert M. Entman, *Media-Power-Politics* (New York: Free Press, 1981).

21. Edwards, *Public Presidency*, 104.

22. See Mark J. Rozell, "Local v. National Press Assessments of Virginia's 1989 Gubernatorial Campaign," *Polity* 24, no. 1 (Fall, 1991): 69–89.

identify key words and phrases used by journalists or to measure degrees of positive and negative news coverage. The approach adopted here suits the objectives of this study well. I am less interested in specific words and phrases than I am in the context of their use. I seek to identify the major themes in journalists' assessments of a president as a means of understanding their underlying leadership values. I want to learn—and to teach—how journalists struggle over the course of an administration's term to understand and define a presidency. The degrees of positive and negative news coverage are not my primary concern. The qualitative approach fosters an appreciation of the context of press evaluations and provides a more complete understanding of the opinion content of these evaluations.

Organization of the Analysis

The main body of this study is a chronological narrative of the journalistic assessments of Ford's presidency. This narrative begins with chapter 2, which covers the press portrayals of Ford's brief vice presidential tenure from October 1973, until August 9, 1974. Chapters 3 through 6 cover the press commentary on Ford's presidency.

In these chapters, I identify and discuss the major themes in the press portrayals of the Ford presidency. These themes are organized into five categories of activities: timing, symbolism and rhetoric, policy agenda, policy development, and staff.

Timing

This category of assessments has two aspects: first, the historic context of the Ford presidency and, second, the different stages of Ford's term in office.

Journalists assessed the Ford presidency at a particular historic period, and this context must be acknowledged in order to understand the press evaluations of Ford. More specifically, Ford came to office immediately in the aftermath of the "long national nightmare," Watergate. The winding down of the U.S. involvement in the Vietnam War also coincided with Ford's term in office. These events profoundly influenced the manner and content of press evaluations of the Ford presidency.

Journalists also assessed the Ford presidency according to their perceptions of how a president should behave during different stages of the term. During the early stages of the term, journalists expected the president to build public and congressional support, articulate a leadership "vision," and communicate a set of policy priorities. Timing helps explain press portrayals of Ford in 1976—an election year. Journalists more often viewed Ford's activities within the context of the presidential campaign and generally characterized his actions as motivated more by electoral politics than by the national interest.

Symbolism and Rhetoric

A second category of journalistic assessments focuses on presidential symbolism and rhetoric. These evaluations concern the president's role as a public leader. Journalists perceive the ability to project a leadership image through the use of symbolism and rhetoric as an important element of the president's leadership task. Leadership, in this view, entails setting the conditions that encourage followership.

During the first month of his presidency, Ford developed quite a following. His symbolic gestures, aimed at portraying the presidency as an institution of the people, received exceptionally favorable press and public notice. His speeches to the public—unpretentious, warm, and even humorous—hit just the right tone. His inaugural "talk," highlighted by the phrase "our long national nightmare is over," began the process of building Ford's "healer" reputation.[23]

Ford's reputation for effective political symbolism and rhetoric did not last. After the pardon of Richard M. Nixon, the press returned to the earlier, negative view of Ford as an ineffective speaker. Throughout his term in office, journalists characterized Ford as incapable of commanding the symbols of the presidency and unable to rouse the public with his words.

Journalists most frequently criticized Ford for failing to articulate a leadership vision. In their commentaries, journalists appeared enamored with the activist-leadership model of the presidency. Ford lacked an overriding theme, such as the "New Deal" or "Great Society," and the press perceived that lack as a failure in visionary leadership. When Ford did employ slogans—"IF" flags for "Inflation Fighters" and "WIN" buttons for "Whip Inflation Now"—journalists mocked these symbolic devices as gimmicky.

Because Ford carried the unfortunate baggage of the "bumbler" image, the press went to great lengths to emphasize every presidential misstatement. Ford's persistent "bumbler" image made White House efforts to portray the president as a national leader commanding respect and deserving public admiration much more difficult.

---

23. Robert Hartmann recalled that this crucial phrase almost did not end up in the final draft of Ford's speech. After reviewing the speech draft that Hartmann had written, Ford commented: "Isn't that a little hard on Dick?" After Hartmann's prodding, Ford kept the phrase that did, indeed, capture headlines and generate favorable press comment (Robert Hartmann, *Palace Politics: An Inside Account of the Ford Years* [New York: McGraw Hill, 1980], 159–60).

Agenda

Journalists also assessed Ford's policy agenda. For this category of assessments, Ford received little favorable comment, particularly in the domestic policy realm. The press viewed the Ford administration as lacking an identifiable policy agenda. In part, this criticism grew out of Ford's conviction to employ market-oriented rather than government-spending policy approaches toward the overriding problem of inflation. Journalists portrayed the lack of a massive government-interventionist policy approach as a lack of a viable agenda to solve the nation's economic woes.

Throughout his term, journalists implored Ford to generously spend governmental resources to solve domestic problems. When Ford vetoed or resisted Democratic party initiatives, journalists said that he did not have an agenda and that he merely "counterpunched" the opposition party.

The press characterized Ford's economic summit and calls for voluntary economic restraint as gimmickry over substance. Journalists often compared Ford's domestic policies to those of former presidents Herbert Hoover and Calvin Coolidge. When criticizing Ford's agenda, they had in mind the far-reaching policies of former Democratic presidents Franklin D. Roosevelt and Lyndon B. Johnson.

In the foreign policy realm, the press viewed Ford's agenda as unimaginative, a Nixon "copycat." Some journalists wrote that Ford did not have his own foreign policy. In their view, Ford merely allowed Nixon's policies to be continued by Secretary of State Henry Kissinger. When Ford embarked upon important diplomatic initiatives, such as the meetings in Vladivostok with Soviet leader Leonid Brezhnev, journalists compared the president's efforts to those of Nixon. According to leading journalists, Ford had to both live down his association with Nixon and he had to live up to his predecessor's foreign affairs acumen.

Policy Development

Journalists tend to define presidential leadership as policy activism. In their assessments, a "leader" articulates an agenda, builds support for it, and gets Congress to move according to his set of priorities. The ability of a president to do these things is what establishes him as an effective leader.

In Ford's case, despite the fact that Democrats dominated Congress and despite the many institutional reforms that made legislative-executive coordination increasingly difficult, the press expected the president to lead according to a notion of leadership more suited to Democratic presidents leading Democratic Congresses during times of governmental expansion. Rather than viewing Ford as a leader—in their sense of the term—journalists said that the president merely "reacted." Although they acknowledged the unquestionable success of Ford's veto strategy, journalists did not characterize that approach to dealing with Congress as true "leadership."

When Ford did initiate major policies to deal with such domestic problems as energy and the economy, the press reported that he did not offer "bold" enough solutions. Journalists asserted that Ford only offered status quo, typically cautious Republican policy initiatives that did not do enough to aggressively tackle problems. They wanted major policy changes from the Nixon years and perceived Ford as offering only the same ideas with some modifications.

Staff

The press viewed the quality of Ford's staff negatively. Journalists reported that Ford brought to the White House staff a strange mixture of Nixon loyalists, Ford loyalists, and people never associated with either president. They viewed Ford's staff as divisive and generally undistinguished. Two aspects of Ford's staffing arrangement led to press image problems.

First, Ford refused to rid his White House of every Nixon Republican. He knew that many Nixon loyalists had served their country honorably, had nothing to do with Watergate, and did not deserve to be stigmatized by the events that led to Nixon's resignation. There may also have been a dearth of good Republicans never previously associated with Nixon. Nonetheless, the press demanded a wholesale cleansing of the White House of all Nixon "holdovers" and criticized Ford for failing resolutely to take such action.

Second, Ford recruited to his White House many former members of his congressional and vice presidential staffs. The press reported that these individuals lacked national "stature" and did not comprise a corps of "distinguished" presidential assistants.

The Ford White House suffered significant staff rivalry, much of which resulted in staffers leaking unflattering stories about each other to the press and, hence, generating negative news stories. Staff infighting perpetuated an image of Ford as not completely in control of his office and substantially hurt his press reputation.

Following the chronological narrative of press reporting and commentary on Ford's presidency, I examine the White House's press relations strategy, as told by leading press office staffers. For chapter 7, I rely on the following sources.

1. Personal interviews with key members of the Ford White House involved in the process of press strategy and presidential imagery. I

interviewed President Ford, Robert T. Hartmann, John W. Hushen, Larry Speakes, William Greener, John G. Carlson, Margita White, Jerald terHorst, Gerald Warren, J. William Roberts, Louis M. Thompson, Jr., and Ronald H. Nessen.

2. The memoirs of Ford White House staffers and other published records of their recollections of the Ford years.

3. Selected documents from the Gerald R. Ford Presidential Library in Ann Arbor, Michigan.

The purpose of chapter 7 is to describe and assess the Ford White House press strategy. The president had a press image problem that profoundly influenced the Ford White House's ability to do its job. White House press office staffers recognized this problem and had to deal with it on a regular basis. Despite their efforts, Ford's basic press image—that of a trustworthy, yet not very commanding, accident prone leader who lacked "vision"— resisted change. The findings discussed in chapter 7 reveal what a modern White House can and cannot do to manage its press relations. It is made clear that a White House cannot easily script its own press coverage and that many contextual factors, beyond the control of image crafters, have a most significant influence on presidential press relations. The comments of Ford press office staffers interviewed for this study reveal that the president entered office with numerous public relations liabilities: the lack of an election mandate, the lack of a regular transition period to plan press strategy, and the post-Watergate environment of press coverage of presidents, to cite just a few such examples. Ford did have a big public relations asset: he was not Nixon. And the White House did employ a conscious press relations strategy to build on that asset. For the most part, however, the Ford White House had to deal with a chaotic, difficult situation in developing a press relationship. Not being Nixon and employing a press strategy to highlight that fact served Ford well for the first weeks of his presidency but could not carry him through the entire term. Journalists looked for other evidence that Ford possessed the "right stuff" to be president.

The concluding chapter reviews the major findings of this study. It also draws together the major themes in journalists' assessments of Ford and identifies the elements of the press's implicit theories of presidential leadership. Chapter 8 concludes with an analysis of the press's leadership criteria and of how leading journalists view the modern presidency. Ford's press relations are considered within the context of the post-Watergate environment of presidential journalism.

The finding of central importance in this study is that journalists have identifiable criteria of presidential leadership. Journalists bring to their evaluations of presidents certain leadership expectations that scholars of presidential journalism need to recognize. These expectations color journalists' perceptions of presidential success and failure. And the modern White House can only do so much to either change journalists' expectations or to present the president in a manner that meets journalists' expectations. A White House cannot script its own press coverage. It can influence some of the press's expectations and improve the president's image to a substantial degree. Creating the correct image of presidential leadership becomes an important factor in determining presidential success or failure.

The findings in this study, therefore, provide an exception to the more common theoretical argument in political science that the White House can generally control its image and that journalists are not independent of the people they cover.[24] My analysis also lends credibility to the belief that journalists have a "herd mentality": the congruity in press assessments of newsworthy events, criteria for judging leadership, and analyses of the president's performance is remarkable. Finally, the data presented here confirm assessments that the press emphasizes personalities, peculiarities, imagery, and political successes and failures at the expense of conveying substantive analyses of issues, public institutions, and processes.[25] For those who believe that the press carries the responsibility of informing and educating citizens about the modern presidency and its occupants, my findings should give cause for concern about the quality of that information and education.

---

24. See W. Lance Bennett, *News: The Politics of Illusion*, 2d ed. (New York: Longman, 1988), xiii, xv, 105; Broder, *Behind*, 194; Thomas E. Cronin, "The Presidency Public Relations Script," in *The Presidency Reappraised*, ed. Rexford G. Tugwell and Thomas E. Cronin (New York: Praeger, 1974), 168–83; Grossman and Kumar, *Portraying*, 253–72; Lewis W. Wolfson, *The Untapped Power of the Press* (New York: Praeger, 1985), 12; Harvey G. Zeidenstein, "News Media Perceptions of White House News Management," *Presidential Studies Quarterly* 14, no. 3 (Summer, 1984): 391.

25. See Broder, *Behind*, 215; Elmer E. Cornwell, Jr., "Role of the Press in Presidential Politics," in *Politics and the Press*, ed. Richard W. Lee (Washington, D.C.: Acropolis Books, 1970), 18–19; Edwards, *Public Presidency*, 151–54; Hess, *Washington Reporters*, 124; Wolfson, *Untapped Power*, 167.

CHAPTER 2

Building the Image: The Vice Presidency

In its October 1, 1973, issue, *Newsweek* speculated that Vice President Spiro T. Agnew might resign his position, and published the results of its vice presidential preference poll. For that poll, *Newsweek* named six likely Nixon choices for vice president and asked respondents to express a first and second preference. Gerald R. Ford was not among the six names mentioned.[1]

At 2:00 P.M. on October 10, 1973, amid growing evidence of his earlier involvement in an illegal kickback scheme as Maryland's governor, Spiro T. Agnew resigned from the vice presidency. Shortly after 9:00 P.M. on October 12, 1973, President Nixon announced his surprise choice of Congressman Gerald R. Ford (R-Mich.) as the next vice president.

Having for weeks expected Nixon to choose John Connally, Nelson Rockefeller, or Barry Goldwater, journalists conducted hasty studies of Gerald Ford's political background and achievements. Most journalists knew little about Gerald Ford, yet the pressures of time and competition compelled them to evaluate Nixon's selection in very short order.

Journalists assessed Nixon's choice of Gerald Ford to be vice president negatively. About the best that journalists would say of Ford was that he was not Agnew. Commentaries pointed out that Ford's personal probity remained untarnished and described the vice presidential nominee as an honest, forthcoming person.[2] In David Broder's words, "His style of politics is open, frank and direct. It is keyed to consultation and negotiation, not confrontation."[3] And William S. White characterized Ford as "quietly competent, unstrident and strictly 'square.'"[4]

For the journalists who evaluated Nixon's choice of Gerald Ford, being an honest, straight shooter did not carry the day. They expected a man of national stature, a charismatic figure capable of carrying the mantle of presidential leadership if called upon to do so. Apparently, Ford did not fit their bill. He was, according to many journalists, a lightweight on the national

---

1. "Spiro Agnew on the Spot," *Newsweek*, October 1, 1973, 27.
2. "A Good Lineman for the Quarterback," *Time*, October 22, 1973, 18.
3. David Broder, "Rating Gerald Ford," *Washington Post*, October 17, 1973, A18.
4. William S. White, "Gerald Ford: The Man to Beat in '76," *Washington Post*, October 20, 1973, A19.

political scene. The *New York Times* called him "a routine partisan of narrow views."[5]

Journalists directed much of their criticism of the selection of Ford at President Nixon. Unconstrained by electoral considerations, Nixon had the opportunity to choose the most qualified person to be vice president. *Time* stated that, instead, "Nixon's choice was safe and unimaginative. . . . Ford would not readily leap to mind as the Republican most capable of leading the nation were Nixon not to finish his term."[6] David Broder agreed that Ford was "obviously not the most distinguished choice Mr. Nixon could have made."[7] A *Washington Post* editorial contended that the vice presidency should be filled by a man of distinction and "it must be said that Gerald Ford is not such a man . . . pedestrian, partisan, dogged—he has been the very model of a second-level party man."[8]

Jules Witcover described Nixon as too insecure to choose a "'superstar' who might outshine him" as vice president. Although Nixon could have showed up his critics by choosing a "superstar,"

> Instead . . . he picked a man nobody had mentioned as presidential timber . . . and whose greatest strength was regarded by many as his party devotion. . . . [T]he choice of Ford is like routine selections of running mates in the past—a personal choice within the prerogative of the party head that satisfies his needs, as he perceives them, more than the country's.[9]

A scathing editorial from the conservative-leaning *Wall Street Journal* perhaps damaged Nixon and Ford the most.

> The nomination of Mr. Ford caters to all the worst instincts on Capitol Hill—the clubbiness that made him the choice of Congress, the partisanship that threatened a bruising fight if a prominent Republican presidential contender were named, the small-mindedness that thinks in terms of who should be rewarded rather than who could best fill the job. . . . [I]t is a blunt fact that in thinking of possible Presidents, few people have even thought of Mr. Ford.[10]

---

5. Quoted in "The Fall of Mr. Law and Order," *Newsweek*, October 22, 1973, 36.

6. "A Good Lineman for the Quarterback," *Time*, October 1, 1973, 18.

7. Broder, "Rating Ford," 18.

8. "The Choice of Mr. Ford," *Washington Post*, October 14, 1973, C6.

9. Jules Witcover, "Ford No Threat to President," *Washington Post*, October 17, 1973, A9.

10. "Squandered Opportunity," *Wall Street Journal*, October 15, 1973, 25.

Many journalists perceived Ford as an accomplished partisan, a Nixon loyalist who lacked charisma, passion, and the ability to inspire. According to *Newsweek*, Ford's "chief distinction in a quarter-century in Washington has been unswerving loyalty to the GOP—and to Richard Nixon."[11] The news weekly added that

> Ford, at 60, remains an oddly elusive personality—a low-profile team player of little color, less humor and no pronounced eccentricities. . . . [A]ny convictions he may hold on his own have been swallowed in his almost total loyalty to President Nixon's policies.[12]

U.S. News and World Report concurred with that evaluation.

> In nominating Representative Gerald R. Ford of Michigan to be his Vice President, Richard Nixon got what he has long admired—a team player right down the line . . . . [Ford] has made his mark as a partisan politician while serving as Minority Leader of the House for almost nine years. Almost invariably, Mr. Ford has championed the Administration point of view on Capitol Hill.[13]

According to David Broder, in choosing a vice president, President Nixon did not want "a partner in policy-making or an apprentice President." Ford became "a perfect choice for the kind of no. 2 man President Nixon" preferred.[14] As House Minority Leader, according to Broder, Ford proved to be the kind of leader of the Republicans that Nixon most liked.

> When President Nixon took office, Ford reverted to being a presidential agent, rather than an independent leader, with an alacrity that made some wonder how comfortable he was in any other role. . . . [Ford's] self-defined goal, has seemed to be to serve the President, not set the legislative policy for his party.[15]

Upon being nominated for the vice presidency, therefore, Gerald Ford carried the burden of proving that he was more than just a narrow partisan, a

---

11. "This Is Your Veep," *Newsweek*, October 22, 1973, 25.

12. "Gerald Ford: The Politics of Loyalty," *Newsweek*, October 22, 1973, 37.

13. "Gerald Ford: A 'Team Player' Gets the Call," *U.S. News and World Report*, October 22, 1973, 20.

14. Broder, "Rating Ford," A18.

15. David Broder, "Always the 'President's Agent,' Ford Now to Get the Title," *Washington Post*, October 14, 1973, A10.

Nixon loyalist. Ford helped himself considerably during his congressional confirmation hearings. During the nearly month-long confirmation process, Ford emphasized that he did not "belong" to President Nixon, asserted that Nixon should have turned over some crucial White House tapes sooner, and characterized the "Saturday Night Massacre" as "an unfortunate incident." Indeed, Ford even distanced himself from some of the Nixon administration's policy positions. In all, Ford not only impressed his former Capitol Hill colleagues (they confirmed him by a vote of 92 to 3 in the Senate and 387 to 35 in the House), but he also received favorable press coverage for his candor and apparent willingness to be an independent-minded vice president.[16]

On December 6, 1973, Gerald Ford was sworn in as vice president. *New York Times* political reporter James M. Naughton characterized Ford's ascendancy to that office as a potential "watershed" event in Nixon's presidency. Also, "it represents escape . . . [for] Republicans from elementary fear of defeat in the 1974 elections."[17] *U.S. News and World Report* declared that, with a new, honest vice president, there was an "atmosphere of change" in the government.[18]

Despite his initially bad press, Gerald Ford appeared to be winning over some of his critics. For the most part, Ford accomplished this feat with a simple strategy: to show that he was his own man and an honest politician. And every time that the new vice president looked different than the former vice president, Spiro T. Agnew, Ford scored points in the press.

Nonetheless, the underlying doubt about Gerald Ford—that he might revert to type and become Nixon's apologist—remained. Among political journalists, there still remained a great deal of sensitivity toward any vice presidential activities that appeared calculated to dissipate press criticism of Nixon administration wrongdoing.

Ford inherited a precarious position. As vice president, he had to be supportive of the Nixon administration. At the same time, he had to distance himself from the Watergate affair. As columnists Rowland Evans and Robert Novak wrote, Ford was "walking a tightrope" as President Nixon's new "front man."[19]

---

16. See, for example, "A Rush to Judgment on Gerald Ford," *Time*, November 12, 1973, 32, 37; "Growing in Stature," *Time*, November 19, 1973, 26–27; "Road Clear for Ford," *Time*, December 10, 1973, 22–23; "The Veep Most Likely to Succeed?" *Time*, December 17, 1973, 12; James M. Naughton, "A Watershed for Nixon," *New York Times*, December 7, 1973, 1, 27.

17. Naughton, "Watershed," 27.

18. "Ford's Job: Heal Split With Congress," *U.S. News and World Report*, December 17, 1973, 23.

19. Rowland Evans and Robert Novak, "Gerald Ford: Walking a Political Tightrope," *Washington Post*, October 13, 1973, A19.

President Nixon did not make Ford's task any easier. A long-standing personal friend and political ally of Ford, Nixon gave the vice president assurances that he [Nixon] had played no role in obstructing justice. Nixon personally assured Ford that the administration had the evidence to exonerate the president. Nixon then dispatched Ford around the country to build public support for the administration against charges of wrongdoing. In Gerald Ford, President Nixon had a new political weapon—a certifiably honest vice president with a strong reputation for believability.

Several themes predominated the press coverage of Ford's vice presidential activities: (1) that Ford lacked charisma and "presidential" stature; (2) that Ford lacked an independent cast of mind and served as Nixon's agent; and (3) that, despite any other flaws, Ford worked hard and was an honest, unpretentious person.

No Charisma, No Stature

To many journalists, Ford lacked such important "presidential" qualities as the ability to lead and to inspire people. Consider, for example, the following evaluations of Ford's political skills.

Wall Street Journal: He is not by any means a spellbinder on the stump. He cannot fashion dreams with words. He has no more charisma than does Mr. Nixon, which is to say he is as plain as bread. He is not creative . . . and there is nothing in his 25 years in Congress that even remotely resembles a Ford Act.[20]

Fred L. Zimmerman: One of his seeming drawbacks as a politician is his weakness as a speechmaker. His standard speech is sprinkled with mispronounced words . . . long and not-too-funny personal anecdotes, and frequent embarrassing pauses.[21]

Newsweek: Ford's political speeches are about as blah as the rubber-chicken dinners he has packed away by the ton. . . . There are those, of course, who believe Mr. Nixon has cleverly removed the subject of his own impeachment from consideration already—by nominating loyal and limited Jerry Ford as his new Vice President.[22]

---

20. "Vice President Ford," *Wall Street Journal*, December 7, 1973, 12.

21. Fred L. Zimmerman, "Man on a Tightrope," *Wall Street Journal*, April 15, 1974, 20.

22. "Gerald Ford: The Politics of Loyalty," *Newsweek*, October 22, 1973, 38.

Richard L. Lyons and Morton Mintz: Ford is not an electric personality, but he works all the time. . . . He isn't a magnetic speaker, but he does his homework.[23]

Adding to the assessment of Ford as lacking in stature and magnetism was the press's perception of him as a not-too-bright bumbler. For a man who had been captain of a Big Ten college football team, drafted by two professional teams, and later graduated in the top third of his class at an Ivy League law school, this perception appears odd, if not unjustified. From where, then, did this perception develop? David Broder maintains that "the seeds of destruction" had been planted, in part, by an October 1973 *New York Times* profile on Gerald Ford. That profile quoted a remark supposedly made by Lyndon B. Johnson that "Jerry Ford is so dumb he can't chew gum and walk at the same time." According to Broder, "Once put in circulation by the *Times* . . . the line was indelible."[24] Quoted in the press with similar frequency was former Detroit mayor Jerome Cavanaugh's quip that, "There's nothing wrong with Jerry Ford except he played football too long without a helmet."[25]

These comments, repeated often in the major news dailies and news weeklies, helped to frame the Ford image. Undoubtedly, much of the business of print reporting and commentary is to reduce complex ideas, events, and personalities to simplicity. But in many cases, simplification is achieved without regard to accuracy. In the case of the not-too-bright bumbler caricature of Ford, journalists seemingly looked for any evidence that confirmed this perception.

More puzzling still was a front-page *New York Times* news story on June 25, 1974. With the headline, "Ford, Teeing Off Like Agnew, Hits Spectator in Head With Golf Ball," the *Times* article reported

Vice President Ford, bringing back memories of his predecessor, struck a spectator in the head as Mr. Ford teed off this morning at a celebrity golf tournament. . . . Later, Mr. Ford, teeing off on the 16th hole, hit a golf cart carrying a policeman.[26]

The article carried a photograph of the grimacing spectator having his forehead examined by a golf tournament official. Under usual circumstances, such

---

23. Richard L. Lyons and Morton Mintz, "The President's Choice: Hard Working, Popular Leader," *Washington Post*, October 13, 1973, A9.

24. David Broder, *Behind the Front Page: A Candid Look at How the News is Made* (New York: Simon and Schuster, 1987), 56.

25. See, for example, William Claiborne, "'Quickie' Book: Wit, Wisdom of Rep. Ford," *Washington Post*, October 28, 1973, F1; "Ford: Politics of Loyalty," 37.

26. Marjorie Hunter, "Ford, Teeing Off Like Agnew, Hits Spectator in Head With Golf Ball," *New York Times*, June 25, 1974, 1.

an incident does not appear to justify front-page coverage in the prestigious *Times*, which boasts "All the News That's Fit to Print." Nonetheless, the incident involved Vice President Ford, the man who already carried the baggage of the bumbler image.

Some of the press stories resurrecting the not-too-bright bumbler theme, though damaging to Ford, were lighthearted. Other stories hit Ford much harder, calling into question the vice president's mental competence and physical prowess. A particularly critical essay was written by *Washington Post* columnist Nicholas von Hoffman after a June 1974 speech by the vice president condemning negative thinking about the U.S. economy. Von Hoffman evidently did not like the tone of Ford's partisan speech.

> Agnew without alliteration, that is Ford tripping over the stumps of dead ideas, giddy with a gaseous sort of attitudinal meanness, which his friends here in Washington apologize for by saying he is dumb but decent. The difference between malice and mental retardation in Mr. Ford's case is 50 points on an IQ test, the results of which are locked up in the White House safe with the truth about Kissinger, and Ehrlichman's notes.[27]

Although journalists revealed their perception of Ford as a stumbler lacking a keen intellect during his tenure as vice president, that perception became a larger theme in the press assessments of the Ford presidency. As Broder noted, the "seeds of destruction" had been planted and Gerald Ford's image became permanently, and unfairly, tarnished.

President Nixon's Agent

When Gerald Ford assumed the vice presidency, there was a great deal of sensitivity among political journalists that Agnew's replacement not resemble his predecessor. From Gerald Ford, journalists expected the kind of sincerity, honesty, and independent thinking they had come not to expect from Agnew.

Despite this expectation, Gerald Ford still had to serve as vice president to a chief executive who was under a cloud of suspicion. Ford faced a most difficult task: critics expected him to be open, honest, and independent, yet his job required that he be loyal to the president. As *New York Times* reporter Marjorie Hunter contended, Ford was forced into "performing a political acrobatic act" by being loyal to President Nixon and trying to protect his own reputation for candor.[28] Vermont Royster believed that Ford's options were,

---

27. Nicholas von Hoffman, "Negative Thinking vs. No Thinking," *Washington Post*, June 14, 1974, B4.

28. Marjorie Hunter, "Ford: Loyalty Conflicts With Unrepressed Candor," *New York Times*, April 21, 1974, IV, 4.

by necessity, limited. "He cannot abandon President Nixon on Watergate, not only because he owes Mr. Nixon his job, but also because if he does he will seem to be betraying the party as well."[29] A *Time* magazine article concurred. "For the good of both the party and himself, Ford must back up the man who selected him—yet he cannot become his puppet."[30] Gerald Ford had commented, "What I have to watch out for is not to become Nixon's apologist. That wouldn't help either of us."[31]

Did Ford succeed at this task? Ford's press critics said "sometimes." During his tenure as vice president, Ford seemingly vacillated between strongly defending the Nixon administration and distancing himself from the Watergate affair.

At first, Ford acted as Nixon's loyal agent, publicly defending the president against Watergate charges. In its December 17, 1973, issue, *Newsweek* quoted a number of Ford's comments in defense of Nixon.

> I can see nothing to justify an affirmative action on impeachment. There is no evidence that would justify it under the Constitution.

> I can assure you the president has no intention of resigning. And I personally don't think he should resign.

> If I was running and the President came to my district, I would be darn glad to have him.[32]

On January 15, 1974, in an Atlantic City, New Jersey, speech before the American Farm Bureau Federation, Ford denounced "powerful pressure organizations" such as the AFL-CIO and Americans For Democratic Action for "waging a massive propaganda campaign against the President." Ford called the impeachment effort a wasteful "political grudge match."[33] One week later Ford publicly declared that the White House possessed evidence that would "exonerate the President" of complicity in any cover-up of the Watergate incident. Ford's confident statement came one day after a nearly two-hour meeting with the president in which Nixon had personally assured the vice president that the White House, indeed, had such evidence. Ford declared that the evidence would "totally undercut the testimony of John Dean." Unfortunately, Ford had not seen the evidence.[34]

---

29. Vermont Royster, "Spring Practice," *Wall Street Journal*, January 30, 1974, 10.

30. "The Vice Presidency: Delicate Balancing Act," *Time*, February 25, 1974, 14.

31. "The Veep," 16.

32. "The New Veep's Real Mission," *Newsweek*, December 17, 1973, 26.

33. Carroll Kilpatrick, "Ford Denounces Critics of Nixon: 'Grudge' Cited," *Washington Post*, January 16, 1974, A1.

34. "Nixon Digs in to Fight," *Time*, February 4, 1974, 13; Lou Cannon, "Ford Convinced Nixon Is Innocent," *Washington Post*, January 23, 1974, A1, 8.

Ford came under heavy press criticism for his defense of Nixon. Conservative columnists Rowland Evans and Robert Novak called Ford's Atlantic City defense of Nixon the "grudge speech," "blooper speech," and "the Atlantic City fiasco."[35] Jules Witcover summarized the press assessments of Ford's pro-Nixon comments.

> An immediate implication was drawn in the press: Jerry Ford was being "Agnewed"—made into an oratorical blunderbuss by the White House in the manner of his predecessor, Spiro T. Agnew.[36]

Against the backdrop of these criticisms, Ford had to reestablish his credibility. The vice president revealed that Nixon speech writers had assisted with the Atlantic city speech. Ford soon brought in his own speech writers to assist in exhibiting his independence from the White House's public relations efforts.

In March 1974 Ford made a speech denouncing the "arrogant, elite guard of political adolescents" who controlled the 1972 Committee for the Reelection of the President (CREEP). Evans and Novak characterized the speech as Ford's "coming of age as the single most influential Republican politician" in the country. With that speech, Ford no longer was "the President's right-hand man." The columnists assessed that Ford had effectively distanced himself from Watergate without appearing to be disloyal to Nixon.[37]

Most important to the vice president, Ford's efforts to display his independence helped to dissipate some of the "president's puppet" charges. In early April 1974, in two public speeches, Ford urged Nixon to release all materials "relevant to the impeachment process." On May 23, in an interview with Bill Zimmerman of ABC News, Ford distanced himself from Nixon.

> It seems to me that a stonewall attitude isn't necessarily the wisest policy. . . . I would hope, if we get down to the final crunch, that the White House would be cooperative if there was relevant information, tapes or transcripts or otherwise, that would be helpful in avoiding a head-to-head confrontation.[38]

---

35. Rowland Evans and Robert Novak, "Gerald Ford: Planning for the Future," *Washington Post*, February 7, 1974, A19.

36. Jules Witcover, "Jerry Ford: Seeking to Be His Own Man," *Washington Post*, February 4, 1974, A1.

37. Rowland Evans and Robert Novak, "The Making of a Republican Leader," *Washington Post*, April 17, 1974, A19; see also, "The President's Strategy for Survival," *Time*, March 25, 1974, 19.

38. William Raspberry, "Gerald Ford: The Best of Intentions," *Washington Post*, June 5, 1974, A27; see also, "Richard Nixon's Collapsing Presidency," *Time*, May 20, 1974, 16.

Although such statements seemed to contradict Ford's earlier defense of Nixon, the vice president's stature grew in the press as a result of these comments.

Fred Zimmerman: [T]he Vice President's comments, taken together, add up to fence-straddling. But considering the constraints of his position . . . Mr. Ford's tightrope-walking has been so skillful that it has won him praise.[39]

William Raspberry: Maybe he is vacillating. . . . What I see in all this is an earnest man in a powerless but highly visible position doing his level best to save the country (and his party) some horrendous grief.[40]

Joseph Alsop: [T]he Vice President has already showed himself a national politician of far greater stature, more long-headed, with a greater sense of strategy and atmospherics, than anyone would have thought a year ago. He has kept apart from Watergate, yet he has been loyal. He has made himself strikingly popular, without taking a single step the remaining admirers of an unpopular President could possibly resent.[41]

Marquis Childs: While he has sometimes seemed to waver on Watergate and the predicament of the President, he has thus far not put a foot wrong. . . . Enter Mr. Clean untarnished by even a trace of the Watergate scandals and at the same time loyal to his party and his President.[42]

The press praise for Ford's handling of his "tightrope act"—keeping clear of Watergate and being vice presidential—did not last. As evidence against President Nixon mounted and Republican electoral fortunes in 1974 looked increasingly glum, the popular vice president traveled around the country pitching the virtues of supporting Republican candidates. As a part of his stump speech, Ford defended President Nixon, the "greatest President for peace in our history," against those critics trying to undermine the president by "innuendo and leaks." The pleas played well to partisan Republican audiences, but, as David Broder pointed out, such defenses of Nixon linked

---

39. Fred L. Zimmerman, "Man on a Tightrope," *Wall Street Journal*, April 15, 1974, 1.
40. Raspberry, "Ford: Best of Intentions."
41. Joseph Alsop, " . . . Gerald Ford: Playing the Odds," *Washington Post*, April 29, 1974, A23.
42. Marquis Childs, "Ford: Collecting Political Capital," *Washington Post*, July 5, 1974, A17.

Ford "to the fate of the Nixon administration, rather than emphasiz[ed] his independence from the scandals."[43]

Within just a few weeks of President Nixon's August 8, 1974, resignation, Vice President Ford stepped up his attacks on Nixon's detractors. At one point Ford went so far as to characterize the House Judiciary Committee proceedings as "partisan" and a "travesty." Ford even traveled to the district of a Judiciary Committee member to inform the Congressman's constituents that, "I can say from the bottom of my heart the President of the United States is innocent. He is right."[44] Evans and Novak commented that such defenses of an all-but-fallen president "could leave Ford a hero with the so-called hard-core but a villain . . . with the rest of the country." The columnists described Ford's rhetoric as out of touch with public and even Republican congressional sentiments, and noted the danger that the man who could become president might undermine his trustworthiness.[45] Indeed, Ford faced a dilemma. According to David Broder, Ford needed "to choose between his obligations as Richard Nixon's Vice President and his responsibilities as the likely next President of the United States."[46] And the *Washington Post* concurred that Ford faced "a tough choice between his duty to the American people and his obvious loyalty to and friendship with Richard Nixon."[47] And to Broder and the *Post*'s editors, Ford could only make one choice.

David Broder: As Sen. Robert C. Byrd (D-W.Va.) said . . . , "the Vice President ought to be preaching unity instead of division." It will be Ford's task to attempt the reconciliation of America after the most divisive experience since the Civil War. Knowing that, he cannot let any obligation stand higher.[48]

Washington Post: [I]f Mr. Ford does inherit the presidency . . . he would have as his first responsibility the highest priority of unifying a deeply divided and troubled America. . . . For Mr. Ford to continue on his current course is to undermine his own presidency in advance. . . . Lest Mr. Ford make the national crisis even graver than it already is, he would do well to leave the defense to Mr. St. Clair and such others as can be

43. David Broder, "Ford's Three Pitches," *Washington Post*, June 23, 1974, C6.
44. David Broder, "Ford's Conflicting Obligations," *Washington Post*, July 31, 1974, A20.
45. Rowland Evans and Robert Novak, "Ford: A Time for Independence?" *Washington Post*, August 1, 1974, A15.
46. Broder, "Conflicting Obligations," A20.
47. "Mr. Ford's Dilemma," *Washington Post*, August 1, 1974, A14.
48. Broder, "Conflicting Obligations," A20.

spared for the task. Mr. Ford's obligations are clearly to the higher cause of the nation.[49]

An Honest Man with Integrity

Journalists generally agreed, therefore, that Ford was an unspectacular choice to be vice president. According to the overwhelming early press consensus, Ford lacked stature and a record of clear leadership ability. Ford received generally mixed press reviews for his delicate "tightrope act"—being a loyal vice president to Richard Nixon and distancing himself from the Watergate scandal.

In one other sense there existed an overwhelming press consensus about Ford: he exhibited the unquestionable qualities of honesty and integrity. This view prevailed throughout Ford's vice presidency, despite journalists' criticisms of Ford's leadership skills and handling of Watergate. During the vice presidential confirmation hearings in Congress a number of journalists called for a favorable vote on Ford primarily because of his known qualities of honesty and integrity.

> *Chalmers M. Roberts*: No one is saying that Gerald Ford is an intellectual genius or that he has the ability to delve into and search out the answers to our current problems. . . . But most everyone expects that he would end the Oval Office isolation. . . . In short, there would be a change in the conduct of the office. But, above all, there would be a restored sense of integrity about the chief executive himself, as a person. And that is why, all other reasons aside, he should be confirmed as Vice President.[50]

> *David Broder*: Whatever his shortcomings, in intellect, oratory, or wit, Gerald Ford is one of the most decent human beings in Washington. . . . Ford does not let partisanship carry to the point of personal enmity. It is inconceivable that his office would compile an "enemies list." . . . What Ford would bring to such a government is the simplicity and honesty that have been missing so long from the White House.[51]

Editorial writers agreed with these assessments. The *Washington Post* found that Ford's strengths included "a record of personal and financial integrity, an open and forthcoming attitude, a real appreciation of congressional

---

49. "Ford's Dilemma," A14.

50. Chalmers M. Roberts, "The Integrity of Gerald Ford," *Washington Post*, December 1, 1973, A18.

51. David Broder, "Gerald Ford: Tradition and Civility," *Washington Post*, November 7, 1973, A24.

and public anxieties about the misuse of presidential power."[52] And the *Wall Street Journal* opined that "against any reasonable yardstick that may be applied to measure political honesty, Jerry Ford seems to qualify for relative sainthood."[53]

The day after the vice president was sworn into office, William Greider described Ford as "a plain man of comfortable familiarity, . . . a reliable lineman in a town where quarterbacks get the headlines." Greider assessed Ford's strongest quality as "the ability to marshal his troops without gathering an army of enemies."[54] Joseph Kraft agreed when he characterized Ford as a "clean turkey." According to Kraft's description of the clean turkey, "these are political figures beyond reproach on moral grounds. They are honorable, decent people of unstained character. Their family and professional backgrounds are wholesome. Unfortunately, they are limited by natural ability or experience."[55]

For the most part, journalists perceived Ford's unpretentiousness as an asset. Marjorie Hunter wrote that "Mr. Ford seems to be a rather uncomplicated man. He may not be brilliant but he is bright, and he is certainly hardworking and sincere. So sincere, in fact, that at times he seems to model his life on the Boy Scout manual. . . . [Ford] isn't stuffy. He can laugh at himself."[56] William S. White concurred that Ford lacked "glamour" and the ability to "wow them in Berkeley," yet "there is an awful lot of country in which a quietly competent, unstrident and strictly 'square' presidential candidate might look pretty good [in 1976]."[57] And four days prior to Nixon's resignation, James Reston praised Ford as "the same open, unspoiled character."[58]

Finally, according to the *Wall Street Journal*'s Fred L. Zimmerman, Ford's attributes carried over to the vice presidential staff.

> As a group, the Ford staff is a lot like the boss: loyal, hard-working, serious, self-effacing and not especially noted for brilliance. . . . It's hard to imagine the Ford men ever running wild, Watergate-style, and the Vice President already has taken steps aimed at preventing that. Mr. Ford's main problem with his staff . . . is more likely to be mediocrity than lawlessness.[59]

52. "The 25th Amendment and Mr. Ford," *Washington Post*, December 3, 1973, A24.

53. "Vice President Ford," *Wall Street Journal*, December 7, 1973, 12.

54. William Greider, "Integrity and Sincerity," *Washington Post*, December 7, 1973, A1, 14.

55. Joseph Kraft, "Political Leaders for '74," *Washington Post*, January 1, 1974, A23.

56. Hunter, "Ford: Loyalty," IV, 4.

57. William S. White, "Gerald Ford: The Man to Beat in '76," *Washington Post*, October 20, 1973, A19.

58. James Reston, "The New Model Fords," *New York Times*, August 4, 1974, IV, 17.

59. Fred L. Zimmerman, "The New Guard?" *Wall Street Journal*, July 10, 1974, 1.

Conclusion

In the public image arena, early impressions often have a lasting, if not irreversible, impact. Indeed, the early assessments of Gerald Ford by leading journalists contributed, in large part, to the creation of his public image as president. Ford clearly began his tenure as vice president with several press relations liabilities. First, his selection to the vice presidency came as a surprise to the leading journalists, who expected someone of "national stature" such as Barry Goldwater, Nelson Rockefeller, or John Connally. Nixon's selection of Ford confounded the leading journalists who already had decided that someone else was more qualified to become vice president. Having already anointed several other Republican leaders to the status of "qualified" candidates, journalists immediately defined Ford as a weak choice.

Second, Nixon's reputation as crafty, deceitful, and insecure fueled intense press speculation over the president's motives in choosing Ford. Journalists concluded that an insecure Nixon could not handle a strong-willed vice president of national stature.

Third, many leading journalists lacked substantive knowledge of Gerald Ford's political background. Nonetheless, given Nixon's unexpected vice presidential nomination combined with the pressures of time and competition, they created a slap-dash Ford portrait that drew heavily on political folklore—particularly the LBJ quip—and from Ford's reputation for strong partisanship as the Minority Leader of the House. Though incomplete, the initial portrait took on a life of its own through constant repetition.

Fourth, Ford served as vice president to an embattled president. Every vice president must deal with the problem of establishing his own identity without appearing disloyal to the president. Ford walked an even more treacherous tightrope: to fulfill his duty as vice president and not be associated with the scandals surrounding the Nixon White House. Nixon clearly made this task more difficult by not being straightforward with Ford about Watergate. Ford's longtime political adviser Robert Hartmann explained Ford's dilemma.

> Ford had been kept in the dark until about two days before President Nixon resigned. In fact, I'm not sure that Nixon ever did tell Ford that he was guilty. And Nixon didn't tell Ford of his resignation decision until about twenty-four hours in advance. Meanwhile, Ford had been out in public beating his brains out for Nixon telling everyone not to prejudge the President.[60]

Fifth, given the temper of the times—especially increased public and press skepticism toward politicians—any person selected to high national

---

60. Author interview with Robert Hartmann, Bethesda, Md., December 15, 1989.

office became "fair game" for intense scrutiny of every aspect of his or her life.

Despite these initial liabilities, Ford came to the presidency with an untarnished reputation for honesty and integrity. In an era of intense public skepticism toward political leadership, that asset became Ford's strongest card in the public image game. For a brief time, at least, Ford's untarnished reputation enabled him to rise above the less flattering aspects of his public persona.

CHAPTER 3

Transition to Power: A Brief Honeymoon

On August 8, 1974, citing a loss of his congressional base of support, Richard M. Nixon announced to a national television audience that he would resign from the presidency, effective at noon the next day. To a nation torn apart by the Watergate scandal, Nixon's resignation lifted a great burden. Gerald R. Ford assumed the presidency at noon on August 9, 1974.

Although he lacked an electoral mandate, Ford came to the presidency with a large reserve of goodwill. Indeed, Ford had some advantages in his efforts to appeal to the nation. First, he was not Richard M. Nixon. Second, Ford's reputation for honesty and integrity suited the needs of a nation left cynical by Watergate, yet eager to believe once again in political leadership. On the heels of the Watergate scandal and an unprecedented presidential resignation, Ford's political style played well not only with the public, but also with a press corps grown weary of conflict with the chief executive. Ford's counselor, Robert Hartmann, made the following comment.

> During the first part of his presidency there was a national euphoria, a honeymoon that the press helped to create, all stemming in part from the fact that Ford was not Nixon and that he was a much more likable personality meriting sympathy and support because of the difficult position he found himself in.[1]

As Richard M. Nixon offered his resignation, journalists evaluated Ford's leadership qualities and liabilities. At this early stage, journalists contrasted Nixon's leadership style and Ford's likely style, a contrast that always flattered Ford. Evans and Novak praised "Ford's new-style government" and "open door" leadership: "This is the death sentence for the royal attributes of the Nixon era with pervasive Oval Office political dominance and remoteness from both Republicans and Democrats on Capitol Hill."[2] *Washington Post* reporter Bob Kuttner assessed: "Certainly, no one expects Ford to conduct a

---

1. Author interview with Robert Hartmann, Bethesda, Md., December 15, 1989.
2. Rowland Evans and Robert Novak, "Ford's 'Open Door' Administration," *Washington Post*, August 8, 1974, A23.

regal, isolated Presidency."[3] A news item from *U.S. News and World Report* inquired about the kind of president Ford would make. "Answer: He'll be *frank, practical*—open to advice but making final decisions himself. *Reliability*, not brilliance, will be his hallmark." And, "the Presidency of Gerald Ford at least offers *a new start*. After months of crushing despair, most Americans will settle for that."[4] A *Washington Post* editorial declared that Ford opened his term with a dual advantage: being able to open a dialogue with people who had given up trying to deal with the Nixon White House and the credibility to address the public "and being believed."[5] Other commentaries expressed hope for a new era under Ford.

> *Vermont Royster*: . . . a Ford administration would try to give the country a time to breathe, a time to recuperate, a time to heal some wounds. . . . [Ford] is basically a friendly, outgoing man. This suggests that he will not retire into isolation, surrounding himself only with cronies and courtiers, the pitfalls of both our last two Presidents.[6]

> *Norman C. Miller*: Mr. Ford seems certain to conduct his presidency much differently from his predecessor. . . . Where Mr. Nixon was a loner who did his decision making in solitude, Mr. Ford is likely to seek out and listen closely to members of Congress and his administration before reaching decisions. . . . Where Mr. Nixon often was devious and secretive, Mr. Ford is direct and open. . . . The Ford White House isn't likely to be the closed, tightly controlled bureaucracy of the Nixon era.[7]

> *Time*: The resignation brought at least the unity of hope for a fresh beginning, and with Ford, the hope for a new style of presidential leadership. . . . Ford promises a new and welcome style in the White House, an openness and candor harking back perhaps to Truman or to the more amiable qualities of Eisenhower. The office will be shorn some of the pretentious Caesarism that has been growing 40 years, and of its imperial paraphernalia and edgy hauteur.[8]

---

3. Bob Kuttner, "Ford Facing Election-Year Legislation, Reforms," *Washington Post*, August 9, 1974, A10.

4. "Newsgram," *U.S. News and World Report*, August 19, 1974, 7–8; italics in the original.

5. "The Next President and Inflation," *Washington Post*, August 9, 1974, A30.

6. Vermont Royster, "What Kind of President Will He Be?" *Washington Post*, August 10, 1974, A22.

7. Norman C. Miller, "President Ford: New Chief to Adhere to Nixon's Programs, But Style Will Differ," *Wall Street Journal*, August 9, 1974, 1, 7.

8. "Time for Healing," *Time*, August 19, 1974, 8, 10.

Clearly journalists began the Ford years with high expectations. After the Watergate scandal, they demanded nothing less than an open, squeaky-clean White House. The Ford White House did nothing to downplay this expectation. The White House communications advisers interviewed for this study emphasized Ford's strategy of capitalizing on the opportunity to provide a strong contrast to the Nixon administration's operations. Hence, Ford chose as his press secretary a respected White House news correspondent, Jerald F. terHorst, in part to signal the administration's trust of and willingness to work closely with the press. In his public appearances and press contacts, Ford stressed the "openness" of his administration and the need for candor in government. The White House fashioned a number of symbolic changes—an informal inauguration, a reformed press conference format, a "fireside chat," and unpretentious White House social functions, just to name a few such innovations—to convey the themes of openness and candor.

Journalists also believed that Ford—despite being a highly partisan Republican and former House Minority Leader—would work constructively with the Democratic-controlled Congress. To these journalists, Ford's open and conciliatory leadership style promised to heal the executive-legislative rift that existed during the Johnson and Nixon years. Anticipating a Nixon impeachment or resignation, a May 27, 1974, *U.S. News and World Report* story assessed that if Ford became president,

> congressional leaders would be consulted more frequently. Mr. Ford . . . would try to take full advantage of the contacts he built up in more than a quarter of a century on Capitol Hill. . . . Roadblocking tactics by Congress, often employed now to embarrass President Nixon, probably would decline. At the outset, at least, Mr. Ford could look for more cooperation on the Hill.[9]

Once Ford became president, *U.S. News*'s assessment mirrored its earlier prediction.

> *Relations with Congress* will be Mr. Ford's strong suit. Lawmakers will be eager to display a spirit of unity in wake of the bitter impeachment fight. . . . Mr. Ford will draw on friendships made in both parties during his 25 years on Capitol Hill. . . . Result: The "honeymoon" of amiable relations between the White House and Congress could last until next spring—maybe even longer.

According to this news story, Ford possessed specific attributes conducive to establishing good legislative relations: a willingness to compromise and to

---

9. "The Nixon Crisis," *U.S. News and World Report*, May 27, 1974, 19–20.

forgo ideology, a keen knowledge of the legislative process, a desire for open consultation with legislators, and an unwillingness to use the veto power as anything more than "an unspoken threat."[10]

Other news stories corroborated the belief that Ford knew the legislative process well and would work effectively with Congress. Bob Kuttner wrote that "Ford, as a skilled legislator accustomed to the arts of legislative compromise, is likely to fill quickly the vacuum which developed during the White House preoccupation with Watergate."[11] *Wall Street Journal* Capitol Hill reporter Albert R. Hunt contended that, as a "longtime GOP House leader," Ford could expect cooperation with Congress on economic policy. Ford as well "enjoys a reservoir of 'goodwill,' which will make it easier to request sacrifices from business, labor and Congress."[12] Murray Marder wrote that, in foreign policy making, Ford held a "special advantage . . . his ability as a legislator to produce compromises for administration programs."[13] And *Time* magazine predicted that the Ford administration

> . . . should be able to develop once again a coherent legislative policy. The leftover Nixon legislative program is a shambles. There is no energy policy. Attempts at a foreign trade bill, welfare reform and land-use legislation have bogged down. In what promises to be a protracted honeymoon period, and the President undistracted by scandal, such programs can presumably be pushed forward again.[14]

Journalists expressed doubts about Ford's ability to exercise foreign policy leadership. In their view, twenty-five years in Congress did not provide sufficient experience for Ford to develop knowledge of international affairs and diplomacy. And following in the footsteps of Richard M. Nixon's masterful international diplomacy did little to enhance the press perception of Ford's capacity for international affairs leadership. Stephen S. Rosenfeld offered the following perspective.

> If Gerald Ford has credibility then he lacks experience, expertise or even a strong interest in foreign affairs. Unlike Richard Nixon, he has never

10. "Newsgram," *U.S. News and World Report*, August 19, 1974, 7–8.

11. Bob Kuttner, "Ford Facing Election-Year Legislation, Reforms," *Washington Post*, August 9, 1974, A10.

12. Albert R. Hunt, "Rx for Inflation: Ford Is Seen Taking Conservative Course in Aiding Economy," *Wall Street Journal*, August 12, 1974, 1. Hunt's colleague, columnist Lindley H. Clark, Jr., offered the opposing viewpoint that "Mr. Ford can look forward to a brief honeymoon with Congress. . . . Personal friends or not, the lawmakers are predominantly Democrats." See Lindley H. Clark, Jr., "Ford and the Economy," *Wall Street Journal*, August 12, 1974, 8.

13. Murray Marder, "Ford's Foreign Policy a Question, but Kissinger is for Sure," *Washington Post*, August 9, 1974, A22.

14. "Time for Healing," 9.

had a defined, if debatable, world view. He does not project a sense of realizing how difficult and painful the choices in foreign affairs are. And his honeymoon can't last long.[15]

A *Newsweek* report disputed Ford's self-assessment as an "internationalist" and instead characterized him as a "cold warrior." This report expressed reservations about "Ford's almost invisible profile on the world stage" and "the meager record of the new President's overseas travel." *Newsweek* did praise Ford's quick decision to allow Nixon's secretary of state, Henry Kissinger, to remain in office.[16] In fact, that decision received widespread praise from journalists concerned with Ford's capacity for conducting foreign policy. Murray Marder wrote:

> He is more of an unknown quantity globally than any incoming President since Harry S Truman. . . . The record is extremely sparse in supplying any clues about Ford's independent approach to world issues, beyond his constant support of Nixon administration policies. . . . [Keeping Kissinger signifies Ford's desire] to assure continuity in American foreign policy.[17]

Norman C. Miller added that keeping Kissinger as secretary of state "should tend to allay uneasiness about Mr. Ford's almost-total inexperience in foreign affairs."[18] A *U.S. News* report concurred: "Foreign affairs will get low priority—too many problems at home. Mr. Ford will rely on Henry Kissinger to carry on what's already under way."[19]

At this stage, the most negative press assessment of Ford's leadership ability concerned his intellect. Citing LBJ's quip that Ford couldn't walk and chew gum at the same time, a *Newsweek* report explained that "although Ford is decidedly more intelligent than reputed . . . he is not an idea man and has scant grounding in economics or foreign affairs."[20] Citing Jerome Cavanaugh's quip that Ford racked his brains by playing football without a helmet, *New York Times* reporter Israel Shenker commented: "No intellectual, he likes to think of himself as a devotee of sensible courses and determination rather than of originality and flair. . . . About Gerald R. Ford there is no wiff

---

15. Stephen S. Rosenfeld, " . . . And the Foreign Challenges Ahead," *Washington Post*, August 9, 1974, A30.

16. "Diplomacy: The New Model Ford," *Newsweek*, August 19, 1974, 62–63.

17. Marder, "Ford's Foreign Policy," A22.

18. Norman C. Miller, "President Ford: New Chief to Adhere to Nixon's Programs, But Style Will Differ," *Wall Street Journal*, August 9, 1974, 7.

19. "Newsgram," *U.S. News and World Report*, August 19, 1974, 8.

20. "The Once and Future Ford," *Newsweek*, August 19, 1974, 23.

of charisma."[21] Norman C. Miller described Ford as "a dull party work-horse," "an aggressive partisan," and "not an idea man."[22] Vermont Royster wrote that Ford, "the practicing politician," developed policy positions "more often from instinct than from profound analysis." Royster further stated that "it is . . . difficult to imagine him brooding alone in deep thought over either philosophical questions of government or over the complexities of economics or foreign policy. None of his long-time associates mark him as an 'intellectual' given to abstract analysis."[23] Lindley H. Clark, Jr., offered the commentary closest to defending Ford's brain power. "He doesn't come across as an intellectual, perhaps, but so far no certified moron has made it through Yale Law."[24]

The Presidential Inauguration and Transition

On August 9, 1974, after taking the presidential oath of office from Chief Justice Warren Burger, Gerald R. Ford spoke to the nation in an informal tone unprecedented in the history of presidential inaugurations. He called his remarks, "Not an inaugural address, not a fireside chat, not a campaign speech, just a little straight talk among friends." Ford's "talk" carefully addressed the sentiments of many Americans left cynical and angry toward government by Watergate.

> I believe that truth is the glue that holds government together, not only our government but civilization itself. That bond, though strained, is unbroken at home and abroad. In all my public and private acts as your President, I expect to follow my instincts of openness and candor with full confidence that honesty is always the best policy in the end. My fellow Americans, our long national nightmare is over. Our Constitution works. Our great Republic is a government of laws and not of men. Here, the people rule.[25]

To the leading journalists, Ford's speech suited the historic occasion perfectly. A *Washington Post* editorial said that Ford's speech "struck precisely the right tone. . . . His words, simple and candid, were a flawless response to an extremely difficult situation." The editorial declared Ford "in

21. Israel Shenker, "Ford a Traditionalist Who Believes in Home, Family, Hard Work and Patriotism," *New York Times*, August 9, 1974, 8.

22. Miller, "Ford: New Chief," 7.

23. Royster, "What Kind," A22.

24. Clark, "Ford and the Economy," 8.

25. Gerald R. Ford, *A Time to Heal* (Norwalk, Conn.: Easton Press, 1987), 40–41.

tune with the country as a whole. A man who deals in so open and honest a manner with the American people cannot fail to retain their support."[26]

The *New York Times*'s editorial on the inaugural speech also said that Ford "comes into office with a huge reservoir of personal good feeling that will constrain even his strongest political adversaries from opposing him." The *Times* added the following evaluation of Ford's speech.

> The simplicity with which Gerald R. Ford addressed the nation as he took the oath of office in the White House yesterday reflects the nature of this unpretentious man. . . . It also suggests the straightforwardness and the humility which may be expected to characterize Mr. Ford's [leadership] approach.[27]

George F. Will commented that the inaugural speech got Ford "off to a splendid start. . . . Like a Spanish galleon under full sail, President Ford is moving with imposing grace through the most difficult period in the history of American government."[28] *Washington Post* reporter William Greider also praised Ford's "straight talk among friends."

> In other times, Gerald Ford's expressions of old-fashioned virtue, honesty and the Golden Rule and a human prayer for help might be pushed aside as political boilerplate. Yesterday, people savored his words and thirsted to believe them. Yesterday, his level gaze and flat Midwestern voice seemed more dramatic than the loftiest rhetoric.[29]

The news weeklies also commented favorably on Ford's talk. *Time* complimented the "soothing, low-keyed speech" and said that "he delivered the kind of inaugural address that the U.S. surely needed—refreshingly candid, sincere, unpretentious and effectively crafted to ease national tension and clear the air of Watergate."[30] *Newsweek* reported that "the modest way Ford began his inaugural day echoed Thomas Jefferson's. . . . Ford's seven minute speech . . . had a gripping eloquence. . . . The promises were accordingly modest, the tone positively deferential."[31] And *U.S. News and World Report* concluded that "the Ford way of governing is clearly to be far different from

---

26. "The Transfer of Power," *Washington Post*, August 10, 1974, A22.

27. "President Ford," *New York Times*, August 10, 1974, 28.

28. George F. Will, "Ford's Search for No. 2," *Washington Post*, August 10, 1974, A23.

29. William Greider, "Plain-Spoken Promises and a Level Gaze," *Washington Post*, August 10, 1974, A1.

30. "The Transition: Enter Ford," *Time*, August 19, 1974, 10.

31. "Once and Future Ford," 23, 27.

the Nixon way. The difference was evident almost from the moment Mr. Ford took office on August 9."[32]

In the initial days after the inauguration, Ford emphasized what people most wanted to hear—that he truly meant to be an accessible and unpretentious chief executive. Given the unusual nature of the presidential transition, the Ford family could not move immediately into the White House residence. The Fords continued to live in their modest, northern Virginia suburban home (the vice presidential residence had not been completed in time for the Fords to occupy it). What a perfect opportunity to portray the president as just an ordinary guy. The day after the inauguration, journalists photographed Ford, pajama-clad, retrieving the early morning home-delivered *Washington Post* from the house's front stoop. Journalists then photographed Ford in the kitchen making his own breakfast. Richard Nixon wanted to clothe his White House guards in formal Prussian military uniforms. Gerald Ford showed that becoming president did not make him enamored of pretentious displays of power and authority. Even the president was not too important to carry out the mundane tasks of everyday life.

Ford adopted even more symbolic changes than I previously identified to convey the changes taking place in the government. Rather than refer to the White House living quarters as the "executive mansion" he chose the word *residence*. He renamed the presidential aircraft *Air Force One* (Nixon had changed it to *Spirit of '76*). Ford chose to have President Harry S Truman's portrait hang in the Cabinet Room because of Truman's reputation as the common man who became president. He also directed the White House band not to play "Ruffles and Flourishes" or "Hail to the Chief." Instead, Ford requested the "The Victors," the fight song of the University of Michigan.

Ford's actions may have been calculated, but they played enormously well with the press corps. Other Ford actions sent a positive message to the press and public. In his first official presidential appointment, Ford named *Detroit News* White House correspondent Jerald F. terHorst as press secretary. The selection of a leading member of the press corps had important symbolic meaning. And at 10:00 A.M. on August 10, President Ford held his first Cabinet meeting. Ford urged Cabinet members to adopt "affirmative" press relations, to be open and accessible to reporters. In the words of *Time* magazine, "It was a remarkable beginning—the beginning, perhaps, of a new style for the presidency."[33]

Many other news stories corroborated this view. *Washington Post* reporters Morton Mintz and Stuart Auerbach described Ford's first days as "a

---

32. "Ford Sets His Course," *U.S. News and World Report*, August 26, 1974, 17.
33. "The Transition," 13.

sharp change in atmosphere and style from the Nixon presidency."[34] A *U.S. News and World Report* article proclaimed in bold print: "It's more than a change in direction—it's also a fresh style—that the new President is bringing to the White House. The first days of Gerald Ford marked a striking departure from many of the Nixon ways and policies."[35] A report from *Newsweek* declared that Ford "brought his own square-cut, straight shooting political style with him, and it swept like a cornfield breeze through the Byzantine corridors of the Nixon White House."[36] Another *Newsweek* report declared that, beginning his term in office, "Ford showed a style that was open, relaxed and impressively self-confident. . . . Ford is a genuine conservative who has been appalled by what he considers to be the excesses of the last two Administrations."[37] The *Wall Street Journal* joined the chorus of praise for Ford. "In this role, Gerald Ford is perfectly cast. Plain. Earnest. Simply spoken . . . an ordinary man. . . . This is a time for stewardship, and Mr. Ford is a man for such times."[38] William V. Shannon noted that Ford's biggest asset "is that he is not Richard Nixon. . . . After so much demagoguery, his dullness is welcome. After so much nervously calculated insincerity, his complacency is comforting."[39] James Reston added another favorable commentary.

> Suddenly, the incessant anxiety and aloof, suspicious, intricate authority of the Nixon Administration has vanished, and something very plain, natural and straight has taken its place. The tone is different. . . . Gerald Ford has demonstrated the force of those principles of open discussion and moral example. His approach is different. His language is different. . . . Nothing fancy, nothing contrived, nothing concealed. . . . He is Main Street and not Madison Avenue.[40]

In the early days of his presidency, it seemed that, from a public relations standpoint, Ford could do no wrong. Time and again Ford made some gesture that demonstrated his differentness from Richard M. Nixon. In particular, Ford extended a welcome to groups shut out of Nixon's White House. Ford

---

34. Morton Mintz and Stuart Auerbach, "Ford Solicits Suggestions On No. 2 Man," *Washington Post*, August 11, 1974, A1, A9.

35. "Ford Sets His Course," 15.

36. "Seven Days in August," *Newsweek*, August 19, 1974, 14.

37. "Once and Future Ford," 23.

38. "President Ford," *Wall Street Journal*, August 12, 1974, 8.

39. William V. Shannon, "The Missing Conservative," *New York Times*, August 11, 1974, IV, 17.

40. James Reston, "Ford's Noble Beginning," *New York Times*, August 11, 1974, IV, 17.

met on one occasion with AFL-CIO leader George Meany, on another occasion with Congressional Black Caucus Chair Charles Rangel, and on a third with approximately three hundred senior appointive officials. The meetings symbolically contrasted with Nixon's refusal to meet labor and Congressional Black Caucus leaders and his efforts to control the bureaucracy. Ford also extended his "open administration" policy to members of Congress, a most important gesture in light of Nixon's efforts to deceive the legislature and impound funds for congressionally enacted programs.

On the evening of August 12, 1974, Ford addressed members of the Congress from the House chambers. The speech received an enormously favorable response from legislators and the press. *Newsweek* reported, in an article entitled "The Sun Is Shining Again," that "in the space of 32 minutes [Ford] reopened relations that had soured in the embittered last days of Lyndon Johnson and had nearly broken off in the Age of Nixon."[41] Once again, Ford responded most effectively to the expectations of his audience.

As President . . . my motto toward the Congress is communication, conciliation, compromise and cooperation. This Congress, unless it has changed, will be my working partner as well as my most constructive critic. I am not asking for conformity . . . I do not want a honeymoon with you. I want a good marriage. . . . My office door has always been open, and that is how it is going to be at the White House.

. . . there will be no illegal tapings, eavesdropping, buggings or break-ins by my Administration. There will be hot pursuit of tough laws to prevent illegal invasion of privacy.[42]

Ford drew enthusiastic applause for what *Time* called these "words of reassurance"[43] and for his professed commitments to the principles of the First Amendment, especially that of a free press. The televised address to Congress also drew enthusiastic press reviews. The *Washington Post* editorialized that Ford "clearly *knew* what Americans wanted to hear. . . . [A]n acknowledgement of what had happened and a pledge that it would not happen again. Mr. Ford has given it."[44] A *Wall Street Journal* news blurb noted that "even if he hadn't referred to Congress as 'co-equal in our constitutional process,' Ford by his warm tone toward his former colleagues would have signaled a reversal of his predecessor's often combative approach to Congress."[45] *Jour-*

---

41. "The Sun Is Shining Again," *Newsweek*, August 26, 1974, 17.
42. Ford, *Time to Heal*, 134.
43. "Gerald Ford: Off to a Fast, Clean Start," *Time*, August 26, 1974, 11–12.
44. "President Ford: A Return to Old Virtues . . . ," *Washington Post*, August 14, 1974, A16.
45. "World-Wide," *Wall Street Journal*, August 13, 1974, 1.

nal reporters Fred Zimmerman and James Gannon commented that "the tone of his address, and the warm manner in which his former congressional colleagues received him, showed that the long bitterness between the White House and Capitol Hill has ended, at least for now."[46] William Greider wrote that, because of the incivility between the White House and Congress during Nixon's administration, "the good humor of [Ford's] speech was almost as significant as the policy points he outlined."[47]

For four weeks after the presidential address to Congress, press plaudits for Ford's leadership continued unabated. Only a few hints of press criticism and negative comments surfaced at this time. Unimpressed with Ford's speech to Congress, *New York Times* reporter Clifton Daniel argued that "they probably would have cheered if he had read them a page from the telephone book." According to Daniel, Ford's speech lacked substance and did not depart enough "from the policies and plans of his discredited predecessor."[48] The editors of the *Wall Street Journal* thought that Ford could not rely on his penchant for compromise in order to lead Congress effectively.

> . . . there also has to be a sense of direction. . . . [Leadership] must come from the President, and the Executive branch must have a blueprint to sell or to impose upon Congress.[49]

> The new President is now in the best position he will ever be in to *create* political reality, to take a blueprint that would have been scorned even a week ago and have the people and the Congress take it seriously.[50]

The *Journal*'s Alan L. Otten asked, "Will the Congress that . . . so loudly applauded Mr. Ford's pledges to cut spending still applaud him when he vetoes some of its pet projects?"[51] Fred L. Zimmerman, though impressed by Ford's first few days as president, added that "whether the down-to-earth Ford style will help him solve tough economic and foreign-policy problems is another matter."[52] The *New York Times*'s Chalmers M. Roberts believed that, to be successful, Ford needed "to show leadership on policy matters." Could

---

46. Fred Zimmerman and James Gannon, "Ford Is Planning 'Summit' to Map War on Inflation," *Wall Street Journal*, August 13, 1974, 1.

47. William Greider, "Something Like a Family Reunion on the Hill," *Washington Post*, August 13, 1974, A1.

48. Clifton Daniel, "Ford's Speech: Same Priorities," *New York Times*, August 13, 1974, 21.

49. "The Dangers of Compromise," *Wall Street Journal*, August 14, 1974, 10.

50. "President Ford and Inflation," *Wall Street Journal*, August 13, 1974, 12.

51. Alan L. Otten, "Can He Do It?" *Wall Street Journal*, August 15, 1974, 10.

52. Fred L. Zimmerman, "In Washington Now, Some Hear 'Sound of Peacefulness,'" *Wall Street Journal*, August 19, 1974, 1.

Ford succeed? "The doubts about Mr. Ford have to do with his brains: Is he smart enough for the job?"[53] Columnists Evans and Novak also offered an uncertain judgment. "Thus besides turning the White House from paranoid hostility to candor and openness, the President must make policy changes. . . . Abandonment of traditional positions and innovation are distinctly out of character for Jerry Ford."[54]

In their largely laudatory articles on Ford's early days as president, the news weeklies also offered some hints of doubt about his leadership capabilities. *Time* magazine wondered "whether Ford offers anything more [than good character] for the most burdensome office in the world." This news article repeated the LBJ quip about Ford's intellect and reminded readers that "Ford's executive abilities have yet to be tested."[55] *Time* added that "some people worry that Ford's plodding, amiable ways and his eagerness for consensus may render him less than decisive in a national crisis."[56] *Newsweek* criticized the lack of "substantive detail" in Ford's first address to Congress and the new president's legislative program that "consisted largely of Nixon leftovers."[57] *U.S. News* only cited Ford's relatively "limited" experience in foreign affairs as a potential leadership liability.[58]

Despite these early indications that Ford's positive reputation among journalists might not last, the early rounds of press commentary hardly could have been more favorable. During the first two weeks of Ford's presidential term, journalists heaped praise on the new leadership for restoring integrity, trustworthiness, and openness to government. Consider this sampling of opinion from columnists featured in the *Washington Post*.

> *Chalmers M. Roberts*: Integrity has been restored to the White House. Gerald Ford's first days in office, especially his inaugural remarks and his first address to Congress, have heralded a total reversal of the secrecy, criminality and introversion of the Nixon years.[59]

---

53. Chalmers M. Roberts, "Under President Ford: A Return to Normalcy?" *Washington Post*, August 15, 1974, A28.

54. Rowland Evans and Robert Novak, "How Tough Is Gerald Ford?" *Washington Post*, August 12, 1974, A23.

55. "The New President: A Man for this Season," *Time*, August 19, 1974, 27.

56. "New President," 33.

57. "Sun Is Shining," 17.

58. "What Ford Will Do As President," *U.S. News and World Report*, August 19, 1974, 17. Some news stories speculated that Ford ultimately would be judged by how well he handled the national economy. These stories suggested that Ford might not be up to the task. See "Seeking Relief from a Massive Migraine," *Time*, September 9, 1974, 22–27; "Ford Confronts Public Enemy No.1," *Newsweek*, August 19, 1974, 64–66.

59. Roberts, "Under Ford," A28.

David Broder: Jerry Ford is the most normal, sane, down-to-earth individual to work in the Oval Office since Harry Truman left. . . . Every instinct in his bones and in his midwestern background rebels against the idea of an "imperial presidency."[60]

Tom Braden: He comes to us in pristine straightness. One can no more imagine him accepting substantial gifts as Eisenhower did than one can imagine him sitting in the White House planning how to misuse independent agencies as Nixon did.[61]

The commentaries of three *Wall Street Journal* reporters corroborate these assessments.

Alan L. Otten: He is a man of integrity. He will work closely and cordially with Congress. He likes a loose, free wheeling staff. He enjoys contact with people, even reporters. He is not a hater; an enemies list is unthinkable in a Ford White House. . . . A proud product of Capitol Hill, Mr. Ford will always be more ready than some of his predecessors to meet with members of Congress, listen to them, compromise with them.[62]

Fred L. Zimmerman: The contrast with the always suspicious and mean-spirited—and finally siege-like—mentality of the Nixon White House couldn't be greater. . . . Richard Nixon's "imperial presidency" of pomp, closed doors, yes-men and executive fiat has vanished in favor of informality, openness and receptivity to a variety of viewpoints.[63]

Vermont Royster: . . . there is something refreshing in the picture of the President of the United States bending over his front stoop to pick up the morning paper and bustling in the kitchen to fix his own breakfast. . . . To most people Gerald Ford represents the hope of a new day.[64]

The three news weeklies presented similar adulatory reviews of Ford's opening weeks in office. *Newsweek* praised Ford's "de-Nixonization" of the government and reviewed the new president's early symbolic activities.

---

60. David Broder, "Giving Mr. Ford a Chance," *Washington Post*, August 14, 1974, A16.

61. Tom Braden, "Welcome to the White House," *Washington Post*, August 17, 1974, A19.

62. Otten, "Can He Do It?" 10.

63. Zimmerman, "In Washington Now," 1.

64. Vermont Royster, "Ford's Problems," *Wall Street Journal*, August 14, 1974, 10.

"Ford's young Presidency was open where Nixon's was insular, straight where Nixon's was devious, plain where Nixon's was imperial, and above all cheery where Nixon's had gone sullen under its long siege."[65] *Time* magazine acknowledged that Ford benefited in press relations by highlighting the differences between his administration's and Nixon's. "To the press, the turnover in the Oval Office already seems like the dawn of a new era, free of the rancor of the Nixon years."[66] *Time* added the following assessment.

> Journalists, who found themselves suddenly popular at the White House again, rejoiced at the minutiae of the New Administration. . . . Gone was the public hostility of yesterday as Nixon's presidency foundered; now there was a new President, totally contrasting in manner, mien and style from his predecessor. . . . Good sense, perspective and proportion were back in fashion.[67]

U.S. News also praised the "new style of openness and informality that Gerald Ford brought to the White House." Impressed by Ford's fast-paced first days in office, the *U.S. News* reporter added that, "At the same time, he kept demonstrating that he was a man—like Harry Truman—with 'the common touch.'"[68]

During these early days of the presidential term, Ford drew favorable press commentaries for proposing a domestic "summit" on the national economy and for publicly rebuking a proposed General Motors price increase of 9.5 percent on 1975 automobiles. The domestic "summit" certainly appeared more symbolic than substantive. And General Motors responded to Ford's rebuke by cutting the price increase to 8.5 percent. Ford later recalled, "Hardly a major victory, but it was significant psychologically."[69] Nonetheless, these presidential initiatives came at a time when Ford seemed to be rewarded with favorable reviews by journalists merely for showing up to work each day.

In the first two weeks of Ford's presidency, no news story received as much attention as the selection of a vice presidential nominee. By the end of

---

65. "Sun Is Shining," 16.

66. "Off to a Helluva Start," *Time*, August 26, 1974, 52.

67. "Ford: Fast, Clean Start," 9–10.

68. "First Whirlwind Week in the White House," *U.S. News and World Report*, August 26, 1974, 18.

69. Ford, *Time to Heal*, 135. For example, the *Washington Post* commented that "President Ford is now moving rapidly and effectively to change that national climate of pessimism. . . . President Ford gave General Motors a well-deserved rap on the knuckles. . . . Mr. Ford is showing a very nice set of orderly tactics" (" . . . And a Summit at Home," *Washington Post*, August 14, 1974, A16). *U.S. News* reported that the GM rebuke proved that Ford "can get tough" when he needs to ("First Whirlwind Week," 18).

his first week in office, Ford had narrowed the list of prospective candidates to five. The individuals under consideration included Republican National Committee Chairman George Bush, former chairman Rogers Morton, House Minority Leader John Rhodes, Tennessee Senator Bill Brock, and former New York governor Nelson Rockefeller. The two leading candidates were Bush and Rockefeller. Ford makes clear in his memoirs that Bush appeared to be the strongest candidate, yet the GOP chairman carried the baggage of holding a highly partisan and visible office during a time in which the president needed to eschew partisanship, to the extent possible, in major decisions.[70] Ford selected Rockefeller, a choice that won plaudits from just about everyone except movement conservatives who had never liked the progressive and feisty New Yorker.

The Rockefeller selection provided an interesting contrast to Nixon's vice presidential selection of Gerald Ford. Nixon, recall, received widespread criticism for the selection of a man who lacked both national stature and a reputation for executive leadership. In contrast, Rockefeller, a giant on the national political scene, could claim substantial executive experience. Ford wrote in his memoirs that some of his staff viewed Rockefeller as "too strong" for such a position as the vice presidency. "That didn't worry me. . . . If Rockefeller was strong, that was all to the good. What the country needed was not just the image but the substance of strength."[71]

The press obviously agreed. The *Wall Street Journal* praised the selection of "a man of national stature," a person whose major virtue was his qualification to be president rather than loyalty to President Ford. "It is reassuring to the nation to have a known quantity as Vice President, and doubly reassuring to learn that a less known President makes his selection on the grounds that the selection bespeaks."[72] The *New York Times* said: "Above all, Mr. Ford's choice of Nelson Rockefeller for Vice President was not only right in that it brought to the office a man of Presidential caliber; it was also a masterly political act."[73] Columnist R. W. Apple, Jr., asserted that Ford's selection of Rockefeller "completes a reversal of national political tides of potentially historic proportions. . . . Republican office-seekers can identify themselves with a popular new President, a pervasive spirit of renewal and candor in the capital and a politically dynamic Vice-President designate."[74] Marquis Childs agreed that Republican party fortunes had improved dramatically with a potential Ford-Rockefeller ticket in 1976 and that Ford had proved "his indepen-

---

70. Ford, *Time to Heal*, 143.
71. Ford, *Time to Heal*, 143.
72. "Mr. Ford Gets Rolling," *Wall Street Journal*, August 21, 1974, 8.
73. "Political Turnaround," *New York Times*, August 25, 1974, IV, 8.
74. R. W. Apple, Jr., "A Turn in G.O.P. Tide," *New York Times*, August 21, 1974, 1.

dence" from ideological and partisan considerations.[75] *Newsweek* applauded Ford's selection, one that allegedly marked

> . . . a profound further shift in the face of American government, and American politics as well. The nomination gave Ford a manifestly well-qualified heir apparent. . . . It brought Ford's homespun Presidency a dash of glamour, a dollop of high style and a direct line to the Rockefeller lode of cash, connections and brainpower.[76]

And *Time* described the choice of Rockefeller as "an indication of [Ford's] own political maturity. A less secure President might have been fearful of naming so dynamic a personality."[77]

Soon after the nomination of Rockefeller to be vice president, journalists contributed more adulatory commentary to the already substantial favorable opinion about the new leadership. A sampling of typical headlines from editorials, opinion columns, and news stories partially conveys the prevailing press view.

> "Ford Seems to Be a Man in Tune With the Times"
> "A Natural Force on a National Stage"
> "Political Turnaround"
> "Mr. Ford's Open Door"
> "Notes From an Open White House"
> "So Like the Rest of America"
> "A Sure Touch in Ford's Second Week"

More revealing still is the content of these news and opinion pieces. *Newsweek* noted that "Nixon's resignation and Ford's surprisingly surefooted beginnings have in fact altered the American political calculus. . . . The first days of Jerry Ford have been an uncontested hit."[78] The *New York Times* claimed that "the country's political prospects—to say nothing of its morale—have undergone a dramatic transformation."[79] In two weekly columns, *Time*'s Hugh Sidey added the following.

75. Marquis Childs, "Prospects for the Ford Team," *Washington Post*, August 31, 1974, A17.

76. "Striking It Rich," *Newsweek*, September 2, 1974, 14; see also James Reston, "Rocky's Rocky Road," *New York Times*, December 20, 1974, 37; "Rockefeller: New Kind of Vice President," *U.S. News and World Report*, September 2, 1974, 12–13.

77. "A Natural Force on a National Stage," *Time*, September 2, 1974, 14.

78. "Striking It Rich," 14–15.

79. "Political Turnaround." The *Times* also praised Ford's meeting with Congressional Black Caucus members as "a refreshing departure" from the Nixon years ("Mr. Ford's Open Door," *New York Times*, August 24, 1974, 24).

The transformation is doing so well, not from mystique but from candor, not from majesty but from plainness. It is everything in those manuals of authority used by Lyndon Johnson and Richard Nixon turned upside down. Ford's first days look like genius because they are so ordinary, so like the rest of America. . . . The adjectives for all this have been extravagant: new wine, fresh breeze, clean broom.[80]

Everywhere there was the feeling that the American presidency was back in the possession of the people.[81]

U.S. News and World Report observed that the Ford presidency marked an end to "conspicuous opulence" in White House social affairs.[82] *Time* magazine was impressed with Ford's "low-key," lack of fanfare announcement that Nelson Rockefeller was his vice presidential nominee, a major contrast with "the East Room extravaganza that Nixon staged for the announcement of Ford as his nominee for Vice President."[83] And *Washington Post* reporter Carroll Kilpatrick wrote that

the contrast between Mr. Ford and his immediate predecessor is staggering, and that may be the principal reason he has so quickly won the plaudits of Congress, the press and Main Street, U.S.A. Now candor and relaxation are words in common usage again.[84]

Newsweek singled out Ford's first press conference on August 28 to emphasize the stylistic differences with Nixon's presidency.

He walked on-camera with no grand entrance, no Pan-Cake makeup, no studio-style backdrop, and above all none of that mutual suspicion that had poisoned relations between President and press in the unhappy years past. . . . [Ford] got across his real message: the further evidence, if more was needed, that he is not Richard Nixon.[85]

---

80. Hugh Sidey, "So Like the Rest of America," *Time*, September 2, 1974, 23.

81. Hugh Sidey, "Notes From an Open White House," *Time*, August 26, 1974, 16.

82. "With New First Family, Style in White House is Changing," *U.S. News and World Report*, September 2, 1974, 15–16.

83. "A Sure Touch in Ford's Second Week," *Time*, September 2, 1974, 11.

84. Carroll Kilpatrick, "Ford Seems to Be a Man in Tune With the Times," *Washington Post*, August 25, 1974, A4.

85. "Touching All the Bases," *Newsweek*, September 9, 1974, 21. The *Wall Street Journal* editorialized that Ford gave an impressive performance, demonstrating the "scope and depth" of his thinking "and the evolving directions of policy." *Time* magazine reported that Ford "seemed relaxed and self-assured" and liked his "informal tone" and dispensing of Nixonian "trappings" ("Ford: Plain Words Before an Open Door," *Time*, September 9, 1974, 11).

This reaction is exactly what Ford and his press secretary, Jerald terHorst, had hoped for. At terHorst's urging, Ford made a number of changes in the press conference format to facilitate a more congenial atmosphere. Ford replaced Nixon's formidable podium with a simpler lectern. The president had the pretentious blue-curtain backdrop that Nixon used removed. Ford spoke from the side of the White House East Room where he could stand in front of an open hallway.[86] As Robert Hartmann commented, the purpose of this innovation was to "have the President stand in the door to give the television a sense of openness, and you looked down the hall of the White House, watched him walk in to the press conference, and I think it did have that effect."[87] *Newsweek* concluded that, with this press conference, Ford had "completed his own disassociation from the Nixon past."[88]

Conclusion: Ford's Association with "the Nixon Past"

Newsweek's reporter failed to recognize that this first presidential press conference would play a crucial role in Ford's reassociation with the Nixon past. Beyond the symbolism of the press conference that earned Ford more press plaudits, the substantive matters raised by reporters had a more compelling impact on his presidency.

Ford entered the press conference expecting a variety of questions on substantive domestic and foreign policy issues. That expectation proved unrealistic. Despite all of the press adulation over Ford's first month in office, journalists still wanted to focus on the fate of former president Nixon. Helen Thomas of the United Press International put the first question, asking Ford about the issue of immunity for Nixon. Subsequent questions also addressed Ford's views on the legal controversy over Nixon's White House tapes, the prospects for a presidential pardon, and other Watergate-related matters. Ford commented in his memoirs that "I was disappointed by the questions that were raised. The White House press corps didn't seem interested in finding out how I planned to deal with the substantive issues that confronted me. They just wanted to know what I was going to do about Nixon, and I thought they had wasted my time."[89]

Despite this disappointment, Ford acknowledged that the reporters' questions "forced me to address the issue squarely for the first time."[90] This press

---

86. Ford, *Time to Heal*, 156–57.
87. Hartmann interview.
88. "Touching All the Bases," 21.
89. Ford, *Time to Heal*, 158.
90. *Ford, Time to Heal*, 159.

conference made Ford realize that the Nixon issue would not go away and that much of his time in office would be devoted to that issue unless he took some forthright action. Less than two weeks after his first press conference, President Ford made a most forthright decision regarding Nixon's fate, a decision that dramatically changed Ford's press relations and profoundly altered the course of his presidency.

CHAPTER 4

The Nixon Pardon and the Fall from Grace

The President . . . shall have power to grant reprieves and pardons for offenses against the United States, except in cases of impeachment.
—U.S. Constitution, Article II, Section 2

Now, therefore, I, Gerald R. Ford, President of the United States, pursuant to the pardon power conferred upon me by Article II, Section 2, of the Constitution, have granted and by these presents do grant a full, free and absolute pardon unto Richard Nixon for all offenses against the United States which he, Richard Nixon, has committed or may have committed or taken part in during the period from January 20, 1969 through August 9, 1974.
—Pardon proclamation of President Ford, September 8, 1974

From a public relations standpoint President Ford achieved great success during his first four weeks in office. Robert Hartmann is correct in his assessment that the White House press corps initially loved President Ford for not being Richard Nixon. But, undoubtedly, Ford won the respect and admiration of the press and public by employing a conscious strategy to have himself presented as a "people's president." This is not to suggest that Ford concocted a slick, phony public relations image. He did not. Instead, he adopted a public relations strategy that suited his own personality, leadership style, and public persona.

The press and public favorably received Ford's efforts to lead an "open" administration. They loved his sense of humor and ability not to take himself too seriously. They perceived his use of political symbolism and frank rhetoric as an important antidote to the effects of the Nixon years, particularly the increase in public cynicism toward government.

Despite these early successes, Ford's public and press standing stood on thin ice. Beneath the surface of the adulatory reviews for Ford's first weeks in office remained a very large reserve of cynicism toward public leaders and institutions. And there remained, particularly within the press corps, an underlying perception of Gerald Ford—formed in his prepresidential years—as a not very intelligent, petty partisan who lacked a leadership vision. An unpopular decision by Ford, a further downturn in the economy, or some other perceived presidential "failure" promised to revive such cynicism and the earlier, negative views of Ford's leadership ability.

In fact, a single, unexpected presidential action—the unconditional pardon of Richard M. Nixon—undermined Ford's reserve of goodwill and image as a politician "indebted to no man." On Sunday morning, September 8, 1974, President Ford issued his pardon proclamation and declared that the unlikelihood that Nixon could obtain a fair trial until considerable time had lapsed justified the pardon. Ford explained that "bringing to trial a former President of the United States" would disrupt the national "tranquility."[1]

The public responded to the pardon swiftly, negatively, and severely. Within one hour of the announcement, phone calls running eight to one against the pardon inundated the White House switchboards.[2] The Gallup Poll reflected a sixteen point decline—from 66 to 50 percent—in the president's public approval rating after the pardon announcement.[3] Ford's press secretary, Jerald F. terHorst, resigned in protest, a most damaging decision for the president given terHorst's popularity with the White House press corps.

Press Reaction to the Pardon

Ironically, by pardoning Richard M. Nixon, President Ford had adopted the kind of decisive, "take charge" action of which many of his critics believed he was not capable. Yet more than anything else that Ford did as president, this one decision influenced the press and public perceptions of his leadership. The pardon of Richard M. Nixon ended President Ford's honeymoon with the press, public, and political Washington. With a single presidential proclamation, the national political landscape had changed fundamentally. TerHorst later recalled the reaction to the pardon.

> What [Ford] had portrayed as an act of mercy for a broken man was bitterly attacked as a betrayal of justice, even as a "deal" secretly arranged in advance with Nixon. Newspapers, network commentators, and private citizens from coast to coast expressed their outrage and dismay. Instead of encouraging the healing process as he had hoped, Ford had reopened the Watergate wound and rubbed salt into the public nerve ends thus exposed.[4]

---

1. Gerald R. Ford, quoted in John D. Feerick, "The Pardoning Power of Article II of the Constitution," *New York State Bar Journal* 47 (January 1975): 8.

2. Jerald F. terHorst, *Gerald Ford and the Future of the Presidency* (New York: Joseph Okpaku Publishing, 1974), 222–23.

3. Clifton Daniel, "Ford's Gallup Rating Off 21 Points after Pardon," *New York Times*, October 13, 1974, A1.

4. TerHorst, *Gerald Ford*, 222.

TerHorst's description of the newspaper, network, and public reactions to the pardon is unarguable. Whether Ford would have fared better with his critics over the course of his term by either offering the pardon at another date or not giving a pardon to Nixon cannot reliably be determined. Nonetheless, the White House communications advisers interviewed for this study emphasized the difficulties they experienced trying to handle this presidential action from a public relations perspective. Only a few people in the White House knew prior to the pardon proclamation that Ford had decided to consider a pardon for Nixon. Ford did not include anyone from the press office in the decision-making process. The press people had no insight into Ford's thinking on the matter, yet they had to explain it to the media. The terHorst resignation left an acting press secretary, John Hushen, suddenly to carry the weight of handling a press corps as puzzled and surprised about the decision as he was.

The immediate press reaction to the pardon could hardly have been more negative. The *New York Times*'s editorial responses to that decision provide a good measure of how strongly press opinion ran against President Ford. Between September 9 and 12, the *Times* featured five editorials denouncing the pardon! The first of these editorials (September 9), entitled "The Failure of Mr. Ford," deserves to be quoted at length.

> In giving former President Nixon an inappropriate and premature grant of clemency, President Ford has affronted the Constitution and the American system of justice. It is a profoundly unwise, divisive and unjust act. . . . President Ford has failed in his duty to the Republic, made a mockery of the claim of equal justice before the law, promoted renewed public discord, made possible the clouding of the historic record, and undermined the humane values he sought to invoke. . . . President Ford speaks of compassion. It is tragic that he had no compassion and concern for the Constitution and the Government of law that he has sworn to uphold and defend. He could probably have taken no single act of a noncriminal nature that would have more gravely damaged the credibility of this Government in the eyes of the world and of its own people than this unconscionable act of pardon. . . . This blundering intervention is a body blow to the President's own credibility and to the public's reviving confidence in the integrity of its Government.[5]

The other *Times* editorials lambasted the pardon. The September 10 editorial, "Pardon For What?" expressed the following view. "There are too many mysterious circumstances surrounding the decision for anyone to have

---

5. "The Failure of Mr. Ford," *New York Times*, September 9, 1974, 34.

confidence that the whole story is out."[6] A September 11 editorial, "Nightmare Compounded," criticized the "untimely" nature of the pardon.[7] A second editorial on that day, "Growing Dossier," offered more criticism. "Hopes for an 'open Presidency,' marked by candor and forthrightness, threaten to become casualties of Mr. Ford's mishandling of the Watergate aftermath."[8] The September 12 editorial, "Back to Politics," denounced the pardon as "premature" and added that "the candor and forthrightness that were so refreshing in the first days of the Ford Administration have now vanished in fog, with public statements becoming inoperative almost as soon as they are issued."[9]

The *Times*'s editorials raised all of the important arguments against the pardon made by the leading national journalists: the pardon (1) undermined the concept "equal justice under the law"; (2) revived public cynicism toward government, thus it destroyed the progress Ford had made in building public confidence in government; (3) proved Ford to be no different than his predecessors; (4) associated Ford with the Watergate controversy; (5) turned out to be an ill-timed, clumsily handled decision; (6) revived speculation of a "deal" between Nixon and Ford.

"Equal Justice Under the Law"

In an article reviewing reactions to the pardon of Richard M. Nixon, *Time* magazine observed that "most critics complained that Ford's action had dealt a devastating blow to the idea that the poorest citizen is equal to a President— or former President—under the laws."[10] This assessment is confirmed by a review of press commentary, including *Time*'s.

> The issue is not whether Nixon has suffered enough. Indisputably, he has suffered, but so have countless other people who have committed wrongdoings—and they have not been exempted from prosecution. Nixon will be free and well pensioned, while those who took his orders are jailed and broken.[11]

The press critics of the pardon included, among others, George F. Will: "Americans will have to eat more bread now that President Ford has drained the nutritional value from the catchwords about 'equal justice under the law.'"[12]

---

6. "Pardon For What?" *New York Times*, September 10, 1974, 40.
7. "Nightmare Compounded," *New York Times*, September 11, 1974, 44.
8. "Growing Dossier," *New York Times*, September 11, 1974, 44.
9. "Back to Politics," *New York Times*, September 12, 1974, 38.
10. "Reaction: Is the Honeymoon Over?" *Time*, September 16, 1974, 12.
11. "The Pardon That Brought No Peace," *Time*, September 16, 1974, 12.

Anthony Lewis concurred that, "in a sudden and ill-considered gesture, [President Ford] has frustrated the process of law and the Constitution. The damage to his own hopes will be grave, perhaps irreparable."[13] And a *Newsweek* reporter thought that the pardon "revived the Watergate furies, raised the most profound and disturbing questions about the equal application of justice and abruptly ended Ford's brief honeymoon with Congress and the nation."[14]

A Honeymoon Ended, Cynicism Revived

According to a *U.S. News and World Report* news story, Ford's pardon of Richard M. Nixon "shattered the national euphoria that had been created by [President Ford's] accession—and squandered much of the goodwill he brought with him to the White House."[15] News stories in the other weekly news magazines articulated similar viewpoints.

> *Newsweek*: American justice has survived worse affronts, and can probably weather this one. But the process of political healing that Ford so earnestly sought in his Presidency may be another matter. At a stroke, he not only ended his political honeymoon but called his own good faith into question.[16]

> *Time*: By taking such sweeping action so soon, Ford damaged his efforts to restore confidence in the U.S. presidency and opened his own credibility gap. . . . Of course, nothing will be easy now, and the furor promises to be intense.[17]

> The Nixon pardon [raised] far graver questions about "the credibility of our free institutions" than would a proper and probably illuminating trial. One of the few consolations in the entire Watergate affair had been that those institutions had persevered against the most calculated cover-up efforts of the highest official in the land; now the judicial process was being aborted in Nixon's favor. . . . In the understandable concern shown by Gerald Ford over Nixon's personal fate, the larger national interest was submerged.[18]

---

12. George F. Will, " . . . Who Has Eroded Respect for Law . . . ," *Washington Post*, September 10, 1974, A21.

13. Anthony Lewis, "The System Scorned," *New York Times*, September 9, 1974, 35.

14. "Was Justice Done?" *Newsweek*, September 16, 1974, 19.

15. "Worries Pile Up For Ford," *U.S. News and World Report*, September 30, 1974, 18.

16. "Was Justice Done?" 23.

17. "Pardon Brought No Peace," 10–11.

18. "The Fallout From Ford's Rush to Pardon," *Time*, September 23, 1974, 14, 22.

A *Washington Post* editorial said that public erosion of confidence in government could "only have been compounded by President Ford's premature pardon of Mr. Nixon."[19] Joseph Kraft agreed, "The sad thing about President Ford's mishandling of the Nixon pardon is that he has blown a big opportunity to end what he called the long, national nightmare. We are now in for a new orgy of moralistic recrimination and corrosive suspicion."[20] Anthony Lewis concluded that "the result must be the opposite of what he hoped for America: More rancor, more division, more cynicism about government and the law."[21]

"Just One of the Boys"

To some journalists, the pardon of Richard M. Nixon proved Ford to be no different than other politicians: no more decent, no more honest, just another crafty and deceitful person. For a president who had worked so ably to project the values of decency and honesty, this assessment proved most damaging. In George F. Will's devastating indictment, "The English Muffin Theory is now just another theory killed by a fact." Will added the following commentary.

> That theory was that a President who toasts his own English muffins for breakfast is somehow different from the general cut of politicians. The lethal fact is that Mr. Ford now has demonstrated that he is just one of the boys: he doesn't mean what he says. . . . [T]he effect of his precipitate action appears rather like the effect of what used to be called, in less polite times, a coverup.[22]

Joseph Kraft likewise thought that "the President is now seen for what he is—an ordinary pol who cannot be deeply trusted, even if he does make his own breakfast."[23] *Time* concurred with both Will and Kraft. "Undermined, too, was the pleasant notion that Ford, a direct, uncomplicated Midwesterner who used to prepare his own breakfast, is wholly unlike those crafty politicians who maneuver for personal prestige and luxuries during careers on either coast."[24]

---

19. "The Presidential Pardon," *Washington Post*, September 10, 1974, A20.

20. Joseph Kraft, "Prolonging the National Nightmare . . . ," *Washington Post*, September 12, 1974, A15.

21. Lewis, "System Scorned," A21.

22. Will, "Eroded Respect," A21.

23. Joseph Kraft, "Gerald Ford: 'An Ordinary Pol' . . . ," *Washington Post*, September 10, 1974, A21.

24. "The Fallout," 13.

The Nixon-Watergate Association

As vice president, Gerald Ford received ample press criticism for defending President Nixon against Watergate-related charges. According to many journalists, by defending Nixon publicly, Ford moved dangerously close to becoming associated with the Watergate controversy. In his first four weeks as president, Ford effectively removed the taint of Watergate from himself. The pardon of Richard M. Nixon changed that. As Anthony Lewis argued, "When he became President, he seemed to understand so well the need to separate himself from the horrors of the immediate past. Now, just a few weeks later, he gives every sign of having lost that understanding."[25] *Newsweek* said that Ford undermined the public's faith in our institutions to survive the scandal and that he "had embraced the demon of Watergate."[26] Joseph Kraft added that "the goal of exorcising the Watergate demon remains. Only now it will be a slower process."[27] R. W. Apple, Jr., wrote that Ford "reidentified himself" and the Republican party with Nixon and Watergate.[28] The *Washington Post* editorialized that Ford had "revived and prolonged," rather than ended, "the Watergate anguish" by pardoning Nixon.[29] Marquis Childs added that the pardon gave "new life to the whole Watergate horror" and ended Ford's "new era of cooperation."[30] And according to *Time*,

> Ford's first major decision raised disturbing questions about his judgment and his leadership capabilities, and called into question his competence. He had apparently needlessly, even recklessly, squandered some of that precious public trust that is so vital to every President. By associating himself so personally with the welfare of his discredited predecessor, he had allowed himself to be tainted by Watergate. . . . It was obvious that Ford, by pardoning Nixon, had failed to achieve his professed desire to end "the bad dreams" of Watergate.[31]

Ill-Timed, Poorly Handled Decision

The timing of Ford's pardon and his method of announcing the decision in a way that surprised nearly everyone angered many critics. The Ford admin-

25. Anthony Lewis, "It's Up to Congress," *New York Times*, September 9, 1974, 43.

26. "Was Justice Done?" 23.

27. Kraft, "National Nightmare," A15.

28. R. W. Apple, Jr., "Cost of Ford's Decision," *New York Times*, September 10, 1974, 28.

29. "The Unfinished Business," *Washington Post*, September 13, 1974, A26.

30. Marquis Childs, " . . . And Reopened the Watergate Scandals," *Washington Post*, September 10, 1974, A21.

31. "The Fallout," 11–12.

istration did nothing to prepare the press for this momentous decision. In fact, in an earlier press conference, Ford had created the unmistakable impression that a possible pardon of Nixon was not on his agenda. Caught off guard, leading journalists responded harshly, denouncing both the pardon and Ford's handling of that decision, including his inability to secure a true statement of contrition from Nixon as a condition for the pardon. *Newsweek* wrote that "Ford seemed to have stampeded himself into a badly timed decision. . . . That Gerald Ford is no superman was bound to come out sooner or later. But both he and the country could have used a longer period free of fresh trauma."[32] A number of the press office staffers interviewed for this study said that Ford made a mistake by convincing the press and public at a press conference that he would not pardon Nixon and then issuing the pardon soon after without any effort to alert people to the decision. They said that Ford had thereby generated comparisons to the Nixon White House, although Ford had worked so hard to prove that the new administration was different.

Some journalists, indeed, thought that Ford's tactics looked Nixonian. In Joseph Kraft's words, "the President acted in a hugger-mugger, hole-in-the-corner fashion. . . . It looked almost like a replay of Mr. Nixon's favorite tactic of government by bombshell."[33] Anthony Lewis wrote similarly.

> What made the pardon so damaging to Mr. Ford . . . was the way it was done: suddenly, secretly, with the minimum of consultation or concern for law. The failure to get any admission of wrongdoing in exchange for the pardon left an aching sense of illegitimacy.[34]

Other journalists thought that the handling of the pardon decision displayed ineptitude and undermined Ford's ability to lead effectively. According to the *Washington Post*,

> Mr. Ford has had his Bay of Pigs . . . : an early and monumental blunder, born of miscalculation, ingenuousness, and a considerable degree of self-indulgent and unpresidential impulsiveness on the part of a new and untested President.[35]

> By acting prematurely and abruptly he has thus not added measurably to anything but Mr. Nixon's immediate ease of mind. And he has done so at a terrific cost.[36]

---

32. "Nixon's Crisis—And Ford's," *Newsweek*, September 23, 1974, 30, 35.
33. Kraft, "Ford: 'Ordinary Pol,'" A21.
34. Anthony Lewis, "Gerald Ford's America," *New York Times*, May 13, 1975, 35.
35. "Unfinished Business," A26.
36. "Presidential Pardon," A20.

Vermont Royster agreed that Ford had "in one ill-advised moment emptied his reservoir of good will. The damage, then, was to the President's credibility and . . . to his political skill. It was unbelievably clumsy." Royster noted that Ford, "like his two predecessors, will hereafter have a credibility problem."[37] The *Journal* columnist also believed that, "by not allowing time to work its healing, the President has lost that universal good will with which he began."[38] The *Wall Street Journal* joined the *Times* and the *Post* in criticizing Ford's handling of the pardon decision.

> In one day, President Ford spent much of the good will he has so skillfully built in his few weeks in office. . . . The danger is that by so quickly taking unto himself a bit of Watergate, Mr. Ford may revive the atmosphere of surly suspicion that has had so little time to subside.[39]

Ford's Motives

Some journalists speculated about Ford's motives in granting a pardon to Richard M. Nixon. Ford had already explained his motives in granting the pardon. He said that Nixon-related matters had dominated too much presidential time that could have been better devoted to the nation's problems; Ford expressed compassion for Nixon and explained that Nixon already had suffered enough; and the president argued that Nixon could probably not receive a fair trial for years.

Nonetheless, a number of journalists remained unconvinced that Ford had stated the "real" reason for the pardon. Most bluntly, Joseph Kraft wrote that "it is hard not to suspect that there was some kind of a deal between the former President and the man now in the White House."[40] Joseph Alsop thought he knew Ford's reason. "As to the President's motives, they are not hard to read. He owes the White House, after all, to the man who appointed him Vice President; and he is the kind of politician who remembers and acknowledges political debts."[41] The *Washington Post* argued that if you perceived Watergate as a breach of public office and not merely a private criminal matter, "then this newest use of the powers of the presidency to curtail inquiry and to relieve Mr. Nixon of responsibility for this action will strike you as nothing less than a continuation of a cover-up."[42] George F. Will

---

37. Vermont Royster, "A Bitter Spirit That Won't Die," *Wall Street Journal*, September 18, 1974, 16.

38. Vermont Royster, "The Second Month," *Wall Street Journal*, September 11, 1974, 24.

39. "Mr. Nixon Pardoned," *Wall Street Journal*, September 10, 1974, 28.

40. Kraft, "National Nightmare," A15.

41. Joseph Alsop, "The Case for Moving Quickly," *Washington Post*, September 11, 1974, A29.

42. "Presidential Pardon," A20.

too suspected that a "cover-up" scheme surrounding the pardon had taken place.[43]

Journalists articulated other positions against the pardon as well. According to one commonly held assessment, Ford had ruined a "good marriage" with his former congressional colleagues by pardoning Richard M. Nixon. A *U.S. News* "Newsgram" warned that "President Ford's pardon of Mr. Nixon means trouble with Congress. Democratic leaders are going to take a tougher line with the White House."[44] A news article in the magazine added the following.

> President Ford, by his surprise pardon of Richard Nixon, has brought a sudden change in the political outlook. The "marriage" with Congress . . . is already in trouble after barely a month. . . . Mr. Ford is going to get less cooperation from his former colleagues in Congress than had previously been expected.[45]

R. W. Apple, Jr., contended that, because of the pardon, Ford's legislative programs "will be subjected to more vigorous criticism than they might have been."[46] Dennis Farney added that "suddenly, Gerald Ford has plunged his new Administration into a crisis of competence. . . . [T]he traditional grace period of a new President has ended for Mr. Ford."[47] Evans and Novak wrote that "by succumbing to emotion . . . President Ford has raised serious questions of his performance in time of crisis. . . . Mr. Ford bloodied his young presidency by issuing the pardon."[48]

Another concern expressed by journalists regarded Republican party fortunes in the wake of the pardon. As Evans and Novak argued, "Mr. Ford shredded his own credibility and put all Republican candidates on the Watergate spot less than two months before the election. His presidency, his relations with Congress and Republican campaign prospects have been damaged."[49] *U.S. News* agreed that "Republican hopes for November . . .

---

43. Will, "Eroded Respect," A21.

44. "Newsgram," *U.S. News and World Report*, September 23, 1974, 9.

45. "Effects of Nixon Pardon," *U.S. News and World Report*, September 23, 1974, 19; see also, "Worries Pile Up For Ford," *U.S. News and World Report*, September 30, 1974, 17–18.

46. Apple, "Cost of Ford's Decision," 28.

47. Dennis Farney, "Under Fire: Pardon Controversy Raises Some Doubts of Ford's Abilities," *Wall Street Journal*, September 12, 1974, 1; see also Mitchell Lynch and Albert Hunt, "Ford Pardons Nixon; Move on Watergate Jolts His Honeymoon," *Wall Street Journal*, September 9, 1974, 1, 21.

48. Rowland Evans and Robert Novak, "Somebody Got to President Ford," *Washington Post*, September 11, 1974, A29.

49. Evans and Novak, "Somebody," A29.

have taken a turn for the worse."[50] And *Time* said that "Republicans, who had delightedly looked forward to the deflation of Watergate as a major issue in November, now dejectedly faced the prospect of defending to the voters Ford's grant of pardon."[51]

Time also believed that Ford's allegedly inept handling of the pardon decision could, in part, be attributed to a White House staff that lacked political experience and savvy. Indeed, oftentimes when Ford received strong press criticism, members of his staff and the White House decision-making process bore the brunt of negative commentary. Regarding the pardon, *Time* made the following statements.

> Neither Ford nor his shaken staff moved effectively to calm the controversy or dispel the doubts about the way in which the President had reached his decision. . . . It was Ford's failure to explain fully the timing of his pardon of Nixon that raised most doubts about Ford's candor and perceptiveness, as well as questions about the competence of his staff in handling a White House crisis. . . . If the political crisis raised troubling questions about Ford and his hastily assembled staff, it may also have performed a costly but positive function in warning of those weaknesses. In a sense Jerry Ford had now experienced his own Bay of Pigs and may have discovered, at considerable cost, the wisdom of consulting more widely.[52]

Within the prestige press, only a few persons said anything positive about Ford's decision to pardon Richard M. Nixon. Some who had criticized Ford balanced their criticisms with favorable acknowledgments. For example, Joseph Alsop argued that there were "strong reasons of national interest" behind the pardon. "It would have been dangerous, in fact, to prolong the Watergate obsession by bringing former President Nixon to trial and perhaps sending him to jail. . . . In short, President Ford has not pleased everyone, but the pardon was not the act of a fool or a knave."[53] Vermont Royster contended that "gone is the image of the unassertive Congressman or the unassuming party leader just following a party line. Gone are those doubts that Jerry Ford would be able to make up his own mind about anything. . . . Mr. Ford, like Harry Truman, has learned where the buck stops. . . . Jerry,

---

50. "Effects of Nixon Pardon," 19.

51. "Pardon Brought No Peace," 12.

52. "The Fallout," 17, 20.

53. Alsop, "Case for Moving Quickly." Alsop also wrote that "but it also seems probable that fear of President Nixon soon slipping over the edge was what led President Ford into clumsily abrupt action last Sunday" (Alsop, "Behind the Nixon Pardon," *Washington Post*, September 13, 1974, A27).

like Harry, is proving to be a pretty gutsy guy."[54] Royster also said, "He showed himself gutsy but exceedingly inept. . . . Hereafter neither politicians nor journalists will draw back from criticizing him on anything."[55] William Raspberry agreed.

> It was a gutsy call, in stark contrast with the Nixon record of temporizing and postponing. . . . Mr. Ford didn't fool around. He did it, and there is nothing that anyone . . . can do about it. But it was a foolish, dangerous and . . . avoidable decision.[56]

Two prominent journalists initially did not find the pardon of Richard M. Nixon objectionable.

> *Hugh Sidey*: In oversimplified terms, the pardon came down to a compromise, the kind he had negotiated as minority leader. The nation's problems needed attention, but they would not have it if everyone was preoccupied with the pardon and the tapes.[57]

> *David Broder*: I am not offended by the grant of pardon to Richard Nixon, because it seems to me essentially a matter of no great public significance what happens to Richard Nixon, private citizen.[58]

These assessments were exceptional. Overwhelmingly, the press corps disapproved of the pardon. Journalists who, for four weeks, had written that Ford did everything right as president immediately revised their interpretations of his leadership. The contrast could hardly have been more stark. A single presidential act fundamentally changed Ford's press image—from that of an honest, open, and accessible chief executive to that of a deceptive, secretive, even Nixonian chief executive. This sudden press image turnaround led Nicholas von Hoffman to lambaste his journalistic colleagues for inconsistency. In his view, the pardon revealed more about Ford than a month of "he's no Nixon" stories.

> It was these same reporters who, but a month ago, tired a skeptical nation with their bad writing about what a good guy Jerry Ford is. That, appar-

---

54. Royster, "Second Month," 24.

55. Royster, "Bitter Spirit," 16.

56. William Raspberry, "Mr. Ford's No-Return Decision," *Washington Post*, September 11, 1974, A29.

57. Hugh Sidey, "Second Sight on the Pardon," *Time*, October 7, 1974, 23.

58. David Broder, "TerHorst: A Resignation on Principle," *Washington Post*, September 11, 1974, A28.

ently, went out the window when Ford, by pardoning Nixon, did something they disapproved of. On the basis of that single act a number of reporters . . . felt entitled to attack Ford's honesty and probity under the guise of questions.[59]

More Press Criticism

The unpopularity of Ford's pardon of Richard M. Nixon opened up the president to press criticism in other areas as well. One related area of contention concerned the issue of "Nixon holdovers." That is, Ford kept on many officials who had worked in the Nixon administration. Never mind that almost every such person had served the president admirably and had nothing to do with the Watergate scandal. In the immediate, post-Watergate months, many critics had a bloodthirst for all persons associated with Nixon. Prominent journalists led in charging that President Ford had failed the country by not purging every person who had a Nixon association.[60] One week after the pardon, the *New York Times* said that Ford's administration provided "mediocre leadership" due to an allegedly undistinguished White House staff and a failure to depose all Nixon administration holdovers.[61] One month later, the *Times* reiterated that "the secrecy with which the pardon was granted and the lingering presence of Nixon personnel and policy holdovers raise the suspicion that there will be little consultation, compromise and consensus in the new President's decisions. . . . Mr. Ford has not yet become his own man, with his own policies."[62] Three *Times* columnists articulated similar views.

Tom Wicker: . . . the pardon and the reluctance Mr. Ford has shown to part with the Nixon holdovers in the Government, make him appear more and more a lineal descendant—"Son of Nixon Administration."[63]

James Reston: His tardiness in weeding out many of Mr. Nixon's aides and his rewarding of other members of the Nixon team with new appointments have also suggested that he has not abandoned the old party ways.[64]

---

59. Nicholas von Hoffman, "Having Jerry Ford to Kick Around," *Washington Post*, September 18, 1974, B1.

60. One such "Nixon holdover," Deputy Press Secretary Gerald Warren, pointed out that a good deal of "Nixon bashing" went on within the Ford White House as well, creating an unpleasant atmosphere for those who had served Nixon honorably (Author telephone interview, March 15, 1990).

61. "Mr. Ford's Priorities," *New York Times*, September 16, 1974, 34.

62. "President and Congress," *New York Times*, October 21, 1974, 32.

63. Tom Wicker, "Hustling on the Hustings," *New York Times*, October 25, 1974, 39.

64. James Reston, "Jerry on the Hustings," *New York Times*, October 13, 1974, IV, 17.

John Herbers: . . . a strong Nixon flavor persists. This is attributed largely to the fact that Mr. Ford is comfortable and at home with Nixonian Republicans and policies. . . . [The] retention of Nixon personnel and many of the old ways has contributed to the lack of focus as to what kind of institution the Presidency will turn out to be under Mr. Ford.[65]

President Ford's handling of the nation's leading problem—the economy—did not win much journalistic praise. Prior to the pardon of Richard M. Nixon, a *Wall Street Journal* news story declared that "he's no deep economic thinker; will his policy be determined by the last man to see him?"[66] A *Newsweek* report said that "it seems highly unlikely that the President will order major changes in economic policy. Those who know him well say that his knowledge of economics is anything but expert."[67] *Time* thought that Ford's proposals of budgetary cuts, reviving the Cost of Living Council, and holding an "economic summit" comprised "a Fibber McGee closet crowded with familiar ideas that have been tried, or at least noisily advocated, before." *Time* also criticized Ford's lack of a "comprehensive program" to revive the economy as "Nixonomics without Nixon."[68] Economic policy columnist Hobart Rowen wrote that "when it comes to positive actions to counter the recession, President Ford has no programs he wants to whip into force." Instead, Ford offers "a deliberately cautious policy."[69] Joseph Alsop ridiculed Ford's proposal for a domestic "economic summit" as "an inherently silly idea." The kind of idea put forth "to avoid painful decisions. . . . So if we are to be honest with ourselves, he has hardly began to tackle the tough parts of his job."[70]

The postpardon reviews of Ford's handling of the economy did not improve. For the most part, leading journalists expected Ford to produce a "new" approach to the nation's problems of increased inflation and unemployment. Yet, as Hobart Rowen observed, "there is nothing to indicate that the

---

65. John Herbers, "Four Months After Nixon, His Legacy Haunts New President," *New York Times*, December 19, 1974, 16; see also Herbers, "Ford People Largely Resemble Nixon People," *New York Times*, December 22, 1974, IV, 1.

66. "Washington Wire," *Wall Street Journal*, August 16, 1974, 1.

67. "Ford Confronts 'Public Enemy No. 1,'" *Newsweek*, August 19, 1974, 64.

68. "Policy and Problems: Ford Confronts the Deadliest Danger," *Time*, August 26, 1974, 30; see also, "Seeking Relief from a Massive Migraine," *Time*, September 9, 1974, 22–27.

69. Hobart Rowen, "Economic Outlook Grim, But Ford Moves Slowly," *Washington Post*, September 1, 1974, G1.

70. Joseph Alsop, "Mr. Ford: Facing Major Problems . . . ," *Washington Post*, September 9, 1974, A23.

Ford administration is ready to abandon the substance of the 'old time religion' as it applies to a tight budget."[71]

On October 8, 1974, President Ford addressed a joint session of Congress on the nation's economic problems. He proposed a series of measures designed to deregulate certain industries, decrease foreign oil dependency, increase food production, stimulate the housing industry, and raise government revenues through a one-year, 5 percent tax increase on corporations and individuals with incomes above $15,000 per year. Ford also proposed that citizens voluntarily exercise financial austerity to lower inflation and he displayed a "WIN" lapel button—"Whip Inflation Now"—that became the most mocked symbol of his presidency. In the speech, Ford likened his program to a "declaration of war" against the nation's economic woes.[72]

In his memoirs, Ford refers to the press reaction to the speech as "frustrating." Ford cited the opinions of the *Wall Street Journal*, which referred to the economic program as "neither surprising nor bold," and the *New York Times*, which said that

> the overall impact of Mr. Ford's speech was weak, flaccid and disappointing. While some of his measures are good and some are questionable, they in no sense add up to a program for an emergency, and it is an emergency that confronts the nation and the world.[73]

Many others agreed. James Reston wrote that "personal honesty, good intentions, locker-room exhortations and WIN buttons won't solve the economic crisis."[74] George F. Will added that

> as an anti-inflation weapon, the buttons will be about as effective as a policy of exhorting sacrifices while promising subsidies. . . . The fact that they call their new program a "war" proves that their language, like our currency, is suffering from inflation.[75]

Chalmers M. Roberts also mocked the WIN campaign and repeated a joke that the buttons should read BATH—"Back Again To Hoover." Chalmers at

---

71. Hobart Rowen, "Economy: More 'Old Time Religion,'" *Washington Post*, September 12, 1974, A15.

72. Gerald Ford, *A Time to Heal* (Norwalk, Conn.: Easton Press, 1987), 194–95.

73. Ford, *Time to Heal*, 195.

74. James Reston, "Don't Sell Ford Short," *New York Times*, October 18, 1974, 41.

75. George F. Will, "Putting Ford's Economic Program Into Perspective," *Washington Post*, October 11, 1974, A25.

least conceded that Ford's program did not resemble former president Herbert Hoover's policies.[76]

Newsweek called Ford's program "a committee-designed package of economic compromises with something for everybody and . . . very little hard action against inflation." The program "was designed to be weak—a placebo to ease the pain of stagflation while the tight-money and spending policies begun by Richard Nixon do their work." *Newsweek* concluded that, by pardoning Richard M. Nixon, Ford had wasted a great deal of political capital needed to persuade Congress on the economic recovery program.[77] *U.S. News* similarly thought that Ford's program would not immediately turn the economy around and would bring about economic changes "only over a substantial period of time."[78] *Time* said that "the [economic] package is not very remarkable. . . . As the program stands, it is not likely to do much to immediately deter inflation."[79] *Time* added that "the program . . . was essentially unchanged from that which Ford inherited from Richard Nixon." *Time* praised Ford for not offering unrealistic solutions to complex problems, yet

> the fact that the policy is not new does not make it wrong, but it is a poor standard round which to rally a people to change the habits of a lifetime. . . . [T]he Ford program, taken as a whole, represents a modest package.[80]

Postpardon press reviews of Ford's capacity for leadership were also low. Despite the fact that Ford's pardon of Richard M. Nixon displayed a propensity for take-charge leadership, journalists criticized the president for not offering vigorous, visionary leadership. The *New York Times* led in making that charge.

> At a time that calls for resolute action, the President's priorities . . . are primarily negative, commending for "immediate action" a long roster of appropriations he would like to see canceled.[81]

> Many of the crucial issues requiring his leadership run counter to the parochial conservatism of his prepresidential years in the House. . . .

76. Chalmers M. Roberts, "Ford Is No Hoover, But . . . ," *Washington Post*, December 8, 1974, B6.

77. "Ford's Rx: A Placebo," *Newsweek*, October 21, 1974, 34.

78. "Ford's War On Inflation: A Losing Battle?" *U.S. News and World Report*, October 21, 1974, 19.

79. "Ford's Plan: (Mostly) Modest Proposals," *Time*, October 14, 1974, 28; see also "Gerald Ford: Wrestling with Inflation," *Time*, October 7, 1974, 12–13.

80. "Small Weapons for the Two-Front War," *Time*, October 21, 1974, 41–42.

81. "Ford's Priorities," *New York Times*, September 16, 1974, 34.

President Ford appears generally to have been slow to understand that he is not the routine inheritor of a departed Administration. . . . Mr. Ford has been suggesting by his actions that he is perpetuating a discredited regime.[82]

The conservative-leaning *Wall Street Journal* agreed that Ford had failed in his duty "to impose some strategy of leadership." The *Journal* identified the following view of presidential leadership.

Leadership, intellectual direction that imposes some coherence on the system, can only come from the President. And in supplying that leadership, he must inevitably confront, affront and battle the claims of the special interests, meaning Congressmen and Executive bureaucrats. Faced with this presidential challenge, Mr. Ford has been acting like a consummate Congressman.[83]

Evans and Novak assessed the impact of "the premature Nixon pardon" and observed that President Ford "simply has not taken hold of the presidency and its problems."[84] Joseph Alsop wrote that, whereas President Ford wisely rejected imperial presidential trappings, "he cannot jettison the increased power of his office. . . . The outlook for his presidency is not bad just because he showed himself a bad tactician in the manner and the timing of his predecessor's pardon. Instead, the outlook is bad . . . because President Ford has not prepared himself for all the difficult actions which he will surely have to take."[85] Chalmers M. Roberts compared President Ford's leadership acumen to former president Harry S Truman's. "President Ford has yet to fight, indeed to give us a sense that he knows beyond generalities what he would fight for if he did. He has yet to show that, unlike Truman, he does not feel overwhelmed by his job."[86] Joseph Kraft argued that "the President's men are going to have . . . to make time for him to concentrate on the truly difficult problems which face the country."[87]

Two of the national news weeklies summarized the opinion makers' major criticisms of President Ford's leadership.

---

82. "Ford vs. Ford," *New York Times*, October 24, 1974, 40.

83. "Stand Up, Mr. President," *Wall Street Journal*, October 4, 1974, 8.

84. Rowland Evans and Robert Novak, "Ford: At the Crossroads," *Washington Post*, September 30, 1974, A27.

85. Joseph Alsop, "The Ford White House: A Crisis of Authority," *Washington Post*, September 18, 1974, A27.

86. Chalmers M. Roberts, "Comparing Presidents: Truman and Ford," *Washington Post*, November 28, 1974, A30.

87. Joseph Kraft, quoted in "In Quest of a Distinctive Presidency," *Time*, October 21, 1974, 20.

U.S. News: Mr. Ford is accused of spending too much time campaigning. He's criticized for having a weak staff, taking part in too many
ceremonies, seeing a stream of visitors instead of devoting his time to
making policy decisions.[88]

Time: . . . his whirlwind pace has . . . led to criticism that he spends too
much time on the unimportant details of the presidency and not enough
on the tough and complex decisions that he now must make. . . . Ford
encountered mounting criticism from political pundits who accused him
of talking too freely to reporters, allowing policy-making in the White
House to become chaotic and not properly rationing his time.[89]

Prior to the pardon of Richard M. Nixon, President Ford adopted a
controversial yet firm stance on the issue of amnesty for Vietnam War draft
resisters and military deserters. On August 19, 1974, Ford addressed the
seventy-fifth annual Veterans of Foreign Wars (VFW) convention in Chicago,
Illinois. In that address, Ford announced his decision to offer what he called
"earned reentry" into the United States for the draft resisters and military
deserters. Ford did not outline all of the details of the proposal, but he
believed that he could best "indicate strength" by announcing his decision to
an audience unlikely to favorably receive such a plan.[90] The press reaction to
this proposal eventually became clouded in the controversy over the pardon of
Richard M. Nixon. After the pardon, *Newsweek* declared that "the surprise
proposal for limited amnesty for Vietnam War resisters now could be inter-
preted as a cynical show of leniency to pave the way for Nixon's pardon."[91]

Ford did not detail his amnesty plan until September 16, 1974, one week
after the pardon of Richard M. Nixon. The plan called for a clemency board to
review each case. In brief, "earned reentry" meant that draft dodgers had to
pledge their allegiance to the United States and perform two years of national
service. Military deserters also had to take the pledge and then provide two
years of military service.[92] A *U.S. News* headline identified the political
problem posed by the proposal: "Ford's Amnesty Plan—Will It Satisfy Anybody?"[93] Many conservatives preferred former president Nixon's hard-line,
no clemency stance. Many liberals could not understand a full, unconditional

88. "Newsgram," *U.S. New and World Report*, November 4, 1974, 7–8.
89. "Distinctive Presidency," 18–20.
90. Ford, *Time to Heal*, 141.
91. "Was Justice Done?" *Newsweek*, September 16, 1974, 23.
92. Ford, *Time to Heal*, 181–182.
93. "Ford's Amnesty Plan—Will It Satisfy Anybody?" *U.S. News and World Report*,
September 9, 1974, 24.

pardon for Nixon and an "earned" clemency for Vietnam draft evaders and military resisters. The press also criticized this alleged inequity.[94]

September 16, 1974, became important to Ford's presidency for another reason. On that date, the president held his second news conference. President Ford wanted to lay to rest the pardon controversy by explaining his action. Instead, he confronted a cynical press corps anxious to get the "real" story behind the pardon. According to *Time*'s report, "Inevitably, Ford was asked why he gave a full pardon to Nixon and only conditional amnesty to Vietnam War evaders. Ford said that he saw no real connection between the two— hardly a convincing reply. Overall, it was a gutsy performance under fire, although Ford's explanation of the timing of the pardon remained thoroughly unsatisfying."[95] Ford determined that he had to present his case through a different format.[96]

Ford decided to go to Congress to explain his rationale for pardoning Richard M. Nixon. On October 17, 1974, Ford appeared before the Subcommittee on Criminal Justice of the House Judiciary Committee. He explained to the committee members that he issued the pardon "to change our national focus. I wanted to do all I could to shift our attentions from the pursuit of a fallen President to the pursuit of the urgent needs of a rising nation."[97]

From the press, Ford received high marks for agreeing to testify in such a fashion before a congressional subcommittee. Tom Wicker wrote that "President Ford has set a notable example, and taken a long step toward an 'open presidency' by his appearance before a Congressional subcommittee."[98] *Newsweek* agreed that, by testifying before the congressional subcommittee, "Ford may restore some of the luster to his tarnished reputation for openness."[99] Editorial writers applauded the move.

New York Times: By volunteering to appear before a committee of the House of Representatives to answer questions about the pardon he granted to Richard Nixon, President Ford has set an admirable example of open and responsive government. Such readiness to be accountable to Congress gains in significance by its contrast to the Nixon Administration's defiant custom of hiding behind the stone wall of executive privilege.[100]

---

94. See "Next, A Vietnam Amnesty," *Newsweek*, September 16, 1974, 26–33; "Jerry Ford Faces Life," *Newsweek*, September 30, 1974, 26–27; "Amnesty At Last," *Newsweek*, September 30, 1974, 30–32.

95. "Taking the Heat on Nixon Pardon," *Time*, September 30, 1974, 30.

96. Ford, *Time to Heal*, 180.

97. Ford, *Time to Heal*, 198.

98. Tom Wicker, "The 'Pulpit' Magnified," *New York Times*, October 18, 1974, 41.

99. "A Ford With Loose Steering," *Newsweek*, October 14, 1974, 37.

100. "Responsive President," *New York Times*, October 2, 1974, 46.

Washington Post: There is a stunning directness about President Ford's offer to go before a House Judiciary subcommittee to respond to questions about his pardon of former President Nixon. . . . One can easily imagine how Mr. Ford's predecessor might have replied to a similar request initiated by two very liberal Democrats seeking details concerning his exercise of power assigned explicitly and exclusively to the *President*.[101]

James Reston also contrasted Ford's move with the Johnson and Nixon "coverups. . . . President Ford, when he got into trouble on the pardon, at least had the gumption to face the opposition."[102] Regarding the substance of his congressional testimony, Ford received mixed press reviews. Reston thought that "he proved in the Nixon pardon hearings that he is not to be underestimated." The public "caught his integrity, which has been the missing element in Washington for too many years."[103] *U.S. News* called Ford's testimony "a daring gamble. . . . First reactions indicated Mr. Ford had won his gamble. He impressed viewers as unflustered, forthright, a man with nothing to hide."[104] The *Washington Post* was very impressed with Ford's testimony.

The President was categorical and compelling, in our view, in refuting the allegation that his pardon of Richard Nixon was part of a prearranged "deal." His mere presence, as well as his ease and good temper, said a lot about the restoration of civil relations and a sensible balance between the executive branch and Congress.[105]

Despite these favorable assessments, one problem remained for Ford: according to many journalists, he failed in his effort to put the pardon controversy to rest. *U.S. News* reported that "Watergate wouldn't go away. Not even Mr. Ford's appearance before a congressional subcommittee . . . could kill all suspicions that there was more than met the eye in his pardon of Richard Nixon."[106] Haynes Johnson contended that the Ford testimony did not change many opinions and that major questions about the pardon remained as "unresolved as before."[107] *Newsweek* noted that Ford "left signifi-

---

101. "President Ford Goes to Congress," *Washington Post*, October 3, 1974, A18.

102. Reston, "Don't Sell," 41.

103. Reston, "Don't Sell," 41.

104. "Ford's Own Story of the Nixon Pardon: 'No Deal—Period,'" *U.S. News and World Report*, October 28, 1974, 20.

105. "The President's Testimony," *Washington Post*, October 18, 1974, A24.

106. "Long Wait For a Quiet Time," *U.S. News and World Report*, October 28, 1974, 19.

107. Haynes Johnson, "Ford's Historic Visit: Questions Remain," *Washington Post*, October 18, 1974, A1.

cant questions unanswered, about the pardon itself and his judgment in grant-ing it, and the daily newspapers were otherwise rich with evidence that he had not yet put Watergate behind him."[108] *Time* said that "the session left trou-bling questions unanswered, doubts unresolved, and Ford still struggling to find a way of exorcising the wrath of Nixon that haunts his presidency."[109] The *Washington Post*, despite a favorable view of Ford's congressional testi-mony, offered the following observation.

> Far from putting the Watergate "nightmare". . . behind him, he quite obviously miscalculated the public mood, misread the true meaning of the Watergate trauma and contributed measurably to a weakening of his own power and capacity to deal with the urgent national problems to which he supposedly was redirecting the country's attention and energies.[110]

And William Raspberry echoed other journalists' perceptions.

> Anybody who previously had suspicions about a "deal" between Presi-dent Ford and his predecessor has exactly the same suspicions now. There is no way that [the] namby-pamby session between the President and the House Judiciary subcommittee could have eased anyone's doubts.[111]

The Midterm Elections

President Ford's pardon of Richard M. Nixon also had important partisan implications. The unpopular pardon came at a time when congressional candi-dates nationwide were campaigning for office. For Republican candidates, the timing of the pardon could hardly have been worse.

The president tried to mitigate the partisan fallout from the pardon by traveling nationwide to campaign on behalf of Republican congressional and gubernatorial candidates. Nobody could dispute the importance of the 1974 elections to a president whose party held only 42 Senate seats and 187 House seats. Nonetheless, Ford received widespread journalistic criticism for cam-paigning. The *New York Times* maintained that

> at this juncture in history, there could hardly be a worse use of his time. . . . President Ford would be much better advised to stay at his

---

108. "Campaign for Confidence," *Newsweek*, October 28, 1974, 24.

109. "The Pardon: Questions Persist," *Time*, October 28, 1974, 16.

110. "President's Testimony," A24.

111. William Raspberry, "Mr. Ford's Testimony: The Suspicions Remain," *Washington Post*, October 21, 1974, A23.

desk coping with the knotty personnel and policy problems that require his attention.[112]

Marquis Childs wrote that, rather than stumping for Republican candidates, "[Ford] should be taking the high road of unity to pull people together for the common goal of fighting inflation."[113] James Reston agreed that Ford's campaign traveling "seems a little excessive. . . . For the more he gets involved in the rough and tumble of the Congressional and gubernatorial races, the more he is likely to weaken his position as a President who is trying to unite and heal the country."[114] Reston also argued that

> he is getting into trouble now because he is talking like a party leader instead of like a President. . . . [Ford's] real power lay in the fact that he was the opposite of Messrs. Nixon and Johnson, a plain, honest and uncomplicated man. The country was sick of partisan politics, but lately he has insisted on the ridiculous thesis that peace and economic stability depend on electing Republicans next month.[115]

Marquis Childs also argued that Ford risked his presidential stature by associating himself so closely with the electoral fortunes of Republican candidates.[116] If true, then the voters dealt Ford a major rebuke on November 5, 1974. The Republicans lost four Senate seats and forty House seats. A postelection analysis in *Time* clearly blamed Ford for the Republican electoral disaster.

> The direct causes of that beating were easily stated, indeed inescapable: the public outrage over Watergate, Ford's pardon of Richard Nixon, double-digit inflation and worsening unemployment. . . . Ford's prodigious efforts seem to have done next to nothing to help Republican candidates. The Nixon pardon . . . cut off any coattails that his accession might have offered to beleaguered Republicans.[117]

---

112. "America Adrift . . . ," *New York Times*, October 15, 1974, 38.

113. Marquis Childs, "Come Home Gerald Ford," *Washington Post*, October 29, 1974, A19.

114. Reston, "Jerry on the Hustings," IV, 17.

115. James Reston, "Forgetting You Are President," *New York Times*, October 25, 1974, 39.

116. Childs, "Come Home," A19.

117. "Democrats: Now the Morning After," *Time*, November 18, 1974, 8, 10–11; see also "After Elections: Problems for Ford," *U.S. News and World Report*, November 11, 1974, 19–21; "Real Meaning of Democratic Sweep," *U.S. News and World Report*, November 18, 1974, 20–24.

The First Hundred Days

Since Franklin D. Roosevelt's presidency, journalists customarily review each president's performance after one hundred days in office. FDR's first hundred days set a standard of early presidential activism that no subsequent president could measure up to. In fact, given the extraordinary circumstances surrounding Roosevelt's early months in office, it seems highly unfair that subsequent presidents have been evaluated against the backdrop of FDR's activities.

The contrasts between FDR's and President Ford's political circumstances after a hundred days in office could hardly be greater. In 1933, FDR could claim a resounding electoral mandate; Ford did not seek the presidency. FDR worked with large Democratic party majorities in both Houses of Congress; the 1974 elections gave Republicans only 147 of 435 House seats and 38 of 100 Senate seats. During a time of crisis, FDR sought to lead a Congress willing to defer enormous authority to the chief executive; during a time of cynicism toward executive branch leadership, Ford had to deal with a combative Congress that wanted to seize power from the presidency.

None of that convinced the press to forego a hundred-day assessment of Ford's presidency. *U.S. News* even carried an article entitled "It Was FDR Who Set the Record for Action" along with its hundred-day evaluation of Ford.[118]

According to leading journalists, Ford failed to capitalize on the opportunities created by his accession to the presidency. Despite the lack of an electoral mandate and of the traditional eleven-week transition period, journalists expected Ford to articulate a set of goals early in his term and to cleanse the government of all vestiges of Richard Nixon.

James Reston criticized Ford for a "limited vision" and wrote that "[Ford] gives the impression that we are not living in a revolutionary age, and don't have to make fundamental changes in the lives of families and nations, but that we must merely be patient and sensible and all will go back to the old affluent days and be well in the end."[119] Anthony Lewis added that "there is very little sign that Gerald Ford has any idea of the seriousness of the times, or a clue to any way out of our difficulties."[120] Dennis Farney referred to the Ford White House as "a makeshift team in search of a theme. That's the Ford administration . . . a presidency without unifying strategies or a clear set of

---

118. "It Was FDR Who Set the Record for Action," *U.S. News and World Report*, November 25, 1974, 19.

119. James Reston, "Mr. Ford On His First 100 Days," *New York Times*, November 10, 1974, IV, 15. In his memoirs Ford rebutted this column by Reston: "Reston didn't quite understand that we had to consolidate and pull things together before we could begin to make those 'fundamental changes' he was talking about" (Ford, *Time to Heal*, 207).

120. Anthony Lewis, "Nixon's Last Election," *New York Times*, November 7, 1974, 45.

priorities. Beyond a repeated commitment to economy in government, it has yet to evolve a central theme."[121] The *Washington Post* thought that "he has yet to take hold of the large questions of policy . . . . [I]t is . . . appropriate to ask when he proposes to take command of his own administration—when, in other words, he proposes to start acting like a President in 1974." The *Post* complained that Ford offered "shifting and vague [policy] pronouncements" rather than a clear leadership direction.[122] George F. Will referred to "the astonishing incongruity between Mr. Ford's words and deeds." According to Will, "Gerald Ford, after 100 days in office, is not yet a convincing President. . . . Mr. Ford's words treat inflation as a threat comparable to 'an armed enemy' attacking our liberty. But his actions treat inflation as a homecoming football game, an occasion for buttons and banners."[123] David Broder wrote that

> after 100 days in the presidency, Gerald R. Ford is still very much the man of Congress. . . . He is surely the simplest man to occupy the White House in modern times, but the times are not simple. And after 100 days, there is still a question of whether Mr. Ford can develop a method of presidential leadership that suits both his character and the national situation. . . . What he has not yet discovered is how to convey to the Democrats who control Congress or to the voters who elected them what it is that he perceives about the toughness of the problems and the choices facing this country.[124]

James Reston once again wrote that Ford needed "to give a sense of order after an age of violence and faction, which he has not done." Reston further commented that

> President Ford has not yet provided this sense of a new beginning in his first three months. He has tried to deal with a revolutionary situation with the old team and with traditional partisan arguments, and it is not working.[125]

121. Dennis Farney, "Uncertain Course: After First 100 Days, Ford's Ship of State Mostly Keeps Drifting," *Wall Street Journal*, November 15, 1974, 1.

122. "Mr. Ford and the Energy Crisis: Abroad . . . ," *Washington Post*, November 17, 1974, C6.

123. George F. Will, "An Unconvincing President," *Washington Post*, November 15, 1974, A27.

124. David Broder, "Mr. Ford's First 100 Days," *Washington Post*, November 13, 1974, A24.

125. James Reston, "Ford's First Three Months," *New York Times*, November 3, 1974, IV, 19.

According to Reston, as a product of Congress, the new president—despite partisanship, legislative assertiveness, and antipresidential power sentiments—had an even better opportunity "than Richard Nixon, or John Kennedy, or even Lyndon Johnson . . . to bring the two branches together" to achieve policy goals.[126]

Evans and Novak critiqued Ford's "disappointing first hundred days." Even these conservative columnists agreed that successful presidential leadership entailed initiating fundamental change.

> It is the President's tragic failure that he has not replaced cabinet members hired by his repudiated predecessor. . . . The clear indication is that President Ford appears far more content with the established order in his inherited administration than in boldly striking out for new faces and policies essential to give it a uniquely Fordian quality.[127]

Anthony Lewis boldly concluded that "it would be an overwhelming piece of optimism to place any reliance on President Ford for leadership . . . He has not even had the sense or the courage to clear many Nixon holdovers out of his Government."[128]

Despite his negative assessment of Ford's capacity for visionary leadership, James Reston rated the president's style and character favorably.

> The contrast between this and the Nixon White House is startling. The Ford White House is now almost as open and casual as a Congressman's office. No show or pretense or fake dignity. . . . In short, the upstairs-downstairs division of the Nixon days is gone. . . . Not since Ike have we had a more decent man in the White House, or anybody so open and relaxed.[129]

The hundred-days assessment of Ford's leadership contained in *U.S. News* contrasted significantly with the prevailing press opinion. *U.S. News* acknowledged that Ford's "almost euphoric 'honeymoon'" had been "shattered" by the pardon of Richard M. Nixon. Nonetheless, this news analysis did not find Ford's leadership wanting.

> The nation can expect activist leadership from Gerald Ford—and a willingness on the part of the President to make unpopular decisions when he

---

126. James Reston, "After the Cheering . . . ," *New York Times*, November 6, 1974, 45.

127. Rowland Evans and Robert Novak, "President Ford's First 100 Days," *Washington Post*, November 20, 1974, A27.

128. Lewis, "Nixon's Last Election," 45.

129. Reston, "Ford On First 100 Days," IV, 15.

believes them to be in the best interest of the public. The President recognizes the gravity of the problems he faces at home and around the world, but is in no way intimidated by them. He likes his job, is stimulated by challenges, doesn't brood over his setbacks . . . [130]

Foreign Travel

On his 101st day in office, November 17, 1974, President Ford departed on official visits to Japan, Korea, and a summit meeting with Soviet leader Leonid Brezhnev in the Siberian port city of Vladivostok. Ford thus became the first U.S. president to visit Japan when *Air Force One* landed at Tokyo's Haneda International Airport on November 18. During the next few days, Ford met Emperor Hirohito and held official talks about trade policy with Prime Minister Kakuei Tanaka. Ford traveled to Kyoto and Osaka on November 21, and then to Seoul, South Korea, the following day. There Ford met with South Korean President Park Chung Hee to discuss U.S. troops in South Korea and human rights concerns. On November 23, Ford went on to Vladivostok to meet Brezhnev and Foreign Minister Andrei Gromyko. Ford held a series of wide-ranging talks on arms control, Soviet emigration policies, and Middle East policy with his Soviet counterparts.

In his memoirs, Ford recalled that the accomplishments of the Far Eastern trip "exceeded my expectations."[131] Yet Ford acknowledged that the trip's "timing couldn't have been worse. Congress hadn't yet confirmed Nelson Rockefeller as Vice President. Inflation and unemployment were worsening, and there was a new threat of war in the Middle East. 'Jerry, stay home,' one newspaper implored."[132]

Indeed, as *Time* magazine reported, "many people questioned whether he should be making the trip at all."[133] *U.S. News* called Ford's trip "a dramatic move" because of all the press and partisan criticism of him for traveling at a time of serious domestic problems.[134] In a column entitled "A Time to Put the Big Jets to Rest," Hugh Sidey wrote that

> a nervous, though tentative worry began to build as Ford flew on. It was that the President, just like Nixon, was finding international junketeering far more pleasurable than the grind in the Oval Office. Perhaps he was beginning to succumb to the illusion that he could outrace domestic

---

130. "Ford's First 100 Days: Clues to the Future," *U.S. News and World Report*, November 25, 1974, 19.

131. Ford, *Time to Heal*, 219.

132. Ford, *Time to Heal*, 209.

133. "Ford Makes His First Foray Overseas," *Time*, November 25, 1974, 14.

134. "Ford as a World Leader," *U.S. News and World Report*, December 2, 1974, 15.

difficulties and bring home enough of the foreign huzzahs to dispel the leadership malaise.[135]

In a subsequent column entitled "Look Homeward, Gerald Ford," Sidey iterated the point.

At the end of his Asian adventure, Ford was tempted to do just what his predecessor had done—use the summit euphoria to salve the domestic disruptions and the growing White House leadership malaise. It did not work, and it will not work. The domestic problems that this country faces are for the most part a good deal more complex than the foreign dilemma. . . . [N]ew directions for American life. That is what the U.S. needs and what Ford, resisting the siren call of foreign horizons, must concentrate on.[136]

Lou Cannon wrote that "President Ford is demonstrating that he is as fully infatuated with foreign policy as his predecessors."[137] And the *New York Times* lambasted Ford for traveling too often.

During his first four months in office, Mr. Ford has continued almost nonstop and frequently pointless travel. . . . Aside from Mr. Ford's habitual restlessness, there is an element of public relations fakery in his dashing about the country and the world. . . . The country does not need a "red-eye President." Mr. Ford should stop soaring into the jetstream and heading for faraway places. He should be putting his feet under his desk and learning his job.[138]

Press Secretary Ron Nessen recalled that the Far Eastern trip marked the beginning of the deterioration of his own relationship with the press corps. According to Nessen, despite the diplomatic and symbolic importance of the trip, many reporters emphasized "inconsequential matters" in their reporting.[139] In particular, a number of journalists seized on President Ford's appearance before the Japanese leaders. Apparently, Ford wore an ill-fitted suit with too-short pant-legs. To some journalists, Ford looked comical. Hugh Sidey reported that "the big, comfortable American galumphed over the red

---

135. Hugh Sidey, "A Time to Put the Big Jets to Rest," *Time*, December 2, 1974, 17.

136. Hugh Sidey, "Look Homeward, Gerald Ford," *Time*, December 9, 1974, 19.

137. Lou Cannon, "Ford to Make China Visit In New Year: Foreign Policy Echoes Nixon's," *Washington Post*, November 30, 1974, A1.

138. "Red-Eye Special," *New York Times*, December 14, 1974, 28.

139. Ron Nessen, *It Sure Looks Different From the Inside* (New York: Playboy Press, 1978), 44.

carpets as if he were out rabbit hunting, unconcerned about his too-short pants."[140] Nessen protested the reporting, only to be lectured by United Press International's Helen Thomas. "The president's pants being too short was a big story . . . and you can't expect us not to write about it."[141]

Despite Nessen's protests, Ford did receive a few favorable press comments for the Far Eastern trip. *U.S. News* commented that "in a historic journey . . . Gerald Ford achieved the primary goal of his first venture in global diplomacy. The President proved that he was ready to take over in his own right the world-leadership role Richard Nixon held until he was toppled from office."[142] *Time* also praised Ford's efforts.

> The point of Gerald Ford's journey halfway round the world last week lay chiefly in its symbolism. He sought no major new agreements with leaders of Japan, South Korea and the Soviet Union. He offered no change in U.S. foreign policy. But as he traveled, he was visibly performing as a global leader and dramatizing the fact that on the world stage, no one is more important than the U.S. President.[143]

End of Year Reviews

President Ford referred to the Far Eastern trip as "a high-water mark" in his presidency. He described the following five and a half months as "the most difficult of my Presidency—if not my life. It was a period during which Murphy's Law prevailed. Everything that could go wrong did go wrong, and on almost every front the nation took quite a battering."[144]

In late November, a worsening economy and a combative, lame-duck Congress greeted the president at home. Congress had not acted affirmatively on an anti-inflation package that Ford proposed on October 8, it refused Ford's request to defer federal pay increases for three months, and it overrode the president's vetoes of the Railroad Retirement Act and a veterans' benefit bill.[145] *Time* called the latter veto, overridden 394 to 10 in the House and 90 to 1 in the Senate, a "smashing defeat" for the president.[146] Congress did not confirm Nelson Rockefeller for the vice presidency until December 19, nearly

---

140. Sidey, "Put the Jets to Rest," 17.

141. Nessen, *It Sure Looks Different*, 53.

142. "Ford as World Leader," 15; see also, "Off to Asia—President Gets His First Test Abroad," *U.S. News and World Report*, November 25, 1974, 31–32; "How U.S. Really Came Out In Summit Bargaining," *U.S. News and World Report*, December 9, 1974, 27–28.

143. "President Ford's Far Eastern Road Show," *Time*, December 2, 1974, 13.

144. Ford, *Time to Heal*, 219.

145. Ford, *Time to Heal*, 219–220.

146. "Heading for Stalemate in Congress," *Time*, December 16, 1974, 17.

four months after Ford announced the nomination. In mid-December, Ford convened meetings with scholars to discuss the problems of asserting leadership during an era of pessimism.[147] Clearly, Ford understood the troubles he faced.

Near the end of the calendar year, a popular time for journalists to assess a president's political standing, the press criticized Ford's leadership. *U.S. News* noted that Ford had "to convince the public and Congress that he can be an effective leader. Throughout the government there is a sense of drift, of tough decisions being put off, of policies being announced and then abandoned. Few things seem to be going well." *U.S. News* also identified the economy—particularly the automobile sales and housing slumps—as Ford's major problem. The news weekly criticized Ford's WIN program, which "lacked dramatic appeal," and his approach to the national energy problem, where "no clear program has emerged."[148] *U.S. News* added that "policies and programs clearly identified with Mr. Ford have been slow to emerge. Except for a 31-point economic proposal that has been given a chilly reception by a hostile Congress, very little has been suggested that bears the 'Ford Administration' stamp."[149]

According to Alan L. Otten, Ford failed to project a forceful demeanor. Instead, the president behaved like a conciliatory legislator. Otten maintained that "[Ford] must unlearn habits acquired in a lifetime as a legislator and legislative leader. The habits of the career lawmaker aren't the best habits for a President. . . . As legislative leader, Mr. Ford was Mr. Nice Guy. . . . A President must often be more of an SOB—get tough, chew people out, even fire them."[150] John Herbers contrasted Ford to former president Harry S Truman and concluded that "the main difference in the two men is that Mr. Truman was more decisive, more imaginative than the good-natured Mr. Ford."[151] Joseph Alsop also made the Truman-Ford distinction. "Admittedly, Gerald Ford is not the same sort of combative, picturesque fellow that Truman was."[152] Both James Reston and Anthony Lewis respected Ford's integrity, yet doubted the president's capacity for leadership.

---

147. "The Education of Gerald Ford," *Time*, December 23, 1974, 10–11.

148. "Can Ford Pull Things Together?" *U.S. News and World Report*, December 9, 1974, 19–20.

149. "'Watergate Paralysis' Past, Government Gets Going Again," *U.S. News and World Report*, December 23, 1974, 17.

150. Alan L. Otten, "Bad Habits," *Wall Street Journal*, December 19, 1974, 14.

151. John Herbers, "Behind Ford's Veto Spree Is Trumanesque Strategy," *New York Times*, December 8, 1974, IV, 1.

152. Joseph Alsop, "A Pleasant Plainness," *Washington Post*, December 20, 1974, A27. Dennis Farney also wrote that "Mr. Ford is not, by temperament or political instinct, a Harry Truman. He's a Gerald Ford, conditioned by a quarter-century in Congress to try to work things

James Reston: He has not defined policies equal to his problems, or stated clearly where he is going or who is going with him, but he has restored at least some respect for the integrity of the Presidency, and whether he is right or wrong on his policies, this is a big advance over the last few years.[153]

Anthony Lewis: Gerald Ford remains . . . a decent human being. That is still a nice change, too. But in terms of today's economic and political realities, he is simply irrelevant. . . . A President who whistles his way past profound threats to our society, assuring us that all will turn out for the best, is unnerving. . . . The curious thing is that Mr. Ford seems to like the trappings of the Imperial Presidency without the substance of power and responsibility.[154]

Ford did win press plaudits for changing the tone of political Washington. Despite the criticisms of Ford's leadership acumen, few journalists accused the president of Nixonian tactics despite their earlier hostile evaluations of the pardon of Richard M. Nixon. By the end of 1974, Ford received widespread praise for leadership integrity. Joseph Alsop explained that

what is now called "the imperial presidency" is plainly dead and buried. . . . Under President Ford, there is no pomp at all. A pleasant plainness is the general style—and if you think about it, an American President could hardly choose a more suitable style. . . . The blandishments, the false reverence, the prostrations in all but physical act—all these are now things of the past, thank God.[155]

James Reston and John Herbers corroborated Alsop's view.

James Reston: . . . whether he is right or wrong in what he does, he is at least beginning to restore belief. He is available to his critics in the

---

out with his Democratic adversaries, to compromise, to settle for half a loaf" (Farney, "Ford's Initiation Enters Phase II," *Wall Street Journal*, November 7, 1974, 22). C. L. Sulzberger agreed with Farney. "He has not yet proved as tough or original minded as Truman nor as intellectual as Hoover. . . . What we have now is a Ford. So far the average man, he has yet to make his mark on destiny" (Sulzberger, "Not Hoover, Not Truman," *New York Times*, February 12, 1975, 37). William Safire wrote that "The President . . . is a Truman-style scrapper: Like his hero, he is a man of the Congress thrust into the Presidency unexpectedly, who knows the ploys that Congressmen play" (Safire, "Ford's 'New Direction,'" *New York Times*, January 16, 1975, 41).

153. James Reston, "In Defense of Mr. Ford," *New York Times*, December 11, 1974, 45.
154. Anthony Lewis, "Room at the Top," *New York Times*, December 5, 1974, 47.
155. Alsop, "Pleasant Plainness, A27."

Congress and the press. . . . [I]t is a big change in Washington, after the last few years. . . . Mr. Ford is different [than Presidents Johnson and Nixon in that] he knows the difference between right and wrong.[156]

John Herbers: Mr. Ford's four-month presence in the White House has brought a distinct change of mood. . . . Now everyone seems relaxed. . . . No one thinks of moving against Congress, the press or the regulatory agencies. A conscious effort is being made to restore credibility to a damaged institution.[157]

Joseph Alsop penned three columns in late 1974 defending Ford against the many press accusations of ineffectual leadership. Alsop attributed the nation's problems to a loss of will due to the Vietnam War, a shaky economy, a decline in patriotism, a decline in U.S. military power, and a Congress "dominated by blatherskites." Given this context, "President [Franklin D.] Roosevelt could not have 'led.' The truth is that the country and Congress, in their present state, do not want leadership." Yet "everyone blames President Ford for not leading."[158] Alsop expressed unease with the perception that presidential success entailed vigorous, confident leadership. "It is far better to have a man who knows what he does not know and sets out seriously to find out, than to have a man who mingles little knowledge and excessive self-assurance."[159] And Alsop reiterated the view that Ford could not be properly blamed for the nation's problems.

Our squalid political community, our intellectual community sunk in sordid self admiration, all the other American communities that matter—nowadays, all these are more at fault than Gerald Ford. And without their help, he can do little.[160]

Conclusion

Alsop expressed a dissenting viewpoint. By the end of 1974, the four-and-a-half-month stage of Ford's administration, few journalists credited the presi-

---

156. Reston, "In Defense of Ford"; see also James Reston, "Nice-Guy Leadership," *New York Times*, December 4, 1974, 43: "He is so honest that he disarms everybody who lived through the devious Nixon era."

157. Herbers, "Four Months." Alan L. Otten added that "Mr. Ford is not only a decent and honorable man but quite an intelligent one" (Otten, "Bad Habits," 14).

158. Joseph Alsop, "Mr. Ford's Declining Stock," *Washington Post*, November 22, 1974, A25.

159. Alsop, "Pleasant Plainness," A27.

160. Joseph Alsop, "The President's List of Problems," *Washington Post*, December 23, 1974, A15.

dent with effective leadership. And Ford could look forward to more difficulties in 1975 when he faced a new Congress composed of strengthened Democratic majorities in both legislative chambers and a press corps expecting activist leadership from the Republican president.

Many of Ford's communications advisers interviewed for this study stressed that the White House had a number of problems establishing a workable press strategy in the early months of the term. Coming to the White House so suddenly, without the luxury of a regular transition period, an unelected president and a hastily put together staff had to move quickly to establish their legitimacy before the public. They did not have time to plan out a coherent press strategy and, therefore, had to proceed as best they could on a day-to-day basis.

From the time of his selection to replace Spiro T. Agnew as vice president until the end of 1974, Ford's press standing fluctuated considerably. Journalists greeted Richard M. Nixon's selection of Ford with strongly worded, negative commentaries. After Ford replaced Nixon, these same journalists wrote the most adulatory columns imaginable about the new president. Ford's decision to pardon Nixon led to overnight press reassessments of the president's leadership and character.

Despite these fluctuations, certain themes emerged in the press evaluations of Ford during his tenure as vice president and early months as president. I shall review these interpretations according to my five categories of press themes.

Timing

The extraordinary set of circumstances that surrounded Gerald Ford's accession to the vice presidency and then the presidency defined the context under which journalists evaluated his actions. As vice president, Ford received unusually close journalistic scrutiny because of the unprecedented manner under which he assumed that office and because of the well-recognized likelihood that he could become president.

As president, Ford had to deal early on with a press corps consumed by the Watergate scandal and the fate of Richard M. Nixon. White House reporters had been "scooped" on the Watergate story by a pair of *Washington Post* Metro section journalists. White House press corps members determined never again to miss the "big story." They therefore subjected Gerald Ford to an unprecedented degree of press scrutiny. Ford had to operate in an environment of deep-seated press suspicion of wrongdoing by political leaders.

At first, President Ford responded effectively to journalists' high expectations. Unlike other, more traditional "honeymoon" periods, journalists did not expect an immediate outpouring of legislative proposals by the new president.

Instead, they believed that the time called for a president who could build trust once again in the integrity of political leadership. In their view, Ford did exactly that, until the pardon of Richard M. Nixon. That decision clearly undermined Ford's efforts to rebuild trust in government, and the press corps let him know it. Not only did they disapprove of the decision, they criticized Ford's timing, coming only four weeks after Nixon's resignation while the nation's wounds caused by Watergate remained open.

By the hundred-day mark of Ford's term, journalists began to express impatience with what they perceived as Ford's lack of visionary leadership. In their assessment, by the hundredth day, a president should have a clearly articulated set of policy goals and a well-defined political strategy for accomplishing those goals. Despite Ford's lack of both an electoral mandate and eleven week transition period, journalists thought that he had failed to move quickly enough on his goals. By the end of 1974, they perceived Ford's presidency as drifting, lacking direction.

Symbolism and Rhetoric

When nominated for the vice presidency, Ford did not win many press plaudits for either public speaking or the capacity for inspirational leadership. Most journalists contended that Ford lacked such "presidential" qualities. As vice president, Ford received low press marks for style. According to the prevailing press view, he gave uninteresting, "plain as bread" partisan speeches. For much of his tenure as vice president, journalists commented negatively on Ford's partisan rhetoric and most strongly attacked his frequent defenses of President Nixon against Watergate charges. Clearly, journalists expected the vice president to do something quite difficult—to distance himself in public speeches from the activities of the president. When Ford later began openly to express discomfort with the Nixon White House's handling of Watergate, journalists praised him for so doing.

Ford's symbolic actions and rhetoric during his first month as president fared superbly with the press corps. Leading journalists wrote that Ford's unpretentious, plain-spoken style perfectly reflected the nation's mood after the Nixon resignation. The inaugural "talk," first address to Congress, first press conference, and symbolic efforts to "de-pomp" the presidency all received favorable notice from the press and public. Adulatory press commentaries abounded and Ford seemingly could do no wrong. To the nation's leading journalists, Ford embodied the lost public virtues of honesty, integrity, and sound judgment—until he pardoned Richard M. Nixon. Immediately following that decision, many of the same journalists called Ford's public virtues into question and some even characterized him as Nixonian. Many questioned whether Ford could ever be trusted again.

Ford's strong underlying image of being an honest, straightforward politician undoubtedly protected him somewhat from a more severe, long-lasting press lambasting over the Nixon pardon. Without doubt, that decision changed the tone of Ford's press relations and harmed his presidential image for the remainder of his time in the White House. Nonetheless, even by the end of 1974—over three months after the pardon—when everything seemed to be going wrong for Ford and the press called into question his capacity for leadership, a number of journalists remarked that Ford deserved high marks for changing the tone of political Washington and for restoring credibility to public leadership.

Agenda

In his first four months as president, Ford's policy agenda received generally unfavorable press coverage. Journalists particularly disliked the president's economic policies of fiscal austerity. According to the prevailing press interpretation, the times called for a president to offer bold, large-scale government programs to combat inflation and unemployment. Meanwhile, Ford spoke of the need for fiscal conservatism, deregulation, and volunteerism. Journalists strongly criticized Ford's call for an economic summit and the WIN campaign as public relations gimmickry. Ford also received negative press comments for not proposing a major energy program early in his term.

Journalists placed relatively little emphasis on Ford's foreign policy, a reflection of the press's belief in the overriding importance, at that time, of domestic economic issues. Journalists described Ford as inexperienced in the foreign affairs realm and praised him for keeping in the administration an experienced hand and stabilizing influence, Henry Kissinger, as secretary of state. Despite this perception, Ford received negative press marks for having engaged in the kind of diplomatic venture designed to establish the president's leadership in the international realm. Journalists generally assessed the Far Eastern presidential trip as inappropriate during a time of domestic economic problems.

Policy Development

Ford's efforts to build public and congressional support for his programs generated poor press reviews. Journalists believed that Ford lacked the essential ingredients of effective leadership: the ability to articulate a vision, followed by a bold set of policies and a coherent strategy to enact his agenda. According to the press, leadership must come from the top, and Ford had not yet provided it. The times called for a major break from the policies of his predecessor, and Ford allegedly offered only more of the same.

Significantly, journalists expected Ford to have a relatively easy time dealing with members of Congress because, for twenty-five years, he had been one of them. According to this view, as a well-liked and respected former member of Congress, Ford could draw on his old friendships to develop support for his programs. Despite the fact that Ford could claim many friends in Congress, the Democrats dominated both legislative chambers and battled the president for control of the policy agenda. And in the aftermath of Watergate, members of Congress did not display much deference to the chief executive, friend or not. Therefore, Ford battled Congress from the early stages of his presidency, resulting in negative press commentaries on his ability to lead by controlling the agenda and developing support for his policies.

Staff

Journalists portrayed Ford's vice presidential and White House staffs as undistinguished and inexperienced. Much of the problem derived from Ford having drawn a good deal of his staff in both the vice presidency and the presidency from his former congressional office. Journalists contended that these people lacked national stature and experience in executive branch politics.

Early reports of staff conflict in the White House also harmed Ford's reputation for effective leadership. Ford lacked the luxury of a lengthy transition period and, therefore, needed to develop staff relationships and understandings on a more ad hoc basis than usual. Internal squabbles in the White House led *Newsweek* to ask "Who's Minding the New Store?" Such bickering apparently reflected on Ford's failure to establish a clearly articulated direction for his presidency early on.[161]

The so-called Nixon-holdovers controversy also damaged the press reputation of Ford's staff. Journalists skewered Ford for not moving, immediately after assuming the presidency, to rid his administration of all Nixon staffers, even those who had served honorably. In the press's view, Ford did not effect a full-scale changing of the guard and thereby failed to cleanse the government of the Watergate controversy. The press viewed Ford's presidential staff as a strange mixture of Nixon loyalists, Ford loyalists, and people who lacked any previous connection to either president.

By the end of 1974, President Ford had little to celebrate from a press and public relations standpoint. His press relations remained tarnished by the pardon of Richard M. Nixon. Journalists began seriously to doubt Ford's capacity for presidential leadership. And, for the first time, the president's Gallup Poll rating for public approval of his leadership dropped below 40 percent. Ford needed a good start in 1975 to revive press and public faith in his presidency.

---

161. "Who's Minding the Store?" *Newsweek*, September 30, 1974, 28.

CHAPTER 5

Attempting a Comeback (1975)

President Ford began the new year in a politically precarious position. From a positive perspective, Ford already had effectively established a reputation for being a leader of high character. Though stung by the press and public reaction to the pardon of Richard M. Nixon, the president's image remained that of an honest, accessible chief executive, a stark contrast to his predecessor. Yet, Ford had not developed a reputation for effective leadership. The press and public expressed little faith in his ability to command national leadership, turn around the economy, and project U.S. strength abroad.

Journalists opened the year with assessments of Ford's prospects. These assessments mirrored earlier press reviews of Ford's leadership. James Reston commented that,

> at the beginning of the New Year, the most hopeful sign in Washington is the general decline of pretense. . . . Suddenly, all the big shots have been cut down to human size. The President doesn't pretend he has all the answers. . . . Even the press is slightly baffled by the President's informal and disarming ways.[1]

A number of journalists concurred with Reston's view. David Broder described Ford as "a man of admirable character and easy personal style, with an unaffected openness and optimism."[2] John Herbers wrote that "there is no brooding into the night, as Lyndon B. Johnson did during the Vietnam War. . . . There is none of the sullen seclusion of Richard Nixon at his vacation homes."[3] A Ford profile in the *Washington Post* by Haynes Johnson, Lou Cannon, and Carroll Kilpatrick added the following observations.

> It now appears that the Imperial Presidency has died abruptly during his administration. It is a marked change. . . . Where Nixon distrusted,

---

1. James Reston, "The Decline of Pretense," *New York Times*, January 12, 1975, IV, 17.
2. David Broder, "A Chance for Mr. Ford In 1975," *Washington Post*, January 1, 1975, A12.
3. John Herbers, "Critical Test for Ford," *New York Times*, January 2, 1975, 24.

Ford trusts. Where Nixon kept his own counsel, Ford seeks advice. Where Nixon despised the press and disliked the Congress, Ford receives both openly. Where Nixon hated, Ford seeks to unite. . . . His administration truly is an open one, marked by a lack of formality and pompousness that seem to represent the most appealing side of Gerald Ford.[4]

Despite these virtues, the press contended that Ford lacked leadership ability. According to David Broder, effective leadership entails developing policies and "mobilizing public and political support for them." Broder believed that Ford had failed this test of presidential leadership: "What he is not . . . is an original thinker or a policy innovator. Like many other longtime legislators, he finds it easier to react to alternatives than to devise a program of his own design."[5] The *Washington Post* profile of Ford criticized the president for "his inability to provide inspirational leadership." The profile listed among Ford's liabilities: "Slow, plodding, pedestrian, unimaginative. Nonintellectual, lacks conceptual ability. Doesn't want change. Poorly staffed. . . . Lacks sense of communication. Inarticulate. . . . He is not a dramatic individual in any sense of that word."[6]

The *New York Times* criticized Ford's "negative approach to the nation's domestic problems." According to the *Times*, "Government passivity is hardly the most constructive attitude toward the nation's social and economic defects." The *Times* cited the need for affirmative action programs; national health insurance; increases in public-assisted housing funds; additional funding for new environmental, economic, and recreational programs; and a "comprehensive, and inevitably expensive program for the rehabilitation of the railroads."[7] After five months in office, Ford clearly had not lived up to the *Times*'s expectation of activist leadership.

The Economic Program

One columnist found the press wanting Ford to exert strong, visible leadership ironic. As Nicholas von Hoffman noted,

Politicians and commentators who were denouncing the imperial presidency a few months ago are imploring our new President to "electrify" the nation à la Franklin Roosevelt while assuring him the citizenry pines

---

4. Haynes Johnson, Lou Cannon, and Carroll Kilpatrick, "Ford Asks Six Months to Prove Himself," *Washington Post*, January 12, 1975, A10.

5. Broder, "Chance for Ford," A12.

6. Johnson, Cannon, and Kilpatrick, "Ford Asks Six Months," A1, A10.

7. "Two Years of Drift?" *New York Times*, January 16, 1975, IV, 16.

for the strong leader who will achieve national unity through national hardship and national sacrifice.[8]

In early 1975, Ford recognized the need to project decisive leadership. Ford planned two crucial speeches: An "informal address" to the people on January 13 and the State of the Union address on January 15. Ford recalled the importance of these speeches as follows.

I knew much depended on the way I delivered those two speeches. If I came across as a Chief Executive fully in command of the situation, I could win the support I needed to push my programs through the Congress. If, on the other hand, the public viewed me as weak and indecisive, I would decline in their esteem to a point from which I could not hope to recover, and the legislation that the country needed wouldn't stand a chance of passage.[9]

In these two speeches Ford presented a series of economic and energy policy proposals, including tax rebates, import levies on crude oil, a one-year moratorium on federal spending programs (except defense and energy), a 5 percent federal pay raise, and strengthened environmental standards on automobile exhaust.[10] In all, the speeches and proposals received mixed press reviews. As a *U.S. News* story commented, "The cheering up of the nation is going to take more than a TV fireside chat and a state-of-the-union address."[11]

The press watched Ford's State of the Union address most closely. James P. Gannon described Ford's speech as "unusually bleak."[12] Ford, in fact, opened with the statement that "the state of the Union is not good" and added, "I've got bad news, and I don't expect much if any applause."[13] Ford proceeded to outline his politically tough policy proposals and received little applause from the members of Congress.

Nonetheless, Ford did receive some favorable press comment for proposing some controversial policies. The *New York Times* contended that "in his address to Congress, President Ford met the first requirement of leadership,

---

8. Nicholas von Hoffman, "A Man With Get Up and Wait," *Washington Post*, January 20, 1975, B1.

9. Gerald Ford, *A Time to Heal* (Norwalk, Conn.: Easton Press, 1987), 231.

10. Ford, *Time to Heal*, 230–31; "Ford's New Strategy: Can He Restore Confidence?," *U.S. News and World Report*, January 27, 1975, 13–15.

11. "Ford's New Strategy," 13.

12. James P. Gannon, "State of the Union: In Grim Address to Congress, President Asks Action on Economic Recovery Program, Previous Budget," *Wall Street Journal*, January 16, 1975, 3.

13. "Not Good," *New York Times*, January 16, 1975, 40.

which is candor."[14] Haynes Johnson added that "what distinguished his address from many of his predecessors—and most sharply that of the man he succeeded only five months ago—was its sober catalogue of the nation's ills."[15] The *Washington Post* offered a similar perspective.

> After the war and the disorders of the '60s and the scandals and constitutional stresses of the early '70s, what the country may be most in need of is straight talk and realistic ambitions. And that is basically what it got.[16]

Not just straight talk, but Ford's performance won some good press reviews. The *Wall Street Journal* called the address "Gerald Ford's most presidential speech, and his most effective one." The *Journal* also praised Ford for not pandering to political expediency.[17] Norman C. Miller agreed that "as he promotes his controversial program, he is projecting a steady and sure sense of command." Miller added:

> Mr. Ford conveys a sense of command not because of clever public relations but because he clearly grasps the complex issues that he is addressing. . . . Mr. Ford is starting to eradicate the notion that he is just a nice guy who isn't quite up to his job.[18]

Newsweek also favorably responded to both of Ford's televised addresses.

> . . . he got his fundamental message across: that he is aware of the dangers in the economy, that he has a program for dealing with them— and that somebody after all is in charge. . . . [Ford] had at last discovered and tapped one of the real wellsprings of Presidential authority—the power to define the issues and to set the terms in which they are debated.[19]

Despite these positive assessments, the *New York Times* still believed that Ford failed to present a sufficiently comprehensive set of policies. The *Times* described Ford as "a homespun conservative in unconservative times."

14. "Not Good," 40.

15. Haynes Johnson, "President Had Bad News," *Washington Post*, January 16, 1975, A10.

16. Quoted in "Ford's New Strategy," 13–14.

17. "The President Speakes," *Wall Street Journal*, January 16, 1975, 10.

18. Norman C. Miller, "Mr. Ford's Sudden New Forcefulness," *Wall Street Journal*, January 24, 1975, 10.

19. "Ford Makes His Move," *Newsweek*, January 27, 1975, 18–19.

The *Times* thought that Ford had "misfired in his attempt to rally the nation behind a new program to meet the many-sided economic emergency."[20]

To build support for his economic and energy proposals, Ford had a tall order ahead of him. A Harris poll showed that 86 percent of the public did not have confidence in Ford's economic performance, "the lowest rating for any President on any issue since the poll began."[21] *Newsweek* reported that Ford's plan "is so broad and complex that it can sustain just about any interpretation. . . . Ford['s] program represents a series of hard and controversial choices among unpalatable options."[22] *U.S. News* reported that the seventy-five new Democratic House members, "a large crop of young, restive and 'liberal'" legislators, appeared unwilling to work constructively with an unelected Republican president. "In prospect: incessant conflict—between Mr. Ford and Congress, and within Congress itself—that could produce little action unless differences are compromised."[23]

Press criticism of the substance of Ford's proposals also complicated his efforts to deal with the economic and energy problems. Ford's proposal for a tax rebate and his willingness to accept larger budget deficits received an especially negative response. James Reston commented that, regarding economic policy, Ford "swings from one extreme to the other. One day he is the old conservative, budget balancing Jerry Ford out of Grand Rapids, Mich., and the next he is a Keynesian supporting budget deficits."[24] *Newsweek* called Ford's economic program "one of those ideological flip-flops that Richard Nixon had made so familiar: a switch from austerity to prodigality, with a major tax cut and what could be the biggest Federal deficit in U.S. history."[25] Clayton Fritchey described the Ford administration as "going around in circles" on economic policy. "In short to reinvigorate the economy and save the country, the new order is not to sacrifice but to live it up."[26] The *Washington Post* wrote that "President Ford's fiscal policy seems to be based on the supposition that nothing is really wrong with the economy, and that it only

---

20. "Not Good," 40; see also "Mr. Ford's Flawed Plan," *New York Times*, January 22, 1975, 38.

21. "A Race to Prime the Pump," *Newsweek*, January 20, 1975, 16.

22. "Sizing Up the Program," *Newsweek*, January 27, 1975, 19. *Newsweek* also thought that "Ford's options were distinctly unappetizing—a set of trade-offs likely to satisfy nobody" ("Back to the Harsh Realities," *Newsweek*, January 13, 1975, 15).

23. "Rough Road Ahead in Congress for the Ford Program," *U.S. News and World Report*, January 27, 1975, 18.

24. James Reston, "Nobody's Mad at Jerry," *New York Times*, March 9, 1975, IV, 17.

25. "Race to Prime the Pump," 16.

26. Clayton Fritchey, "Loosening That Tightened Belt," *Washington Post*, January 6, 1975, A19.

needs one modest shot of tax-rebate tonic to cheer people up."[27] Joseph Kraft also offered some critical commentary.

> The impression given by Mr. Ford's leadership style is enhanced by his economic ideology. All the evidence suggests that he is a free enterprise ideologue of the old school. . . . The President's basic program for beating recession, inflation and the energy shortage is for the government to slug the consumer, thus freeing up profits so the auto and oil companies can step in. Inevitably, the hands-off ideology combines with the permissive leadership style to raise the question of whether Mr. Ford can handle the country's economic problems.[28]

Ford's economic and energy proposals ran into trouble on Capitol Hill, further damaging his quest to be recognized as an effective leader. On February 1, Ford hiked import fees on imported oil by one dollar per barrel and mandated additional one dollar fee increases for March 1 and April 1. Congress passed legislation to delay the three-stage, three dollar per barrel tariff for ninety days. Ford vetoed the legislation. Nonetheless, Ford worked out a compromise with Congress by agreeing to suspend two-thirds of his proposed import tariff for sixty days. *Newsweek* characterized the compromise as a presidential retreat and "not an encouraging omen for Gerald Ford."[29] The news magazine described Ford's economic and energy proposals as "almost universally unpopular," leaving Congress to try to project national leadership.

> Yet Congress in the end is too divisive and dissonant a body to compete with the White House at governance. It is the President to whom Americans look for leadership . . . it is the President who has thus far disappointed their expectations. He has achieved one considerable victory, simply by stealing a march on Congress and forcing it into action.[30]

A worsening economic situation, including the highest national unemployment rate since 1941, placed considerable "pressure on Gerald Ford to do more and do it faster." Though in many ways Ford seemed "at the mercy of events" beyond his control, opinion leaders demanded more vigorous presi-

---

27. "The Economy, Energy and the President," *Washington Post*, January 15, 1975, A16.

28. Joseph Kraft, "The Ford Presidency After Six Months," *Washington Post*, February 9, 1975, B7.

29. "Ford Concedes the Putt," *Newsweek*, March 10, 1975, 14–15; "You Win Some, You Lose Some," *Newsweek*, March 17, 1975, 20–21; "Tilting to a Compromise?" *Newsweek*, March 3, 1975, 16–17.

30. "An Earful From the People," *Newsweek*, February 24, 1975, 16–17.

dential action.[31] The *Wall Street Journal* called on the president to lead in such a vigorous fashion.

> . . . there's no sense of strategy at all emanating from the Ford administration, only day-to-day coping with events as they occur. . . . At some point the President has to show a greater willingness to play rough-and-tumble political football with his old friends on Capitol Hill. . . . Mr. Ford has to start *creating* the political realities, forcing the issues, throwing the unexpected, letting the public know there is a fight on in Washington that he isn't afraid to lose.[32]

In his memoirs, Ford addressed the substance of the reviews of his presidency made during the first eight months of his term. Ford believed that, by mid-April 1975, his administration had made enough progress confronting public problems that "I could begin to shape my own agenda and define the goals I wanted my fellow citizens to endorse." Ford's goals included "less government intervention in the affairs of citizens and corporations, greater reliance on individual initiative and a free market economy, and increased local responsibility for overcoming adversities." Ford replied to his critics.

> None of these goals sounded particularly dramatic, of course, and that's why some people had difficulty responding to them. Political pundits in the nation's capital said that my ideas were stale and that I lacked "vision" as a President. Ever since FDR, that word *vision* has been equated by the media with new federal attempts to solve new problems. The more costly these attempts, the more "vision" their backers possess. . . . But I have always felt that the real purpose of government is to enhance the lives of people and that a leader can best do that by restraining government in most cases rather than enlarging it at every opportunity.
>
> If "vision" is to be defined as inspirational rhetoric describing how this or that new government program will better the human condition in the next sixty days, then I'll have to confess I didn't have it. As President, it was my job to identify the trends that were emerging in American society . . . and then to determine what decisions could affect those trends and put the country in better shape ten to twenty years from now.[33]

This passage reveals an important disjuncture between Ford's conception of presidential leadership and the expectations of his critics. Ford did not

---

31. "That Sudden Sinking Feeling," *Newsweek*, February 17, 1975, 16, 18.
32. "Football Time," *Wall Street Journal*, April 1, 1975, 20.
33. Ford, *Time to Heal*, 263.

aspire to Rooseveltian, activist leadership, yet the journalists who covered and assessed his presidency criticized him for not responding to the nation's problems in Rooseveltian fashion. That is, journalists evaluated Ford according to an image of presidential leadership that he believed did not suit the times. He wanted to be Ford. They wanted FDR. No matter how well Ford projected his own brand of presidential leadership, he would not be credited with effective leadership by those who wanted either someone else as president or Ford to behave like someone else.

In fairness, Ford received press criticism for lacking "vision" not because he lacked initiative, but, in large part, due to Congress's eagerness to up the ante. Ford presented controversial and wide-reaching energy and economic plans. His critics charged that his plans did not do enough. In early 1975, Ford proposed a $16 billion tax cut package to stimulate the economy. Congress came back with a two-year, $22.8 billion tax cut, the largest ever. The congressional response included "nearly $7 billion in lost revenues and a whole Easter basketful of special-interest benefits that [Ford] considered unwarranted or worse."[34] Despite being angry with Congress for the special-interest add-ons, Ford signed the bill into law and announced on national television that he had reached his limit for allowing increases in the national debt.

Given the largely Democratic composition of Congress, Ford had to accept some tough-to-swallow compromises as president, both in domestic and foreign affairs, and to take a good deal of criticism for not controlling the national agenda. His most difficult battle with Congress concerned U.S. policy toward Southeast Asia.

The Fall of Southeast Asia

The fall of Cambodia and South Vietnam to Communist adversaries became the most divisive, acrimonious partisan debate between Ford and the Congress. The president failed in earlier efforts to secure military aid from Congress for the South Vietnamese. By late March, the cities of Quang Tri and Hue had fallen to the Communists, and Ford learned that Saigon would collapse as well. When the situation at last seemed hopeless, Ford wanted to make a last ditch effort to support the U.S.'s allies in South Vietnam with military and humanitarian aid. Ford announced his plans for that effort in his April 10 "State of the World" address to a joint session of Congress. Ford recalled that "Henry Kissinger had urged me to tell the American people that Congress was solely to blame for the debacle in Southeast Asia. . . . My instinct was that this was not the right approach to take at the time."[35]

---

34. "Ford Signs—And Draws a Line," *Newsweek*, April 7, 1975, 30.

35. Ford, *Time to Heal*, 253–54.

But prior to that speech, on different occasions, Ford did make clear his belief that Congress deserved a large measure of blame for the failure of U.S. policy in Southeast Asia because legislators refused to support administration requests for military aid to the South Vietnamese. Journalists thought that such scapegoating did little to serve the nation's foreign policy objectives and Ford's quest for leadership respect. The *Washington Post* criticized Ford's tactic.

President Ford is making a grave mistake . . . by continuing to invent commitments to South Vietnam that never existed in fact and then blaming the Democratic Congress for not having fulfilled them. In doing so he does enormous violence to the truth and to public confidence in the government's word. Worse, he greatly diminishes the chances of working out a bipartisan and constructive approach to the serious foreign policy problems that will confront him in some part as a consequence of the tragedy now unfolding in Indochina.[36]

Murray Marder wrote in a similar vein.

. . . by reaching back to some of the rhetoric and rationalizations of the Nixon and Johnson administrations, the Ford administration has reawakened traumatic memories of 14 years of involvement in Indochina. In this dual process, the administration has stumbled into some of the same patterns of disputes, contradictions, and credibility challenges that plagued its predecessors.[37]

Ford's speech to Congress contained a mixture of statements both critical of Congress's handling of U.S. Southeast Asia policy and conciliatory toward the legislative branch. Lou Cannon saw the speech as mostly graceful toward the legislature. Cannon praised the "tone" of Ford's speech as "both urgent and conciliatory. It invoked the memory of President Truman's resolution after World War II and was couched in the language of bipartisanship which distinguished the foreign policy of that period."[38]

Cannon expressed an almost exceptional viewpoint. Other journalists charged Ford with inappropriate partisan scapegoating and disliked his request to Congress for $722 million in emergency military aid and $250 mil-

---

36. "Vietnam: The Shell Game Goes On, and On," *Washington Post*, April 4, 1975, A26.

37. Murray Marder, "Administration Trapped by Its Own Domino Theory," *Washington Post*, March 31, 1975, A1.

38. Lou Cannon, "Ford Asks $972 Million Vietnam Aid," *Washington Post*, April 11, 1975, A1.

lion in humanitarian and economic aid for South Vietnam. *U.S. News and World Report* noted that

> the President could hardly have done anything more designed to arouse congressional hostility than resubmitting a request that Congress ignored when it was at a much lower level of dollars—and when it looked as if Saigon still had a fighting chance to survive.[39]

A *Time* magazine news story said that the Ford administration made the travesty of Saigon's fall "worse" by reacting "in a schizophrenic mood, alternating between recrimination and caution." *Time* perceived the President's State of the World address as an opportunity "to fashion a new start" in U.S. foreign policy.[40] Ford's speech disappointed the news weekly.

> . . . once again betraying his ambivalence toward his acknowledged concern for a new "national unity" on foreign policy . . . Ford promptly reverted to recriminations. Once again, however indirectly, he indicated his belief that a major share of the burden of blame for South Vietnam's military debacle rested on the Democratic-controlled Congress. . . . Unfortunately, the net impact of Ford's speech . . . was to maintain the divisive domestic rupture over Vietnam rather than to bridge it. The fissure between the Legislative and Executive branches of Government seemed to have widened rather than narrowed. . . . Responding as he felt he had to, Ford has nonetheless bobbled his first grand opportunity to lead the nation out of its concentration on a lost cause and to heal the wounds of domestic partisanship over Vietnam.[41]

Press criticism of what David Broder called "the President's blame-shifting response to the Indochina crisis" abounded.[42] Hugh Sidey wrote that Ford and Kissinger "have set an example of leadership by blame. If ever there was a time to seize opportunity during crisis . . . and put on a creative foreign policy surge, it is now. The moment cries out for leadership to accept the realities, submerge recrimination and fashion a new view of the future."[43] James Reston charged that "he is as strong and subtle as a bulldozer. He talks as if the fall of Cambodia and South Vietnam to the Communists would be a

---

39. "The American Dilemma," *U.S. News and World Report*, April 21, 1975, 19.

40. "Now, Trying to Pick Up the Pieces," *Time*, April 14, 1975, 6–7.

41. "Seeking the Last Exit from Viet Nam," *Time*, April 21, 1975, 7, 10.

42. David Broder, "The Word From Grand Rapids," *Washington Post*, April 13, 1975, C6.

43. Hugh Sidey, "Big, Bulging and Bogged Down," *Time*, April 14, 1975, 30.

spectacular disaster, and that it is all the fault of Congress."[44] Nicholas von Hoffman said that "a part of him . . . strains to overlook who's to blame for Vietnam. The word is no recriminations, but the other part of him is frantic. It permits the recriminations to bubble out in spite of himself. It's the peace party in Congress that did it, that wouldn't vote the money, that lost us Vietnam to the Reds."[45] The *Washington Post* also responded negatively to Ford's speech.

> The President made his own task no easier by blaming the Congress for denying him both aid funds and authority to re-intervene, even while he insisted that he was not leveling blame and even while he offered a version of Vietnamese events ignoring his administration's own part in failing to urge President Thieu to make the political concessions called for in the Paris agreement. . . . He wants the nation to have but "one foreign policy" but neither events nor the methods he has been employing until now will likely grant him that goal.[46]

With the fall of Cambodia and Vietnam, Ford's presidency had hit a low point. Not only Southeast Asia, but a host of other problems combined to weaken Ford's leadership position and place his intended run for the presidency in 1976 in a precarious position. John Mashek noted that Ford had to deal simultaneously with "the crumbling U.S. position in Indochina, a sputtering economy, an uneasy peace in the Middle East, energy problems, a contentious Congress."[47] *Newsweek* believed that, in 1976, Ford "would, as a candidate, be holding a difficult and possibly unplayable hand: inflation, recession, the energy crisis, the final collapse of the American misadventure in Vietnam. He is . . . a thorough greenhorn at national politics. He is a threatened by a mutiny of the right wing of his own party." The news article speculated on whether Ford really would run for president in 1976, even though he had repeatedly said that he planned to seek election.[48]

With such a list of problems, Ford very much needed a major presidential success, or perceived success, to turn his fortunes around. Not long after the fall of Saigon and evacuation of 6,500 U.S. and South Vietnamese personnel from the roof of the U.S. embassy in Saigon, a crisis situation—the

44. James Reston, "Ford, Lexington and Concord," *New York Times*, April 20, 1975, IV, 17.

45. Nicholas von Hoffman, "Growing Old Believing in the American Century," *Washington Post*, April 25, 1975, B1.

46. "Mr. Ford's Post-Vietnam Foreign Policy," *Washington Post*, April 13, 1975, C6.

47. John Mashek, "A President Under Pressure," *U.S. News and World Report*, April 21, 1975, 29.

48. "The President Faces 1976," *Newsweek*, May 5, 1975, 48–49.

seizure of the U.S. merchant ship *Mayaguez* in international waters by Cambodian "pirates"—provided Ford an unwelcome opportunity to reestablish both his leadership image and the image of U.S. military resolve.

The *Mayaguez* Incident

For political journalists, the seizing of the *Mayaguez* became a major test of President Ford's leadership. Many had doubted his capacity for sound judgment and decisive action, in part due to his reaction to the fall of Cambodia and South Vietnam, and in part due to domestic economic troubles.

When the Cambodians seized the *Mayaguez* on May 12, Ford confronted a delicate situation, given the incomplete, unclear, and often contradictory intelligence reports. Over the course of three days, the White House focused its efforts on saving the merchant ship and its crew. Eventually, Ford ordered a naval destroyer-escort to take back the *Mayaguez*, an aircraft carrier to launch air strikes against the Cambodian port Kompong Som toward which the Cambodians had towed the *Mayaguez*, and the Marines to invade the island of Koh Tang (where Ford had been told that some *Mayaguez* crew members had been transferred). The plan did not proceed perfectly. Three of the helicopters moving the Marines to Koh Tang crashed, and Khmer Rouge troops in Koh Tang outnumbered the Marines who eventually landed. By the time a naval destroyer intercepted a fishing vessel carrying the *Mayaguez* crew of thirty-nine, another forty-one Americans had been killed and fifty suffered wounds. Not a spectacular success, but psychologically an important one given its timing. Ford recalled that "all of a sudden, the gloomy national mood began to fade. Many people's faith in their country was restored and my standing in the polls shot up 11 points. . . . I had regained the initiative, and I determined to do what I could with it."[49]

The *Mayaguez* incident also gave a boost to Ford's press standing. Most leading journalists assessed the incident as a major presidential success, a decisive show of leadership mettle. Evans and Novak even called the White House reaction a "spectacular triumph."[50] Richard J. Levine wrote that the White House's quick response "bolstered President Ford's political stock, lifted military morale and pleased top government officials concerned about America's world image in the aftermath of the Vietnam debacle."[51] James M. Naughton added that "the merchant ship *Mayaguez* . . . serves as a visible symbol of United States resolve to remain an influence—and, if necessary, a

---

49. Ford, *Time to Heal*, 284.

50. Rowland Evans and Robert Novak, "Another Foreign Policy Plus for Mr. Ford," *Washington Post*, May 18, 1975, C7.

51. Richard J. Levine, "Success of Mayaguez Recovery Bolsters Ford's Political Stock, Military Morale," *Wall Street Journal*, May 16, 1975, 4.

military presence—abroad despite the recent debacle in Indochina."[52] Hugh Sidey declared Ford's political rebirth after the *Mayaguez* incident. "Washington is becoming Gerald Ford's town. . . . Ford's new presence has been built on many things [including] his quick and successful response to the *Mayaguez* hijacking."[53] A *Wall Street Journal* "Washington Wire" item proclaimed that "Ford becomes bolder on foreign policy—and not just in Cambodian affair. He aims to reassert U.S. influence after Vietnam."[54] Three different *Journal* editorials praised Ford's reaction to the seizing of the *Mayaguez*.

> It not only succeeded in its immediate purpose, but made the exceedingly useful point that U.S. power is still something to be reckoned with throughout the world.[55]

> . . . the nation has seen another facet of the man. It is not that, like Richard Nixon, he will not permit himself to be pushed around. It is rather that there is a point at which he will not permit himself to be pushed around unnecessarily, and that when that point is reached, he will quietly, methodically, decently put aside compromise and send in the marines.[56]

> . . . the U.S. served noticed that it can still respond promptly and forcefully to acts of aggression.[57]

The three national news weeklies offered glowing praise of Ford's handling of the crisis. *Time* magazine called the event "a dramatic, controversial train of events that significantly changed the image of U.S. power in the world—and the stature of President Gerald Ford." The news magazine boasted about Ford's perceived victory.

> By drawing the line against aggression in the *Mayaguez* incident, he put potential adversaries on notice that despite recent setbacks in Indochina and the Middle East, the U.S. would not allow itself to be intimidated. That action reassured some discouraged and mistrustful allies that the U.S. intends to defend vigorously its overseas interests. . . . Ford acted calmly and confidently. . . . [Ford] made his own proposals, and, most important, he made the hard decisions and then stuck to them.[58]

---

52. James M. Naughton, "Praise for the President," *New York Times*, May 16, 1975, 1.
53. Hugh Sidey, "Courting Bear Hugs and Invitations," *Time*, June 2, 1975, 8.
54. "Washington Wire," *Wall Street Journal*, May 16, 1975, 11.
55. "A Lesson in Foreign Policy," *Wall Street Journal*, May 16, 1975, 10.
56. "Getting Up to Speed," *Wall Street Journal*, May 16, 1975, 10.
57. "*Mayaguez* in Retrospect," *Wall Street Journal*, October 8, 1976, 8.
58. "A Strong but Risky Show of Force," *Time*, May 26, 1975, 9–10.

The other national news weeklies agreed.

> *U.S. News*: President Ford's fast and forceful response to a challenge by
> Cambodia's new Communist rulers was meant as a signal to U.S. allies
> and adversaries. In essence: Don't take us lightly. The humiliating set-
> backs in Indochina, the world was told, have not paralyzed America's
> will to play its role as a global power.[59]

> *Newsweek*: . . . a famous victory . . . a daring show of nerve and
> steel . . . a classic show of gunboat diplomacy. . . . It was swift and
> tough—and it worked. . . . [I]ts underlying spirit was geopolitical, a
> demonstration of U.S. power and purpose to a wondering world. . . .
> [Ford] behaved Presidentially in his first important test of nerve abroad,
> and had won.[60]

Not every journalist praised Ford's handling of the *Mayaguez* incident.
An Anthony Lewis column entitled "Barbarous Piracy" intoned, "Once again
an American government shows that the only way it knows how to deal with
frustration is by force. And the world is presumably meant to be impressed."[61] Joseph Kraft penned columns asserting that too much had been
made of the whole incident.

> Particularly suspect is the claim that the United States proved something
> which ought to make us proud to be Americans. In reality, the *Mayaguez*
> is far too special an incident, and Cambodia far too tiny a country for one
> to believe that anything was proved.[62]

> That an event so trivial in importance and so ambiguous in character
> could have had such impressive public opinion results also says some-
> thing about the general climate. It suggests that the country is hungry for
> leadership.[63]

One month before the 1976 elections, the General Accounting Office
issued a retrospective *Mayaguez* incident report of questionable timing and
strongly debated objectivity. Nonetheless, the report described the Ford ad-

---

59. "New Test for U.S.: Why Ford Moved So Fast," *U.S. News and World Report*, May
26, 1975, 19.

60. "Ford's Rescue Operation," *Newsweek*, May 26, 1975, 16, 18.

61. Anthony Lewis, quoted in Ford, *Time to Heal*, 283.

62. Joseph Kraft, "*Mayaguez* Post-Mortems," *Washington Post*, May 22, 1975, A31; see
also Kraft, "Lessons of the *Mayaguez*," *Washington Post*, May 18, 1975, C7.

63. Joseph Kraft, "The President's Popularity," *Washington Post*, July 22, 1975, A19.

ministration response to the crisis in an unflattering fashion, which led the
Washington Post to declare that

> there was something grossly unbalanced about the way the incident was
> played. To imagine that a nation's prestige and credibility could be
> redeemed, or a President's image meaningfully burnished, by throwing
> the massive weight of American power against a small, war-broken,
> isolated country like Cambodia was pathetic.[64]

Presidential Travels

As vice president, Gerald Ford received ample press criticism for traveling
across the country defending President Nixon and trying to build support for
administration initiatives. Stay home and prepare to become the next president, journalists demanded. During the 1974 campaign, President Ford took
on more press criticism for traveling across the country in support of Republican congressional candidates. Stay home, eschew partisanship, and be presidential, journalists implored. In 1975, every time he traveled beyond the
Washington community, Ford could count on additional press criticism.

In late May and early June, Ford spent one week meeting in Western
Europe with NATO country leaders. A NATO summit meeting in Brussels
highlighted the trip. Hugh Sidey commented that "for all that soaring rhetoric
on peace that comes prepackaged with a presidential tour abroad, the nation's
destiny—and Ford's—ultimately rests on what happens in New York, Detroit, Chicago and even Burbank."[65]

At the end of July, Ford again traveled to Europe. During his ten day trip,
he made stops in West Germany and Poland to hold discussions with national
leaders before heading to a European Security Conference in Helsinki, the
major purpose of the trip. Ford then visited Romania and Yugoslavia. The
Helsinki conference provided Ford an opportunity to engage the Soviet leadership in discussions about arms control and freedom for Eastern European
nation-states. Ford noted in his memoirs that "no journey I made during my
Presidency was so widely misunderstood. 'Jerry, don't go,' the *Wall Street
Journal* implored, and the *New York Times* called the trip 'misguided and
empty.'"[66]

With former California governor Ronald Reagan contemplating a run for
the presidency, conservative criticism of the Helsinki conference particularly
hurt Ford. One month prior to that conference, North Carolina Senator Jesse

---

64. "The *Mayaguez* Test," *Washington Post*, October 10, 1976, C6.
65. Hugh Sidey, "Tackling the Bumbling Bureaucracy," *Time*, June 9, 1975, 14.
66. Ford, *Time to Heal*, 300.

Helms confronted Ford with a letter that indicated Alexander Solzhenitsyn's desire to have an Oval Office meeting with the president. Fearing that such a meeting could jeopardize arms control talks with the Soviets, Ford declined to grant an invitation to the exiled Soviet writer. Conservative writers protested what George F. Will called the president's "snubbing" of Solzhenitsyn.

> Obviously Solzhenitsyn is correct: Détente, as practiced by the United States, prevents even gestures of support for the cause of human rights in the Soviet Union. . . . Détente has conferred upon Brezhnev veto power over the appointments calendar of the President of the United States.[67]

Evans and Novak criticized Ford's decision even more harshly.

> The President's treatment of Solzhenitsyn reflected qualities more typical of Richard M. Nixon than Gerald R. Ford: lack of informed political consultation, gross insensitivity, equivocal explanations, just plain bad manners.[68]

One day before Ford's departure for his ten-day European trip, Carroll Kilpatrick noted the domestic criticism of the trip and said that "part of the President's trouble can be traced directly to his handling of the Alexander Solzhenitsyn affair at about the time the trip was officially announced."[69] *Time* magazine reported that "Ford's advisers, notably Kissinger, unwisely urged him against such a meeting [with Solzhenitsyn]. That made Ford look like someone who had to defer to Soviet displeasure."[70]

Solzhenitsyn's criticisms of U.S.-Soviet détente policy received considerable press attention. In a series of news articles on the Helsinki conference, *U.S. News* also questioned whether agreements with the Soviets furthered U.S. interests.

> It is the pace at which the policy is being carried forward that is being questioned. Is the U.S. moving too fast? That—and the price which is being paid. . . . Diplomatic observers see no corresponding advantages

---

67. George F. Will, "Solzhenitsyn and the President," *Washington Post*, July 11, 1975, A23.

68. Rowland Evans and Robert Novak, "Snubbing Solzhenitsyn," *Washington Post*, July 17, 1975, A27.

69. Carroll Kilpatrick, "Critics of the Trip Put President on Defensive," *Washington Post*, July 25, 1975, A2.

70. "To the Summit After a Stinging Defeat Over Turkey," *Time*, August 4, 1975, 7.

for the U.S. and its NATO Allies in the [agreement] scheduled to be ratified at Helsinki.[71]

There is widespread criticism that the bargain will prove to be heavily lopsided in favor of the Russians when it comes to actual implementation.[72]

Still at question is just how far Mr. Ford is prepared to lean on the Soviet Union to insure that détente turns into a genuine two-way street— benefiting the U.S. and its allies, not just Russia.[73]

Time magazine assessed the Helsinki conference as only marginally important to the president's domestic standing. The article contended that "Ford could count on very few of the personal political gains that customarily follow a presidential trip abroad. His stature at home may, in fact, have slipped a bit. . . . Unfortunately for Ford, the Helsinki conference both coincided with, and helped to inspire, a curious rise in skepticism about the value of détente."[74]

Unfortunately for Ford, of all the events surrounding his two trips to Europe in 1975, one trivial misstep made the largest impression on journalists. On his arrival at Salzburg, Austria, to meet with Egyptian leader Anwar Sadat, Ford slipped on wet stairs when deplaning and fell onto the tarmac. Reporters did not see the presidential slip as trivial. It strengthened the press image of Ford as a clumsy person. The next day's *Washington Post* featured a large, front-page picture of Ford's slip accompanied by the caption "Ford Falls."[75] The *Post* featured a news story entitled "Ford Stumbles 3 Times in Austria" and reported that "he lost the heel of his shoe and a measure of his dignity."[76] Nicholas von Hoffman thought the fall suited the president's trip.

Our Presidents tend to look their worst when they sally forth abroad, but this voyage is more embarrassing than most. When Mr. Ford's old football knee gave way under him and he spilled down the last couple of

71. "Big Push for Détente: Is U.S. Moving Too Fast?" *U.S. News and World Report*, July 28, 1975, 12–13.

72. "Ford Probes Brezhnev's Iron Curtain," *U.S. News and World Report*, August 4, 1975, 14.

73. "U.S. Stand After Helsinki—It's Russia's Turn to Give," *U.S. News and World Report*, August 11, 1975, 12.

74. "Some Cheering, Some Troubles," *Time*, August 11, 1975, 6–7.

75. "Ford Falls," *Washington Post*, June 2, 1975, A1.

76. "Ford Stumbles 3 Times in Austria," *Washington Post*, June 2, 1975, A8.

steps of the plane ramp at Salzburg, the fall summarized the journey. Stumble, fumble, tumble and jumble.[77]

Ford recalled that moment in his memoirs.

From that moment on, every time I stumbled or bumped my head or fell in the snow, reporters zeroed in on that to the exclusion of almost everything else. The news coverage was harmful.[78]

Over the course of the year, Ford continued to generate negative press commentary every time he traveled, whether to build public support for some presidential initiative or to commemorate an occasion. Typical of the species of press criticism is a *New York Times* editorial opinion that "it is questionable whether Mr. Ford, in devoting so much of his time to travel, is doing full justice to the other and more significant duties of his office. . . . None of these more substantive activities can be performed as well on the road as they can in the President's office in Washington."[79]

On two separate trips to California in September, Ford narrowly escaped assassination attempts (one in Sacramento on September 4, the other in San Francisco on September 19). These near catastrophes fueled more press speculation over the wisdom of frequent presidential travels. In the wake of these events, some journalists implored the president to stay home, to stop all the traveling and plunging into crowds to shake people's hands. Somewhat defiantly, Ford told reporters that he had no intention of allowing these events to stop him from interacting directly with the public.[80]

Ford stepped up his travels and the press responded with more criticism. David Broder wrote that "the Michigan Mad-Rush thinks the way to win is to travel farther and talk more than anyone else."[81] The *Washington Post* lambasted Ford's "frenzied travel schedule" and proclaimed "a certain arrogance and insensitivity and something even close to clownishness in the way that Mr. Ford has turned his pursuit of public support into a roadshow Perils of Pauline. . . . [T]here is plenty of work to be done right here in Washington for any President who wishes to be taken seriously—and plenty of evidence that this work is not being properly tended to."[82] *Newsweek* featured a number of stories in October and November critical of the president's travels.

77. Nicholas von Hoffman, "A President Stumbles, Fumbles, Tumbles and Jumbles," *Washington Post*, June 4, 1975, B1.

78. Ford, *Time to Heal*, 289.

79. "On the Road," *New York Times*, September 15, 1975, 20.

80. Ford, *Time to Heal*, 312.

81. David Broder, "Mr. Ford's Big Play: The Michigan Mad-Rush," *Washington Post*, November 12, 1975, A27.

82. "Leaving the Scene," *Washington Post*, October 17, 1975, A22.

The road show has run Ford, his staff, his bodyguards and his logistical train red-eyed and ragged. It has opened him to the charge that he is neglecting the nation's business. . . . His government is beset by high unemployment and resurgent inflation; his jet-hopping and speechmaking, in the absence of any bold programmatic answers, has begun stirring a faint but visible backlash even among friends.[83]

In recent weeks he had often seemed more like a traveling salesman than a President. He had visited more than 40 cities in 30 days, logged nearly 28,000 miles in the last two months.[84]

Ford also continued his journeys abroad. In mid-November he attended what some journalists called the "mini-summit" in Rambouillet, France. The conference involved Ford with Western European leaders in discussions about monetary policy, international trade, and other matters.

More important, Ford departed on November 29 to the People's Republic of China for meetings with Communist party Chairman Mao Tse-tung and Vice Premier Teng Hsiao-p'ing. Given the precarious U.S.-Soviet détente, Ford considered his meetings with the Chinese leadership vitally important. Ford met once with Mao, and several times with Teng to discuss U.S.-China relations and, he hoped, to encourage future dialogues and diplomatic agreements. Ford left Peking, China, on December 5 to fly to Indonesia and the Philippines.

Once again, the president's travels did not win many press plaudits. Consistent with their earlier criticisms, journalists took the president to task for traveling when policy problems mounted at home. *Newsweek* reported that "the President accomplished little of substance during his eight-day absence, and while he was away a host of problems—domestic and foreign alike— piled up on his White House desk."[85] In two consecutive issues, the news magazine keyed in on Ford's alleged "missteps."

. . . the Peking summit inevitably was sprinkled with a few missteps. In his toast at the opening banquet, Ford mispronounced a key word in China's anti-Soviet lexicon: hegemony (HEDGE-a-mony instead of the correct ha-GEM-ony). His visit to see Mao was held up when the Chinese refused to take along two gate crashers—aides Richard Cheney and Ronald Nessen. Then there was the case of the double dinner. After

---

83. "Call of the Open Road," *Newsweek*, October 13, 1975, 28–29.

84. "Ford's First Plank," *Newsweek*, October 20, 1975, 18; see also "Travel Bug," *Newsweek*, November 3, 1975, 16–17.

85. "Now, Ford's Long March," *Newsweek*, December 15, 1975, 22.

attending a ballet . . . Ford wanted a steak. Just as he was about to dig in, his Chinese chefs set out an elaborate meal of their own. (Ford gallantly struggled through both).[86]

His travels, once again, had done little if anything to counter his image as an amiable bumbler. . . . A hapless run of malaprops, faux pas and odd accidents had clearly wounded his dignity—and unnerved some of his staff.[87]

More substantively, the press criticized Ford's trip to China as unmeaningful because the president did not secure a major diplomatic agreement. No doubt summits generally are viewed as a success or failure by the press on the basis of whether some dramatic international breakthrough is achieved—a treaty, an agreement, something. One day before Ford's departure for Peking, the *Wall Street Journal* featured a news story that prejudged the summit.

Instead of political breakthroughs, there will be much ceremony and sight-seeing. Rather than the forging of new diplomatic relations, there will be efforts to keep intact those that already exist. . . . In all, the Ford journey will be more noteworthy for what it won't accomplish than for what it will.[88]

The *Washington Post* editorialized: "The second visit by an American President to China is neither so momentous as Richard Nixon's trip in 1972, nor so theatrical."[89] At the conclusion of the China visit Dennis Farney said that "there weren't any breakthroughs or any startling announcements here. . . . The results don't compare with those achieved by Richard Nixon in his epochal visit here in 1972. . . . The trip was, in a sense, stillborn."[90] *Newsweek* provided a similar perspective.

There was no afterglow from the China trip to tide Ford over. His visit got little more than token attention on television and in the newspapers. . . . [T]he summit produced no new agreements, no diplomatic breakthroughs, not even a communique. . . . [Ford's] China trip, which

---

86. "Ford's Long March," 26.

87. "Ford in Trouble," *Newsweek*, December 22, 1975, 20–21.

88. Robert Keatley, "Politesse in Peking: Ford China Trip Seen as Ceremonial Exercise Without Much Hope of Action on Vital Issues," *Wall Street Journal*, November 28, 1975, 22.

89. "Mr. Ford in Peking," *Washington Post*, December 3, 1975, 14.

90. Dennis Farney, "Ford Concludes Ceremonial Trip Without Pacts or Major Announcements," *Wall Street Journal*, December 5, 1975, 6.

had been conceived as a vintage political plus, turned out to be essentially a non-event.[91]

His Asia trip and new "Pacific Doctrine" drew yawns all over the Op-Ed pages. . . . [Ford's] transcontinental contrails had yet to establish his credentials as a statesman or his stature as an on-the-case Chief Executive.[92]

If, as some journalists suspected, the president wanted to improve his public and press standing by traveling often and looking "presidential," the strategy did not work. Nonetheless, by late 1975, journalists credited Ford with reestablishing the ethical tone of political Washington, even though they still found his leadership lacking in other areas.

First Year Retrospectives

August 9, 1975, marked the first year of Gerald Ford's presidency. The occasion provided a good opportunity to judge Ford's progress in office, and Ford received mixed press reviews at this stage. On the negative side, many journalists thought that Ford had yet to demonstrate convincing leadership. In their view, he still lacked "vision" and a plan to revive the nation's economy and international prestige. Jack Anderson wrote that "he has not displayed the personal equipment usually associated with the modern presidency. He is not bold, innovative, dynamic nor eloquent."[93] James Reston noted that "he is a deeply conservative and national man in an increasingly radical and interdependent world. . . .[Ford] does not really grapple with the perplexing problems of the insurgent hum of the age."[94] David Broder concluded that, after a year in office, Ford had failed to articulate his "larger objectives" and plans for leading the nation.[95] *Time* agreed that "the President has not provided anything resembling a blueprint for the nation."[96] John Mashek declared Ford "no innovator. He tends to shun new ideas" in favor of "conservative answers to national problems."[97] In the foreign affairs realm, Bernard Gwertzman wrote that Ford had failed to leave "a discernable imprint of his own" and,

---

91. "Ford's Long March," 22, 25.

92. "Ford in Trouble," 21.

93. Jack Anderson, "Mr. Ford—Part of the People," *Washington Post*, August 3, 1975, C7.

94. James Reston, "Ford's First Year," *New York Times*, August 6, 1975, 35.

95. David Broder, "Mr. Ford's First Year," *Washington Post*, August 6, 1975, A14.

96. "Ford in Command," *Time*, July 28, 1975, 9.

97. John Mashek, "A 'Nice Guy' As President: His Strengths and Weaknesses," *U.S. News and World Report,* August 11, 1975, 19.

instead, "stressed continuation rather than innovation."[98] And according to the *New York Times*,

> What is lacking as his second year begins is not personal strength and calmness, but rather a well-stated philosophy and a set of relevant goals. Often . . . the President sounds like a man whose real dream is to return America to a simpler, bygone age when laissez-faire was a credible policy. But no such regression is possible. . . . Public problems make public leadership inescapable. . . . Providing leadership on these and other public problems is the highest test of a President. It is that test Mr. Ford has yet to meet successfully.[99]

Ford fared best with those journalists who evaluated the ethical tone of his presidency. George F. Will undoubtedly hit the mark with his comment that Ford "had an easy act to follow." Even so, Will called Ford's "primary achievement"—restoring public confidence in the national leadership—"crucial and marvelous." That coming from a pundit who, less than a year earlier, lambasted the pardon of Richard M. Nixon, said that Ford could not be trusted to "say what he means and mean what he says," and characterized Ford as just another crafty, deceitful politician. Will's perception of the president evidently had changed.

> After one year in office Mr. Ford is what he ought to be, a straight talker served by clear thinkers. . . . Having succeeded the most curdled personality in the history of the presidency, Mr. Ford's first service to the nation was to be himself, applying to the nation's bruised spirit the healing balm of his calm-like-calm. He did this brilliantly, but easily.[100]

Other journalists, some of whom had criticized Ford's leadership acumen, offered similar favorable appraisals. Hugh Sidey noted a number of factors that confirmed Ford's unpretentious manner. According to the *Time* columnist, Ford shied away from the imperial trappings of the White House, maintained the aura of his Middle American roots, and liked to sit in the old family chair from his modest suburban northern Virginia home and read the

---

98. Bernard Gwertzman, "Ford Impact Is Uncertain In Foreign Policy So Far," *New York Times*, August 9, 1975, 1.

99. ". . . Pursuing Détente," *New York Times*, August 10, 1975, IV, 14. The *Times* also criticized Ford's economic, energy and environmental policies; see " . . . Muddled Economics . . . ," *New York Times*, August 10, 1975, IV, 14.

100. George F. Will, "President Ford's First Year," *Washington Post*, July 25, 1975, A25.

Grand Rapids Press for news about hometown friends. In other words, the presidency did not change or distort Ford's admirable personal qualities.[101] Jack Anderson described Ford as neither "manipulative, secretive nor duplicitous." Anderson added that

> his unpretentiousness fits the mood of a country grown wary of world savers. His calm soothes a people recoiling from years of clamor and turbulence. . . . Rarely has the decency, openness and genuineness of one man been so instrumental in restoring to the conduct of national affairs that sense of serenity and trust.[102]

Joseph Kraft declared that Ford brought about a "rebirth of trust" in national leadership.[103] James M. Naughton favorably compared the mood of political Washington in August 1975 to that of one year earlier.[104] James Reston also praised Ford. "His personal conduct has been almost faultless. He has been open, available, candid, and truthful. . . . He removed the atmosphere of conspiracy. . . . This is a big change in the last year and a triumph of Ford's character and personality."[105] David Broder agreed: "Mr. Ford has fully adapted to the demands of the presidency without distorting his own personality in the process." The *Post* columnist elaborated as follows.

> He has done much to relieve the tensions in this capital and the world by making the generous personal gestures that indicate understanding of the other person's situation. To a nation cynical beyond belief about politics and politicians, Mr. Ford has applied the healing balm of his own calm and candor.[106]

The *New York Times*, which had been consistently critical of Ford's leadership, nonetheless agreed with the press consensus.

> Mr. Ford moved promptly and effectively to end the rancor, distrust and governmental paralysis that marked the last month of his predecessor's scandal-stained Administration. . . . No scandal has marred his Administration.[107]

---

101. Hugh Sidey, "He Has Not Deserted the Old Haunts," *Time*, July 28, 1975, 8–9.

102. Anderson, "Mr. Ford, C7."

103. Joseph Kraft, "Ford's Second Year," *Washington Post*, August 10, 1975, B7.

104. James M. Naughton, "President Marks a Year In Office; Hails Astronauts," *New York Times*, August 10, 1975, 1, 32.

105. Reston, "Ford's First Year, 35."

106. Broder, "Ford's First Year, A14."

107. "Mr. Ford's First Year," *New York Times*, August 10, 1975, IV, 14.

U.S. News favorably assessed Ford's political style. "Mr. Ford has brought considerable change to the Presidency and the way it is run. . . . Mr. Ford's operating style as President is seen as a reflection of his personality—open and friendly. He is far more accessible than most Presidents have been."[108] *U.S. News*'s John Mashek declared Ford's "major success" as "re-establishing the legitimacy and dignity of the office of the President." Mashek opined:

> "Decency," "integrity," "uncomplicated" are words heard so frequently in describing Mr. Ford that they have become clichés. Yet, as with most clichés, there is considerable truth underneath those words. . . . Mr. Ford has been successful in "opening up" the White House. . . . [A] sense of isolation and of an "imperial" Presidency have disappeared with Mr. Ford in office.[109]

Time added to all the praise of Ford's political style.

> . . . he is approachable, conciliatory and not consumed by personal ambition. He has divested the presidency of its imperial trappings. . . . Ford is obviously at home in the White House; more important, he seems to be at home with himself, secure enough to take criticism and attack without resorting to the vengeful tactics of previous Chief Executives, much less the illegal activities of Richard Nixon. His enemies' list, if he has one, must be the shortest on record. By his own behavior, he has blotted out the sordidness of the Nixon years.[110]

Many journalists also described Ford's leadership position as increasingly formidable. *Time* magazine noted that the expectation that Ford would be a "caretaker" in the White House "did not prove to be the case." Instead, "Ford's current stature is based partly on his successes: his series of vetoes of Democratic spending measures, his rescue of the *Mayaguez* from the Cambodians, his growing forcefulness in dealing with world leaders."[111] Citing the *Mayaguez* incident, perceptions of an improving economy, and respect for the president's "open" leadership style, R. W. Apple, Jr., asserted that "President Ford ended his first year in office . . . in a stronger political position than he

---

108. "Start of Second Year—The Big Changes at the White House," *U.S. News and World Report*, August 11, 1975, 15.

109. Mashek, "'Nice Guy' As President," 19.

110. "Ford in Command," 7.

111. "Ford in Command," 7, 9.

began it."[112] *U.S. News* reported that "Mr. Ford clearly likes his job, despite its burdens. . . . What strikes those who have watched Mr. Ford closely in the past is the heightened sense of confidence he projects."[113] Marjorie Hunter agreed that "nearly a year in the Presidency has changed Gerald Ford in one notable way: He is far more sure of himself. . . . [Ford] speaks confidently and without hesitation. . . . [Ford] and many of his top aides are far more accessible than those of previous Administrations."[114] And John Mashek observed that

> twelve months ago, Mr. Ford seemed unsure of himself. . . . Today, things are far different. Mr. Ford now is a man confident of his capacity to serve as President. . . . [Ford] looks and acts like a President. Plainly, Gerald Ford is a man happy in his job.[115]

Despite the favorable commentaries about Ford's ethical presidency and new leadership stature, his administration's handling of the economy continued to receive harsh criticism. Some journalists expressed philosophical differences with Ford over how to revive the economy; others portrayed him as insensitive to the plight of suffering poor people. As Hugh Sidey observed, "The great sympathy that was extended to him in a trying time of transition has apparently run thin. . . . [Although] Americans like him better than ever as a man, there are growing doubts about his ability to lead. These doubts center on the economy."[116] Economics columnist Hobart Rowen wrote that "the Nixon-for-Ford trade provided no magic solution for the economy."[117] Other columnists offered more harsh evaluations.

> *Joseph Kraft*: His do-nothing approach to managing the economy did not exactly work to head [the recession] off. . . . [I]t is a question whether Mr. Ford's conservative bias will allow him to support the programs required to help the cities and the poor.[118]

---

112. R. W. Apple, Jr., "Politicians Find Ford Stronger Than Year Ago, but Are Unsure About Prospects in '76," *New York Times*, August 10, 1975, 33.

113. "Start of the Second Year," 15–16.

114. Marjorie Hunter, "President, Now Confident, Shuns Isolation," *New York Times*, July 25, 1975, 11.

115. Mashek, "'Nice Guy' As President," 19.

116. Hugh Sidey, "The Days of the Dog Star," *Time*, August 25, 1975, 17.

117. Hobart Rowen, "Mr. Ford's Economic Record," *Washington Post*, August 7, 1975, A15.

118. Kraft, "Ford's Second Year," B7.

Russell Baker: . . . he has gone back to policies that have lain in rusty disrepute for half a century. . . . Faced with the worst depression since the nineteen-thirties, he has taken a line that makes Herbert Hoover seem like a New Dealer. . . . It is the rectified essence of old-fashioned conservatism. . . . Government nods until the market shakes itself out.[119]

William V. Shannon: Mr. Ford rocks no boats, offers no challenges to the conventional wisdom. . . . He does not care very much. He does not care, for example, about the many forms of misery that create social problems in America and in the world.[120]

At the end of one year in office, therefore, Ford could claim some progress in generating a favorable press image. For the most part, Ford still suffered press criticism for a lack of "visionary" leadership and for failing to be a policy innovator. Yet Ford effectively reestablished his reputation for integrity and had moved away, somewhat, from the press recriminations over his pardon of Richard M. Nixon.

Despite these public image gains, the nation's economic situation plagued the administration's efforts to enhance Ford's leadership stature. Whether justified or not, Americans equate their economic situation with the president's leadership.

Ford could attribute his somewhat improved press image to the *Mayaguez* incident and his success at sustaining a number of vetoes. But his press image remained in a tenuous position. Most important, journalists still questioned his leadership ability, they still operated in an environment of suspicion, and the economy had not turned around. For the remainder of 1975, Ford had to overcome a number of serious problems before he could build up his presidential stature.

The Economy

Throughout the year, Ford received significant press criticism for his handling of the economy. In 1975, the Democratic Congress attempted to take control of the economic policy agenda by seeking to enact a number of domestic spending programs, including a $5.3 billion jobs bill. Conscious of the budget deficit and unconvinced that the opposition policies would work, Ford vetoed a number of measures, and congressional minorities sustained most of his vetoes. Clayton Fritchey reported that "while the impasse is commonly called

---

119. Russell Baker, "Backward Reels Time," *New York Times*, August 2, 1975, 21.
120. William V. Shannon, "The Happy Traveler," *New York Times*, August 8, 1975, 27.

'government-by-veto,' it is more like stalemate-by-veto."[121] And the *New York Times* wrote that "a string of vetoes does not add up to an action program."[122]

Most important, the press viewed Ford's economic approach as outdated. The *Times* called Ford's approach "stark negativism" and "stolid, unvarnished conservatism." The editorial critically asked, "Are those who fail in a competitive market economy to be thrown on a human scrap heap called a slum and forgotten—unless they rob, mug, or riot?"[123] James Reston described Ford as "a dead honest conservative confronted with radical problems . . . and he gives the country locker-room pep talks on the glories of fiscal responsibility."[124] Clayton Fritchey thought that Ford's policies recalled Hoover's.

> Today, Gerald Ford, another depression President, takes up where Hoover left off. He too, assures us that renewed prosperity is about to break out any minute. . . . So, like Hoover, he thinks the best way of getting the country back on its feet is to rely on nature rather than intensive care or artificial respiration. . . . [Ford's] artificial optimism is no substitute for authentic action.[125]

Linking Tax Cuts and Spending

Ford's critics complained that while the president vetoed one Democratic measure to restore the economy after another, he offered no plausible policy alternative. On October 6, 1975, Ford announced, on national television, an economic plan that he believed would answer the critics. The president proposed a $28 billion tax cut to stimulate the economy, thereby far outbidding the tax cut proposals of congressional Democrats. The catch? This tax cut would be approved only if Congress also approved $28 billion in spending cuts. The *Wall Street Journal* loved the idea of linking tax cuts to spending reductions. "The President's surprising leap is a smart one politically because the economics are sound. . . . [Ford] has finally staked out some commanding political terrain."[126]

Unfortunately for Ford, most of the press dissented from the *Journal's*

121. Clayton Fritchey, "The Vetoes and the Votes," *Washington Post*, July 1, 1975, A19.

122. "Government Disorder," *New York Times*, June 8, 1975, IV, 16.

123. "Government Disorder," IV, 16.

124. James Reston, "Mr. Ford's Bad Politics," *New York Times*, September 26, 1975, 37.

125. Clayton Fritchey, "Happy Days Are Here Again," *Washington Post*, June 28, 1975, A11.

126. "President Ford Does It Right," *Wall Street Journal*, October 8, 1975, 18.

view. By the time Ford announced this proposal, it had become clear that Ronald Reagan planned to challenge the incumbent president for the Republican party's presidential nomination. Therefore, many journalists evaluated Ford's official decisions in light of his political aspirations. In reaction to the Ford economic plan, Hobart Rowen commented that "Mr. Ford is playing election year politics with the tax issue."[127] David Broder wrote that the "spending ceiling is as artificial as a Halloween hobgoblin. . . . Mr. Ford's demand that Congress enact it now, as a condition for his signing a needed tax-cut bill, is pure political showmanship."[128] The *Washington Post* also reacted critically to Ford's tactic.

> The tax cuts may make him popular, but they go well beyond the stimulus that the country now requires. . . . The attempt to corner Congress into a pledge on spending is merely polemic, and promises to make his relationship with the Capitol less productive than ever.[129]

Hobart Rowen agreed with the *Post*'s assessment.

> What comes through clearly is that the President has fashioned an elaborate political ploy. He is playing louder tax-cut music to drown out the Democrats, and sounding elaborate "knock out Big Government" themes to please the Republican right wing.[130]

> . . . one wonders whether Mr. Ford wanted the budget limit, or a political issue with which to hit the Congress. . . . Mr. Ford's maneuvering is a tip of the hat to Reagan, and the result a high-water mark for economic mismanagement by the Ford administration.[131]

Journalists' reactions to this alleged "political ploy" could not measure up to their reactions to Ford's handling of another controversial economic issue—New York City's possible financial default.

---

127. Hobart Rowen, "Tax-Cut Politics," *Washington Post*, October 30, 1975, A27.

128. David Broder, "Mr. Ford's Fall Follies," *Washington Post*, October 15, 1975, A18.

129. "The President and Taxes," *Washington Post*, October 8, 1975, A10; see also "Right and Wrong on Taxes," *Washington Post*, December 15, 1975, A14.

130. Hobart Rowen, "A Ford Tax Cut Offer Congress Should Not Accept," *Washington Post*, October 12, 1975, A27.

131. Hobart Rowen, "Tax Tug of War Symbolizes Politics, Bad Economics," *Washington Post*, November 20, 1975, B7. Yet several weeks later Rowen disputed the assessment that Ford adopted economic policies as part of an election strategy and argued that "the timid fiscal and monetary policies being pursued are not contrived—they are basically what an instinctively right-wing President believes in" (Rowen, "Super Cautious Economics," *Washington Post*, January 8, 1976, A18).

New York City's Fiscal Crisis

In 1975, New York City faced a deteriorating financial situation. In May, Mayor Abraham D. Beame and New York Governor Hugh Carey requested Ford's support of a federal ninety-day credit of $1 billion. Ford rejected the proposal outright as a bad precedent. In September, the mayor and the governor visited the White House and Capitol Hill seeking support for federal aid to the city and still received no presidential support for their proposal. Ford recalled: "As the city's woes multiplied, I maintained a tough line against aid for New York in all my public remarks."[132] Ford believed that the city had to get its own fiscal house in order without expecting federal assistance. He thought that federal aid would only encourage the city to engage in spendthrift activities, knowing the federal government could come to the rescue. He also believed that helping the city in such a fashion would open the "floodgates" to other cities and localities lobbying the federal government for aid. These arguments did not impress many leading journalists. James Reston wrote that "New York is drowning and [Ford] gives it a lecture and throws it an anchor."[133]

On October 29, as the city was on the verge of bankruptcy, Ford addressed this issue before the National Press Club. In a more public forum, and in even stronger terms, Ford iterated his earlier reasons for not supporting a federal bailout of New York City. He further stated that "when New York City now asks the rest of the country to guarantee its bills, it can be no surprise that many Americans ask why."[134]

Ford's rebuke of New York City, once again, led a number of journalists to question whether the president had acted out of political motives. The *Washington Post* denounced Ford for his alleged "icy indifference" to the city's plight and for "gratuitously denouncing" New York's leaders for "fiscal mismanagement." The *Post* speculated that Ford had consciously adopted a position that would "play in Peoria."[135] David Broder explained that Ford had treated the city's problem "as the last act of a morality play." In Broder's view, "It's a play well-tailored to the antigovernment sentiments of the national audience. It's also a way for the President . . . to conceal from the country the reality that we face."[136] The *New York Times* accused Ford of "exploiting nasty anti–New York sentiment around the country" and called Ford's rhetoric "demagogic." The *Times* elaborated: "He has put the manufacture of a propa-

---

132. Ford, *Time to Heal*, 316.
133. Reston, "Ford's Bad Politics, 37."
134. Ford, *Time to Heal*, 318.
135. "The New York Gamble," *Washington Post*, October 21, 1975, A22.
136. David Broder, "Urban Ills," *Washington Post*, November 5, 1975, A27.

ganda theme ahead of governing the nation."[137] Furthermore: "The President has clearly been mixing election politics with macroeconomics—to the detriment not only of New York but of the entire nation."[138] Both a column by Evans and Novak and a news report from *Newsweek* said that Ford had scored a major political victory with his rebuke of the city's finances.[139] The most scathingly critical commentary on Ford's speech came from Anthony Lewis's sarcastically entitled column "Good Old Gerry Reagan."

> Why should a pleasant, open man play to the country's prejudices against New York City? Why take a problem, complex in origin, and misrepresent it, in demagogue's style, as the result of the bad guys' sins? . . . The explanation is not obscure. Peel Gerald Ford, layer by layer, and you find nothing but politician. . . . Political necessity, as his limited vision perceives it, has determined the way he is playing the New York crisis. Mr. Ford has one big thing on his mind right now: beating Ronald Reagan for the Republican Presidential nomination. The way to do that, in the Ford canon, is out-Reagan Reagan.[140]

Other journalists offered unflattering assessments of Ford's action on New York City. James Reston referred to the President's speech as "Nixon talk" and added that "[Ford] sees the New York crisis only in the narrowest terms. He has no general philosophy about the nation as a whole."[141] The *Washington Post* also lambasted the president's actions.

> Undoubtedly there have been presidential speeches more outrageous than the one President Ford delivered on New York City's financial problems. But it is hard to remember one. Mr. Ford used all the demagogue's tricks: misstating the problem, distorting the facts, running down the critics, resorting to pious platitudes and appealing to prejudice.[142]

The most famous press account of Ford's speech came from the tabloid *New York Daily News*'s October 30 headline: "FORD TO CITY: DROP DEAD."[143] The bold-print headline certainly captured a strong New York City sentiment that the president did not care about that city's problems.

137. "Bankruptcy Politics," *New York Times*, November 2, 1975, IV, 14.

138. "Scare Story," *New York Times*, October 31, 1975, 32.

139. Rowland Evans and Robert Novak, "Ford Peels the Big Apple," *Washington Post*, October 30, 1975, A27; "The Birth of an Issue," *Newsweek*, November 10, 1975, 18–20.

140. Anthony Lewis, "Good Old Gerry Reagan," *New York Times*, November 3, 1975, 35.

141. James Reston, "Ford's Limited Vision," *New York Times*, November 2, 1975, IV, 15.

142. "The President and New York City," *Washington Post*, October 31, 1975, A26.

143. *New York Daily News*, October 30, 1975, 1.

Ford's speech did elicit favorable commentary from an unsurprising source—the *Wall Street Journal*:

> President Ford's Dutch uncle lecture to past and present managers of New York's finances yesterday was highly appropriate; anyone who thinks it was political opportunism should reexamine the issue. . . . The refusal . . . to give New York a federal bailout loan or loan guarantee is not based on rednecked prejudice. Washington has been more than generous to New York over the last decade—that's one root of the city's problems.[144]

Significantly, the city government accepted Ford's position and adopted a series of expenditure cuts as well as a package of $200 million of new local taxes. As a compromise, the Ford administration agreed, after all, to loan money to the city when it needed cash, with the stipulation that New York would pay back the cash advances with interest at the end of each fiscal year. This compromise prompted the *Washington Post*, which had been so critical of Ford's position on the city's finances, to comment that "it seems to us that Mr. Ford has handled the problem of New York City in a remarkable fashion. . . . [Ford] has executed that policy well, despite his verbal excesses. . . . By being so hard-nosed . . . Mr. Ford has forced action. . . . And by doing so, he has reduced substantially the amount of federal funds New York City now needs."[145]

Most journalists did not portray this compromise in such a favorable fashion. Instead, they believed that Ford had hurt his leadership image by changing his position. A *Wall Street Journal* news story reported that "Ford's vacillation on aiding New York worsens his competence crisis. . . . He stumbles into a no-win position."[146] Dennis Farney et al., reported for the *Journal* that "[Ford] did force the city and the state to make a series of sacrifices that the mayor and governor had insisted couldn't be made. But by finally promising the aid he had seemed determined never to give, Mr. Ford probably reinforced his national image as a weak and indecisive President."[147] Evans and Novak noted that "Mr. Ford again is seen zigzagging on a nationally spotlighted issue."[148] And Hobart Rowen agreed that "Mr. Ford did a 180-degree turn . . . that brings his credibility into serious question. . . . Now

---

144. "The Dutch Uncle President," *Wall Street Journal*, October 30, 1975, 20.

145. "Mr. Ford and New York City," *Washington Post*, December 1, 1975, A14.

146. "Washington Wire," *Wall Street Journal*, November 21, 1975, 1.

147. Dennis Farney, et al., "Ford's Turnaround: New York City Wins Aid From Washington, But Everybody Loses," *Wall Street Journal*, November 28, 1975, 1.

148. Rowland Evans and Robert Novak, "Mr. Ford and New York: Polls, Politics and Problems," *Washington Post*, November 22, 1975, A15.

that Mr. Ford has done his flip-flop, one shouldn't assume that the crisis is over."[149]

Indeed Ford's new policy position on the city's finances had not ended the problem for him. But a different crisis faced the Ford administration in November, a crisis that also exacerbated Ford's leadership image problems.

The Cabinet Shake-Up

In early November, President Ford made a number of major changes in his cabinet that clearly took the press by surprise. Most important, Ford fired Secretary of Defense James Schlesinger and replaced him with Donald Rumsfeld, who had been serving as the White House chief of staff. Rumsfeld's chief deputy, Richard B. Cheney, moved up to the chief of staff position. Firing Schlesinger caused a major political problem for Ford because the secretary of defense had won over the support of hard-line conservatives. Henry Kissinger, the nemesis of the political Right, stayed on as secretary of state but did not retain his position as national security adviser. That post went to Air Force Lieutenant General Brent Scowcroft. Rogers Morton left the secretary of commerce post for health reasons, and Ford appointed Ambassador Elliot Richardson to the position. Ford also replaced Central Intelligence Agency Director William Colby with George Bush.

Ford's most dramatic move concerned Vice President Nelson Rockefeller's plight. The political Right despised the progressive New York Republican. Clearly, many conservative activists would support a Reagan candidacy over a Ford candidacy with Rockefeller running on Ford's ticket in 1976. Ford chose the politically expedient course of action and capitulated to the political Right. In his memoirs, Ford recalled that he approached Rockefeller on October 28 to discuss "the growing strength of the GOP's right wing." Ford explained to Rockefeller that he could undermine the Ford nomination campaign and the vice president withdrew from the ticket.[150]

After announcing the personnel changes on November 3, the press, in Ford's words, "had a field day."[151] Or, as the *Wall Street Journal* reported, "Ford's shake-up fails to attain its goal of showing strong leadership. . . . Press reaction to the shake-up, from both liberal and conservative pundits, is highly critical."[152]

Unarguably correct. The *New York Times*'s James M. Naughton called

149. Hobart Rowen, "Ending Game of Financial Chicken," *Washington Post*, December 7, 1975, B7.

150. Ford, *Time to Heal*, 328.

151. Ford, *Time to Heal*, 330.

152. "Washington Wire," *Wall Street Journal*, November 7, 1975, 1.

the cabinet changes "the Byzantine reorganization,"[153] and a *Times* editorial characterized Ford's actions as "unpresidential behavior."[154] George F. Will called the Schlesinger firing "a foolish thing done in a foolish way. Gerald Ford the itinerant incumbent, has seemed less than presidential recently."[155] Evans and Novak wrote that the Schlesinger firing indicated "that the Ford White House, which advertises openness and candor, closely resembles the Nixon White House in abhorring dissent and diversity."[156] Lou Cannon referred to the cabinet shake-up as "the Byzantine battle for power that went on behind the closed doors of the supposedly open Ford administration."[157] Joseph Kraft wrote that the changes "stimulated new doubts as to whether he has the brains to be President. For the Sunday Massacre advertised disarray in a way that makes Mr. Ford easier meat for his political foes. . . . The seemingly arbitrary decisions, moreover, betray a President who seems not to know what he's doing."[158] The *Washington Post* said that the effect of the cabinet changes "has been to present the unfortunate image of a weak caretaker, presiding over a divided and unruly government."[159] Dennis Farney speculated that the changes, rather than make Ford look "presidential," would "contribute to the opposite impression of a weak and floundering President."[160] David Broder compared the cabinet changes to the pardon of Richard M. Nixon. "Once again, the decision was made in secret and sprung as a Sunday surprise at an awkward moment. . . . [Ford] has tried to sweep the problem aside by clearing the players off the board."[161] Stephen S. Rosenfeld acknowledged that Ford had a "right" to change administration personnel, but that right seemed unimportant compared to "the apparently unwitting trifling with the national interest which he has now done."[162] James Reston wrote two columns denouncing Ford's personnel changes.

---

153. James M. Naughton, "Mr. Ford's 'Guys' Turn Out to Look Like Everybody Else's," *New York Times*, November 9, 1975, IV, 1.

154. "Abdication," *New York Times*, November 9, 1975, IV, 14.

155. George F. Will, "Dampening Dissent . . . ," *Washington Post*, November 5, 1975, A27.

156. Rowland Evans and Robert Novak, "Schlesinger: Intolerable Dissent," *Washington Post*, November 6, 1975, A27.

157. Lou Cannon, "Rumsfeld: Silent Architect," *Washington Post*, November 4, 1975, A1.

158. Joseph Kraft, "The Crumbling Administration," *Washington Post*, November 4, 1975, A27.

159. "The Shake-Up," *Washington Post*, November 5, 1975, A26.

160. Dennis Farney, "Worried Candidate: Ford's Election Fears Helped Set the Stage for Shake-Up of Staff," *Wall Street Journal*, November 4, 1975, 1.

161. David Broder, "A Glimpse at White House Realities," *Washington Post*, November 9, 1975, D5.

162. Stephen S. Rosenfeld, "Dissolving the Kissinger-Schlesinger 'Partnership': A Mistake," *Washington Post*, November 7, 1975, A27.

He is not trying to compose the honest differences among his Cabinet members but getting rid of the characters who get in his way, and disrupting his Administration when the new men have no time to learn their jobs.[163]

He didn't reorganize his Administration but disorganized it. . . . The country has lost by trading an experienced team for an inexperienced team. . . . [Ford] has proved his machismo and evidently feels liberated and even exhilarated by throwing his bombs. The only trouble is that it was all so sudden, personal and even capricious. Now all he has to do is live with the consequences.[164]

Additional commentaries from the *New York Times*, Nicholas von Hoffman, and Evans and Novak constituted some of the most harsh assessments of Ford's action. Evans and Novak called the cabinet changes an "incompetent execution of an ill-conceived project to reinvigorate Gerald Ford's leadership." Ford had "succeeded only in presenting an administration in utter disarray and making the Reagan challenge more viable than ever." The columnists intoned that Ford's action "gave the nation a picture of Byzantine intrigue and ruthless personal treatment" comparable to "Richard Nixon's Saturday Night Massacre of 1973."[165] The *New York Times* called Rockefeller's withdrawal "the central event in a power shake-up that leaves the Ford administration looking weak and beleaguered."[166] The *Times* also compared Ford to his predecessor.

. . . after this promising start in which he reopened blocked lines of communication and encouraged diverse viewpoints, President Ford began to retreat toward a fortress mentality. He has increasingly resorted to old Nixon strategies and campaign themes.[167]

Nicholas von Hoffman thought that the press had perhaps overstated the case regarding Ford's political motives.

Enormous expenditures of ink and ingenuity have been committed to making the Sunday Night massacre look dishonestly evil instead of stone

---

163. James Reston, "Ford's Narrowing Base," *New York Times*, November 7, 1975, 37.
164. James Reston, "Mr. Ford's Machismo," *New York Times*, November 5, 1975, 43.
165. Rowland Evans and Robert Novak, " . . . and Miscalculating at the White House," *Washington Post*, November 5, 1975, A27.
166. "Rockefeller Down," *New York Times*, November 4, 1975, 34.
167. "The Ford Strategy," *New York Times*, November 5, 1975, 42.

stupid. Surely his sharper advisers—assuming he has some—would also prefer to have their leader regarded as malevolent rather than dumb. We respect the wicked but we laugh at the inept. [168]

End of Year Reviews

The year ended badly for Ford. Ronald Reagan had decided to challenge Ford for the Republican presidential nomination. The Far Eastern trip did not win many press plaudits and did not interest the American public a great deal. Although the economy had shown some improvement, Ford's policies did not receive much of the credit. The cabinet shake-up, designed to demonstrate the president's forcefulness and decisiveness, ended up being perceived as what *Newsweek* called "hastily planned, badly timed and clumsily executed, and in the end it only inflamed the doubts it was intended to settle: whether he really is in control of his unelected Presidency and his uncertain political fortunes." [169]

In the wake of the cabinet shake-up, journalists presented highly negative reviews of Ford's leadership at the end of the 1975. Lou Cannon pronounced that "after 16 months as President, Mr. Ford's basic style both at home and abroad remains that of a House minority leader accustomed to unrelenting Republican fund-raisers." [170] Evans and Novak proclaimed that "he is no political high roller but a true son of Congress inclined to the most cautious route." [171] George F. Will made the following comments.

Mr. Ford not only became President by accident, but has only prospered as President by fortuities—by having an easy act to follow, and by having had an easy war to win (the war against Cambodian kidnapping). . . . After 500 days in office Mr. Ford is widely regarded as a caretaker. And in presidential politics, a synonym for "caretaker" is "lame duck." [172]

No news story so dominated the press during this stage of Ford's term than what *Time* called "The Ridicule Problem." The *Time* news story re-

---

168. Nicholas von Hoffman, "Our Top Fall-Down Comic," *Washington Post*, December 2, 1975, C1.

169. "Ford's Big Shuffle," *Newsweek*, November 17, 1975, 24.

170. Lou Cannon, "Asian Trip Suffered From Political Trivia," *Washington Post*, December 9, 1975, A10.

171. Rowland Evans and Robert Novak, "Procrastination on the Energy Bill," *Washington Post*, December 27, 1975, A15.

172. George F. Will, "A Caretaker in the Oval Office," *Washington Post*, December 17, 1975, A19.

counted: "As an accident-prone President with an amiable but bumbling style, Ford has become a straight man for columnists, gagwriters and partygoers." *Time*'s news story included a number of jokes about the president and quoted several columnists' unflattering commentaries on the "bumbling" president.[173]

The so-called bumbler image problem had been a common part of the press's profile of Ford ever since the early days of his vice presidency. Why so much press attention in late 1975 to this aspect of Ford's image? Primarily because the president took a one-week skiing vacation to Vail, Colorado, during the Christmas season. Ford did what all skiers do—he fell down occasionally. Only unlike other skiers, Ford had a legion of photographers to capture the event. And capture the event they did. Newspapers coast to coast carried unflattering pictures of the president's falls. *Newsweek* ran a Ford profile in which a news story discussed the president's "Bozo the President" image. The story declared that "whether the President has been playing the clown or whether he has become the victim of a cycle of downbeat and trendy journalism remains very much an open question."[174]

Some journalists had fun with Ford's misfortune. William Safire wrote a comical essay describing fictitious presidential thoughts.

> The comedians are clobbering me on television, making me look like a clumsy oaf, and from now on every time I don't move like a ballet dancer the picture will be in every living room. Even Betty says I should spit out my gum before I come to bed. Very funny.[175]

Columnists Tom Braden and George F. Will repeated the antics of television comics to convey the point that people no longer took the president seriously.

> *George F. Will*: On a recent television show Rich Little, the comedian, was doing his familiar impressions of politicians. . . . But in his impression of Mr. Ford, Little did not speak. He just backed up five paces, and then strode forward until he stumbled smack into the microphone. That brought down the house.[176]

> *Tom Braden*: Johnny Carson advised his audience the other night not to worry about Gerald Ford getting a job. "If Reagan beats him," Carson explained, "the Timex watch people want him for commercials. He's going to put the watch on and then walk down the stairs."

---

173. "The Ridicule Problem," *Time*, January 5, 1975, 33.
174. Quoted in Ron Nessen, *It Sure Looks Different From The Inside* (New York: Playboy Press, 1978), 191.
175. William Safire, "Oval Ruminations," *New York Times*, December 18, 1975, 45.
176. Will, "A Caretaker," A19.

When the nation's end men begin to treat a serious politician as a joke, he is through. Gerald Ford is through, and the problem for the Republican party now is how to avoid holding a referendum on Ronald Reagan. . . . As Gerald Ford becomes more and more of a joke, why shouldn't they turn to a serious man?[177]

Nicholas von Hoffman referred to Ford as "Old Bungle Foot" and as "someone catastrophically close to making himself into a national clown." The *Post* columnist further mocked the president.

Whether or not Mr. Ten Thumbs becomes the first President to be laughed out of office, matters have reached the point that one Washington newsie assigned to cover the Great Flub-Dub was heard to complain that ineptitude on such a scale is beginning to reflect unfavorably on those who have to report it.[178]

A number of other journalists also drew attention to Ford's alleged "bumbling."

Newsweek: Ford reading a speech can be a painful experience. . . . He fumbles words. He drifts from his text and loses his place. He butchers gags and blows punch lines. He enjoys a pre-prandial drink with the boys, like any politician on the road, and occasionally shows it in his post-prandial speeches.[179]

Evans and Novak: That Mr. Ford's worst problems concern image rather than substance is no consolation. Indeed, policy positions can be changed more easily than public perceptions. . . . Why does the President stumble? How come his words get mixed up? Irrelevant and unfair as these questions may be, they invite brutal speculation about whether he has wits enough to be President.[180]

Wall Street Journal: Ever since President Gerald Ford became President, he has been haunted by an aura of clumsiness. The American people have seen him falling down airplane ramps, bumping his head on doors, banging into the side of a swimming pool, falling down the ski slopes, getting tangled up in his dogs' leashes, calling Anwar Sadat President of

---

177. Tom Braden, "Possible Alternatives for the Republican Ticket," *Washington Post*, December 27, 1975, A15.

178. von Hoffman, "Top Comic," C1, 5.

179. "Can Reagan Stop Ford?" *Newsweek*, November 24, 1975, 32.

180. Rowland Evans and Robert Novak, "Mr. Ford and Politics: A Terminal Illness?" *Washington Post*, December 16, 1975, A15.

Israel, and suffering from other embarrassments. The subject has become a focus of jokes from all sides.[181]

Presidential Press Secretary Ron Nessen disliked this kind of negative press and decided, unwisely, to fight back. As a former newsman, Nessen should have realized that a defensive posture would contribute to the image problem rather than overcome it. Nonetheless, Nessen reacted to the "bumbling" stories with a "set the record straight" campaign. That is, he expended extraordinary effort protesting the news coverage of Ford and lecturing reporters on Ford's athletic prowess. From Nessen's point of view, such an athletic president as Gerald Ford did not deserve to be lampooned as a klutz and such news coverage demeaned the presidency. Undoubtedly true, but stating the case in an angry, defensive manner failed to change the tone of news coverage. Nessen's lecturing of journalists about his boss's physical prowess itself became a news item and object of ridicule. The *Journal* wrote that Nessen "has shown the real clumsiness here."

He has taken what is essentially a joke and turned it into a serious matter on which he cannot hope to win. To sensible people, the whole idea of a presidential press secretary bragging about his boss's gracefulness makes the whole team look comic. A free suggestion to Mr. Nessen—let the jokers make jokes and encourage Mr. Ford to show us he can stand up on the real issues.[182]

Conclusion

By the end of 1975, the Ford White House staff had failed to turn around their negative press. The year began with a favorably received State of the Union address and concluded with press commentaries mocking the president's alleged clumsiness. Evans and Novak undoubtedly stated the problem accurately when they wrote that such a presidential image would be more difficult to alter than administration policy positions.

How did the press view Ford's successes and failures in the first full calendar year of his brief term? In what follows, I review Ford's press coverage during the year according to the five categories of press evaluations.

Timing

In 1975, journalists looked to the president to provide decisive national leadership, to overcome the political stalemate with the Democratic Congress, and

---

181. "Bumbling on a Bum Rap," *Wall Street Journal*, December 30, 1975, 8.
182. "Bumbling on a Bum Rap," 8.

to make progress on a host of policy problems, particularly the faltering economy. Ford, in their assessment, had several months of presidential training and, therefore, needed to take control of the policy agenda, first with the State of the Union address and then with a coherent plan to enact administration policies. Journalists did not credit Ford with having seized the initiative in such a fashion. At this early stage of his presidency, they expected more activist, interventionist leadership from the Republican president.

Journalists also continued to emphasize the demands of the times for leadership integrity, for moving beyond the recriminations and the cynicism of the Nixon years. In this regard, journalists portrayed Ford as the right man for the times. Joseph Kraft wrote that "I think he has made genuine progress in making government more honest and the White House more open."[183] John Herbers maintained that "he has restored a degree of openness and a higher standard of ethics to the institution he inherited from Richard Nixon."[184] Alan L. Otten observed that "he's managed to remain an honest, open, decent human being. . . . [Ford's] also an unusually honest and straightforward man, of considerable personal and professional integrity."[185] James Reston noted that "he has restored a sense of fairness, respect and decency to the White House."[186] The *Times* columnist also wrote that "he does not shut himself off in the White House, but brings everybody in. . . . He has no enemies list. . . . [Ford's] strength is that he is honest, and after the last few years in Washington this is a big change."[187]

Symbolism and Rhetoric

Journalists still portrayed Ford as a president who lacked vision. In their view, Ford failed to convey an identifiable theme or message that summarized his administration's goals for the future. After the WIN campaign failure, the Ford administration did not unveil another simplifying slogan. The Ford administration did consciously seek to capitalize on the important symbol of an honorable, decent president. That strategy undoubtedly worked because it suited Ford's personality and his public image built over many years in politics. With less success, the administration tried to market Ford as a modern-day Harry S Truman. Yes, journalists said, Ford could claim some noted Truman traits: open, straightforward, and unpretentious. Yet, they claimed, Ford lacked Truman's leadership traits: decisiveness, combativeness, and vision.

---

183. Joseph Kraft, "Rebuilding Confidence," *Washington Post*, June 29, 1975, C7.

184. John Herbers, "Ford Now Is a President In the Recent Tradition," *New York Times*, May 18, 1975, IV, 4.

185. Alan L. Otten, "A Decent Man," *Wall Street Journal*, February 27, 1975, 10.

186. Reston, "Ford, Lexington and Concord," IV, 17.

187. Reston, "Nobody's Mad," IV, 17.

Ford continued to receive negative press commentary for public speaking and political rhetoric. According to the press, Ford failed to use the power of the "bully pulpit" effectively. He lacked the ability to rouse an audience behind his leadership. He did not inspire people with his words. Journalists generally characterized Ford as a poor public speaker, a perception underscored with greater frequency once Ronald Reagan entered the presidential contest. Journalists began to emphasize the inevitable occasional misstatements in presidential speeches, given Ford's continuing image problem as a "bumbler." With this image problem becoming so pervasive, Ford simply had a great deal of difficulty conveying the symbols of his presidency and having his words taken seriously by the press. Ford's many attempts to turn the image problem around in 1975 did not come to fruition.

Agenda

Given the faltering economy, journalists expected Ford to focus his attention on domestic policy issues. They criticized Ford for placing a great deal of emphasis on foreign policy and international travel. Many journalists portrayed Ford's interest in the foreign affairs realm as a form of escapism from domestic economic and energy problems. They defined a set of policy priorities different than the Ford administration's.

Journalists perceived Ford's foreign affairs activities—particularly his travels—as more political and symbolic than substantive. They assessed his trips abroad as unsuccessful when his efforts did not bring home major diplomatic agreements or breakthroughs. From the press's standpoint, Ford's travels abroad lacked the drama and significance of former president Nixon's earlier travels.

In the domestic realm, journalists saw Ford's policy agenda as too cautious, too conservative, and not bold enough to meet the demands of the times. Many journalists dearly wanted FDR-style policy activism from this Republican president who had to deal with a strong opposition party–led Congress. Some journalists compared the domestic economic situation to that of the Depression and called for dramatic policy interventions by the president. Even when Ford proposed a sweeping tax cut as an economic stimulus, journalists thought that the proposal did not go far enough. When Ford later presented a much bigger tax cut proposal tied to budget cuts, journalists called the idea gimmickry. Then, when Ford adopted tax cuts and some spending measures that allowed larger budget deficits, journalists criticized him for policy inconsistency.

Policy Development

According to the leading journalists, President Ford lacked a well-thought-out strategy to build public and congressional support for White House initiatives.

Norman C. Miller blamed the Ford White House for a "lack of comprehensive policy direction [that] cedes many initiatives to Congress."[188] The *Wall Street Journal* declared: "Creating new realities rather than responding to obsolete ones, after all, is what political leadership is all about." The *Journal* thought that Ford had not fulfilled this leadership task.[189] The *New York Times* characterized Ford's political philosophy as "do-nothingism,"[190] and stated its complaints in an editorial entitled "Abdication."

> What the country would like to have is a President who thinks about major policy questions, who formulates consistent domestic and foreign policies and who seems to know where he and his Administration are going. Mr. Ford is in deep political trouble because he thus far fails to satisfy these expectations of the Presidency.[191]

The press perceived the Ford White House as usually reactive to events such as economic downturns. The press did not believe that Ford succeeded at articulating goals and implementing plans to achieve those goals. Journalists saw no clear policy direction emerging from the Ford White House and wondered whether that failure consigned Ford to the status of a caretaker president. In some cases, the press characterized Ford's efforts to build support for his administration's goals as counterproductive. Ford's criticism of Democratic members of Congress for not funding administration efforts in Southeast Asia particularly fueled the perception that the Ford White House had little idea how to build a base of congressional and public support.

Staff

President Ford's White House staff continued to receive press criticism. Journalists perceived Ford's staff members as second rank, lacking in national stature, still composed of too many Nixon "holdovers," and much too inclined to infighting. On New Year's Day 1975, David Broder wrote that "his Hill staff people were rarely more than mediocre, and he has improved the quality only in a few places in his move to the White House."[192] At the end of the year, Broder wrote that Ford needed to end the "tolerance of a White House and campaign staff whose mediocrity sabotages his every effort to exert effective leadership. He could clean house of the bumblers he brought from his

---

188. Norman C. Miller, "Taking Charge: Vietnam Woes Aside, Ford Restores a Sense of Purpose to Office," *Wall Street Journal*, April 16, 1975, 27.

189. "On the Road With Jerry Ford," *Wall Street Journal*, September 22, 1975, 8.

190. "The Two Messrs. Ford," *New York Times*, August 26, 1975, 30.

191. "Abdication"; see also Joseph Kraft, "The Ford Presidency After Six Months," *Washington Post*, February 9, 1975, B7.

192. Broder, "Chance for Ford," A12.

days in Congress and the vice presidency, and give himself a 'team' that is competent for the political and governmental challenges ahead."[193] Joseph Kraft also wrote near the end of the year that "the quality of the men Mr. Ford has with him as his closest advisers is so low, and his own perception of the country's problems so dim, that the chances for a much better record in 1976 have to be rated very low indeed."[194] Lou Cannon added that "the staff remains basically a congressional staff, attuned to the needs of 'good old Jerry Ford.'"[195] *U.S. News* featured a news story, "Disputes that are Splitting the Ford Team," that analyzed the implications of the White House's well-known staff infighting.[196] John Herbers made the following assessment.

> . . . in the two most vital policy areas, foreign and economic affairs, Mr. Ford continues to depend largely on those associated with the Nixon Administration. The limited number of new faces and new ideas reinforce the impression that Mr. Ford, as President, is not the departure he once seemed to be.[197]

Going into the last year of his short presidential term, Ford had a number of problems to overcome: the troubled economy, an unflattering presidential image, a negative press, staff infighting, a combative, opposition party–controlled Congress facing an election year, and the Ronald Reagan challenge for the Republican presidential nomination. Ford recalled that troubled time.

> All of the problems that confronted me were serious, but I made up my mind that I wasn't going to let them get me down. Despite some setbacks, 1975 was nothing to be ashamed about. We had healed the wounds of Watergate, moved the economy from the depths of the recession to more jobs and less inflation, and our basic strengths remained intact. We could look forward to the future with renewed confidence.[198]

---

193. David Broder, " . . . A Prescription for Mr. Ford's Recovery . . . ," *Washington Post*, December 17, 1975, A19.

194. Joseph Kraft, "Self-Imposed Problems," *Washington Post*, November 29, 1975, A17.

195. Cannon, "Asian Trip," A10.

196. "Disputes that are Splitting the Ford Team," *U.S. News and World Report*, August 25, 1975, 19–20.

197. Herbers, "President In the Recent Tradition," IV, 4; see also Herbers, "Ford People Largely Resemble Nixon People," *New York Times*, December 22, 1974, IV, 1.

198. Ford, *Time to Heal*, 346–47.

CHAPTER 6

Campaigning for Election (1976)

The Gallup public opinion poll released on January 8, 1976, noted a mere 39 percent national approval rating for Ford's presidential performance. Ford attributed the poor showing to image more than to substance and said that "we simply hadn't done a good job of communicating what I had done and why over the last seventeen months."[1] David Broder agreed that Ford had failed "to express his vision of America's future or to convey the larger design of what a full four-year Ford administration would seek to achieve. The inspirational dimension of presidential leadership still seems beyond his reach."[2]

The ridicule problem did not subside either. At the beginning of the year, Lou Cannon and David Broder reported the following.

> In the last few weeks, President Ford has become the butt of a hundred jokes and cartoons, all embellishing the theme that he is what *Newsweek* called "an amiable bumbler."
>
> The problem has been building since the President took his first well-publicized pratfall, coming down the steps from *Air Force One* in Salzburg, Austria, last year. There have been other public stumbles—tripping on a dog leash, over a wheel-chair, bumping his forehead on the edge of the swimming pool.[3]

Hugh Sidey believed that Ford's "bumbling" symbolized the president's leadership problems. Sidey believed that the image problem stopped many people from taking the president's substantive activities seriously.

> Ford's sallies into international diplomacy have been marred by little things like tripping on the airplane ramp in Salzburg, or finding himself yucking it up with a Geisha named Honorable Treasure Pleasure in Japan

---

1. Gerald R. Ford, *A Time to Heal* (Norwalk, Conn.: Easton Press, 1987), 347.

2. David Broder, "A President With His Chin Out, Defiantly," *Washington Post*, January 4, 1976, F7.

3. Lou Cannon and David S. Broder, "Ford Hopes For Last Laugh," *Washington Post*, January 5, 1976, A1, 3; see also "Image Maker With His Hands Full," *U.S. and World Report*, January 12, 1976, 27.

while the U.S. Stock Market plummeted and Chrysler Corp. announced it was closing five plants.[4]

Joseph Kraft could not resist plugging another comic Ford anecdote in an Op-Ed column about the presidential budget, further evidence of the president not being taken seriously even on serious matters.

Just before the President presented his budget at a press conference last week, a reporter asked a White House aide whether Mr. Ford was going to have to stand through the full 90-minute session. "Why don't you get him a stool?" the reporter suggested. "Because," the aide laughed, "he might fall off."[5]

The January 19 State of the Union address provided Ford an important opportunity to overcome his image as lacking in vision and constantly stumbling. He made a fluid, if unexciting, presentation characterized by a conservative tone. Ford emphasized the need to balance government programs and individual freedoms and explained that big government had trampled the rights of citizens. He called for a large-scale reduction in government growth, a $10 billion tax cut, an increase in Social Security taxes to help eliminate the budget deficit, private industry incentives, and a catastrophic health plan for the elderly. The president even tried his hand at creating a slogan, and called for a "new realism" in dealing with the economy and foreign policy.[6]

Ford later described the press reaction to his speech as "mixed."[7] Lou Cannon reported that Ford presented an "optimistic" speech, "delivered forcefully and with only an occasional verbal stumble."[8] U.S. News reported that, by emphasizing the need for government restraint, Ford had made "the biggest gamble of his Presidency" and set the stage for presidential-congressional combat.[9] The Washington Post reacted: "Mr. Ford has offered the country a clear description of sharply limited government. . . . Mr. Ford's style of government is one that works best in quiet times."[10] Philip Shabecoff thought that "it was the kind of rhetoric that the public has become accustomed to from Mr. Ford and that Mr. Ford feels suits him best; generally

---

4. Hugh Sidey, "Beyond the Facts and Figures," *Time*, February 2, 1976, 11.

5. Joseph Kraft, "The Politics of the Budget," *Washington Post*, January 26, 1976, A15.

6. Lou Cannon, "President Urges 'New Realism' on Defense, Welfare," *Washington Post*, January 20, 1976, A1, 12.

7. Ford, *Time to Heal*, 351.

8. Cannon, "President Urges 'New Realism,'" A1; see also "State of the Union: I'm an Optimist," *Time*, January 26, 1976, 9–10.

9. "State of the Union: Ford's Formula—Will It Work?" *U.S. News and World Report*, February 2, 1976, 11.

10. "The State of the Union," *Washington Post*, January 21, 1976, A14.

simple, straight-forward, serious and bland. And like the contents of the speech, the rhetoric, too, was cautious and unexciting."[11] The *New York Times* offered a critical view.

There is no cause for surprise at Mr. Ford's go-slow, do-little approach. As a member of Congress for a quarter century, he voted against virtually every social program proposed during that period. His budget and economic projections are framed in terms of his commitment to diminished government rather than of the fiscal realities of government or of the human needs of society.[12]

A number of journalists perceived largely political motives in Ford's emphasis on limited government. Dennis Farney generally described Ford's speech as "aimed at American voters—particularly those in coming Republican primaries."[13] Richard J. Levine characterized Ford's budget proposals as "tailored to undercut Ronald Reagan's conservative appeal in the GOP primaries."[14] David Broder asserted that "Mr. Ford attempted in his speech to preempt the middle-ground conservatism . . . and to leave his challengers . . . on the political fringes."[15] And the *Washington Post* noted that

President Ford in this year's State of the Union Message, drew the portrait of the voter to whom he means to address himself in the coming months' campaign. That voter is fed up with Washington and doesn't really believe that it can do much to improve his . . . life.[16]

U.S. News predicted that election-year politics would dominate the governmental agenda throughout 1976. In bold type, the news weekly declared: "From start to finish, election-year politics will color the second session of the 94th Congress. Result: plenty of stalemates, a few compromises on major national issues." The article projected that "in 1976, every issue will be overshadowed by the race for control of the White House and Congress in 1977 and thereafter."[17]

---

11. Philip Shabecoff, "Mr. Ford in Search of the Right Speech," *New York Times*, January 25, 1976, IV, 2.

12. "Ship of State," *New York Times*, January 21, 1976, 36.

13. Dennis Farney, "State of the Union: Ford Charts Austerity, Merged Programs; Presses Tax Cuts, Plan to Reduce Jobless," *Wall Street Journal*, January 20, 1976, 3.

14. Richard J. Levine, "Frugal Facade? Ford's Budget Slates More Fiscal Stimulus Than Officials Admit," *Wall Street Journal*, January 22, 1976, 1.

15. David Broder, "Ford Seeks Middle Ground," *Washington Post*, January 20, 1976, A12.

16. "State of the Union," *Washington Post*, A14.

17. "President vs. Congress—Endless Feud?" *U.S. News and World Report*, January 5, 1976, 19–20.

Democrats in Congress did not waste much time combating the president. They controlled 290 of 435 House seats and 61 of 100 Senate seats. Nonetheless, Ford had compiled an impressive record of sustaining his many vetoes. In 1975, congressional Democrats had set the stage for conflict with the president by enacting a series of sweeping procedural reforms, including a weakening of the filibuster rule. In unprecedented fashion, a group of liberal reformists changed the entrenched committee seniority system and ousted three powerful committee chairmen. In 1976, the Democratic Congress clearly did not want to practice politics as usual and prepared to challenge Ford's initiatives while trying to take control of the agenda-setting process.

In January 1976, Congress denied a Ford administration request to fund U.S. operatives in Angola. According to *U.S. News*, "This signaled that Congress will insist on writing its own rules to avoid international tangles." Congress then overrode Ford's veto of a $45 billion appropriations bill, "a sure indication the President will face further difficulties in holding down spending."[18] *Time* called the veto override a "startling defeat for Ford [that] set the mood and the stage for what promises to be a congressional session full of tough, partisan politics and bitter confrontations with the White House."[19] Congress then defiantly passed an emergency $6.2 billion public works bill against the president's objections. Ford vetoed the bill and the Senate sustained the veto by just a three-vote margin.[20] *U.S. News* declared, "Troubles are just beginning for Mr. Ford in Congress."[21]

Ford faced even more trouble from outside Congress: a charismatic Republican primary opponent, Ronald Reagan, who had an impressive campaign organization and the fervent support of movement conservatives nationwide. Ford could not afford to concentrate all of his efforts on the duties of the presidency. He had to expend enormous effort just to secure his own party's nomination, an unusual position for an incumbent president. Given its love of "horserace" politics, the press paid increasing attention to the Republican and Democratic presidential primaries.

The Reagan Challenge

Ever since Ford capitulated to party conservatives by encouraging Nelson Rockefeller not to stay on the Republican ticket in 1976, journalists believed the president's decisions were motivated primarily by electoral politics. After

---

18. "Ford Against Congress: The '76 War Begins," *U.S. News and World Report*, January 9, 1976, 11.

19. "Mr. President, We're in Trouble," *Time*, February 9, 1976, 16.

20. "Ford Wins a Fight over Jobs," *Time*, March 1, 1976, 9.

21. "Ford Against Congress," 11.

Rockefeller withdrew in November 1975, Ronald Reagan quipped, "I'm certainly not appeased." The *Washington Post* reacted to Reagan's declaration.

> Mr. Reagan's announcement underscores the failure of Mr. Ford's efforts to preempt conservative support. . . . Mr. Ford's policy of appeasement of the Republican right, it seems to us, is likely to be self-defeating not only for him, but also for the party as a whole.[22]

In December 1975 and again in January 1976, Ford appealed to Congress for funds to send to pro-Western groups in Angola to fight off a communist-led movement. Ford said that he wanted to avert a communist takeover of the country. Congress said that it did not want to involve the United States in "another Vietnam." Some journalists said that Ford adopted this anticommunist posture politically to outflank Reagan on the right.

> *Clayton Fritchey*: Since the administration's determination to continue somehow its involvement in Angola is self-defeating diplomacy, it must be concluded that it is motivated by other considerations, such as domestic politics. . . . [Ford and Kissinger] feel an urgent need to put on a show of "standing up" to the Soviets, especially to protect themselves from charges of being soft on communism. It won't appease Ronald Reagan, though.[23]

> *Washington Post*: President Ford . . . accused congressmen who differ with him on Angola of having "lost their guts"—a tasteless and tactless charge made, one is forced to suspect, to protect his right flank against Ronald Reagan's New Hampshire [primary] onslaught. Why else would Mr. Ford so needlessly further antagonize his congressional adversaries.[24]

Lou Cannon reported that, as the presidential primary and caucus season opened, Ford had "moved closer" to Reagan on a host of policy issues. "At times last week there seemed to be two Ronald Reagans running around New Hampshire—and one of them was named Gerald Ford."[25] Joseph Kraft argued that Ford's "swerve to the right" had destroyed the president's credibility. "The upshot is a kind of schizophrenic presidency. Mr. Ford has to keep

---

22. "The State of the GOP," *Washington Post*, November 22, 1975, A14.

23. Clayton Fritchey, "Angola and U.S. Politics," *Washington Post*, January 3, 1976, A19.

24. "The Next Phase in Angola," *Washington Post*, February 15, 1976, K6.

25. Lou Cannon, "Ford Talks Have Familiar Ring," *Washington Post*, February 10, 1976, A1.

interrupting his management of great affairs to play parish politics."[26] Economic affairs columnist Hobart Rowen saw government spending proposals dictated by party politics. "President Ford has presented the nation with a budget that has been honed and polished to meet the right-wing challenge of Ronald Reagan—but still leaves a significant gap between them."[27]

Evans and Novak noticed that, during the early primary and caucus contests, Ford "seemed on the defensive over the Reagan attacks on détente."[28] Reagan made criticism of détente policies the hallmark of his foreign affairs campaigning. The message played well with conservative activists. In early March, Ford and Kissinger displayed what *U.S. News* called "a new and distinctly tougher attitude towards relations with Moscow." The news weekly reported that

> a significant change is now taking place in U.S.-Soviet relations. The Ford Administration has lost its illusions about the meaning of détente. It has discovered that the Soviet drive for a global empire, far from abating, is still moving relentlessly ahead.[29]

Ford, in fact, declared that the word *détente* no longer could be used to describe his administration's policies toward the Soviets. *U.S. News* wondered, "Why has the Ford Administration shifted to a tougher stand with Moscow? Domestic politics is part of the answer. Ronald Reagan [and Democratic presidential candidates] have attacked Mr. Ford's conduct of foreign policy in general and détente in particular."[30] A host of journalists blasted Ford for having, in Clayton Fritchey's words, "banished 'détente' from his vocabulary." Fritchey thought that Ford had pandered to the political right and thereby invited "further attacks."[31] George F. Will mocked: "Gerald Ford, the semanticist, has announced that never again will the word 'détente' pass his lips. Henceforth, that word is as unwelcome at the White House as, oh, Alexander Solzhenitsyn."[32] David Broder maintained that "Ronald Reagan

---

26. Joseph Kraft, "Mr. Ford's Trips to the Provinces," *Washington Post*, February 22, 1976, F7.

27. Hobart Rowen, "Ford Edges Reagan In Battle of the Budget," *Washington Post*, January 25, 1976, C10.

28. Rowland Evans and Robert Novak, "Dealing With Discredited Détente," *Washington Post*, January 24, 1976, A15.

29. "Why U.S. is Suddenly Getting Tougher With Russia," *U.S. News and World Report*, March 29, 1976, 17.

30. "U.S. Suddenly Tougher," 17.

31. Clayton Fritchey, "The Helsinki Pact: Ford Didn't Sign Alone," *Washington Post*, October 16, 1976, A15.

32. George F. Will, "A Farewell to 'Détente,'" *Washington Post*, March 7, 1976, C7. Will is referring (somewhat sarcastically) to Ford's decision not to invite the Soviet dissident and

washed the word 'détente' out of President Ford's mouth and guaranteed that the policy it represents will be part of the political debate in the coming months."[33] Joseph Kraft criticized Ford for dropping the term *détente* and for proposing additional defense spending increases. "Mr. Reagan, in other words . . . sets the pace for a national security debate. The President of the United States, in keeping with the post-Vietnam mood, is on the defensive."[34] Kraft offered a similar assessment.

> Shallow electioneering figured importantly in the way the President has dropped the word "détente" from his political vocabulary, for clearly Mr. Ford has acted less out of conviction than in response to popular demand.[35]

Throughout the primary election season, journalists took Ford to task for running a reactive campaign and for letting opponent Reagan define the terms of the Republican party debate. The *New York Times* wrote that "the President has hardly given progressive and centrist Republicans much to cheer about. Instead, he has allowed Governor Reagan to push him steadily to far-right positions."[36] Joseph Kraft thought that "in fighting the challenge of Ronald Reagan for the Republican nomination, Mr. Ford has been reacting all the way."[37] Kraft accused Ford of conveniently switching policy positions to appeal to conservatives and wondered "what is one to think of a President who moves at such a dizzying pace from one position to another—who is a budget cutter one day and a defense spender the next?"[38] The *Washington Post* responded to an apparent policy move by Ford on the Panama Canal. "Mr. Ford errs in terms of both policy and politics, we believe, by trying to move to his right on this issue to soften the Reagan attack. He should move back to the center."[39] After Ford won a much hyped primary in his home state of Michigan, the *Post* reasoned that the president prevailed "by playing his strongest card which is the presidency. Mr. Ford has been letting his own campaign

---

author Alexander Solzhenitsyn to the White House. To many conservatives such as Will, that decision was evidence of Ford's unwillingness to adopt a strong posture against Soviet human rights abuses.

33. David Broder, "Foreign Policy Upheaval," *Washington Post*, March 24, 1976, A15.

34. Joseph Kraft, "A Year After Vietnam: The Fixation Continues," *Washington Post*, May 2, 1976, C7.

35. Joseph Kraft, "Détente: The Public's Codeword for Vietnam," *Washington Post*, March 9, 1976, A17.

36. ". . . the Ford Response," *New York Times*, May 30, 1976, IV, 14.

37. Joseph Kraft, "Forget the Alamo," *Washington Post*, May 4, 1976, A19.

38. Joseph Kraft, "The President and the Secretary," *Washington Post*, April 11, 1976, C7.

39. "Panama and Troublemaking," *Washington Post*, May 5, 1976, A22.

strategy be defined by his opponent. Worse, he was letting Mr. Reagan define the issues as well. Wisely, we think, the President got off his defensive kick— the petulance and the retorting and the small bore resentment."[40] Finally, Tom Wicker penned a column entitled "Just a Candidate in Office?"

> Throughout the primary season Mr. Ford has rushed around in Mr. Reagan's wake, shouting after him that the nation does too have more military strength than the Soviet Union. This has only tended to let Mr. Reagan make still another issue out of misstatements and jingoism, and may even have led Mr. Ford into actual budgeting decisions. . . . Mr. Ford could hardly do worse politically by being more Presidential than that. . . . One way he could do it would be to abandon the practice of reacting to Mr. Reagan.[41]

Ford and Reagan competed in an extraordinarily close nomination contest. Neither candidate could secure enough delegates by the end of the primary and caucus season to wrap up a first-ballot party nomination. Ford recalled that "by July 18, when the last of the convention states had selected their delegates, I had a total of 1,102; Reagan had 1,063. I was 28 short of the number needed to win and he trailed me by only 39. And 94 delegates were still uncommitted."[42]

The inability decisively to defeat the Reagan challenge did nothing to enhance Ford's press image. In part that could be attributed to the press's low opinion of Reagan: many journalists still did not take Reagan seriously. David Broder wondered how Ford could be "having a tough time beating a 65-year-old former movie actor."[43]

Some journalists attributed the nearly successful Reagan challenge to the different political styles of the two Republican candidates. Evans and Novak explained that Ford gave a poor performance on the political stump when compared to Reagan's charismatic speeches. "If Jerry Ford's 20-month tenure as President has not transformed him into a finished platform performer, neither has it destroyed the impression given of a nice, plain, decent Midwesterner."[44] Lou Cannon also explained that, whereas Reagan used effective, rhetorical flourishes, Ford delivered his message "in the flat, unmodulated style that has become the President's trademark."[45] *Newsweek* agreed

40. "Michigan and Maryland," *Washington Post*, May 20, 1976, A18.

41. Tom Wicker, "Just a Candidate in Office?" *New York Times*, May 9, 1976, IV, 15.

42. Ford, *Time to Heal*, 393.

43. David Broder, "A Tough Struggle Ahead for Mr. Ford," *Washington Post*, May 5, 1976, A23.

44. Rowland Evans and Robert Novak, "A Sense of Foreboding in the Ford Campaign," *Washington Post*, April 27, 1976, A19.

45. Lou Cannon, "A Question of Style: Lively Reagan Outflanks Ford," *Washington Post*, June 1, 1976, A1, 4; see also Cannon, "Ford Talks," A1, 4.

that "the President has generally been a lackluster contrast to Reagan on the road."[46] *Time* called Ford's campaign style "reassuring but plodding and predictable."[47] *Time* pointed out that

> the Reagan crowds respond to his smooth style. Ford, on the other hand, often gets a rousing reception when introduced as the President, but audiences lose enthusiasm as he reads his speeches—actually more thoughtful and more varied than Reagan's standard pitch.[48]

David Broder wrote a column entitled "How Did He Get Into Such a Predicament?" Broder's answer reflected a widespread journalistic interpretation: "It is the inability of Mr. Ford to define the goals, the vision and the purposes of his presidency in a way that gives coherence to his administration and his campaign."[49] Dennis Farney wrote that "from the beginning, President Ford has been a candidate without a real theme or a real constituency. Lacking a vision or an agenda for the nation, he has tried to rely upon his 'decency.'"[50] A *Wall Street Journal* editorial explained: "The President's problem is to draw attention to where we are headed, to persuade the nation that the trends are indeed solidly established and will be carried on in a new term."[51] James Reston asserted that "he seems to have no consistent philosophy, no connecting rod between one day and another."[52] *Newsweek* reported that "his own political habits were formed in 23 years as a minority member of Congress, reacting to rather than controlling events, and his people now worry at his apparent incapacity to convey that sense of motion and of vision required of Presidents."[53] Vermont Royster acknowledged that Ford had "grown into the job" of president. Nonetheless,

> Gerald Ford doesn't exude the commanding presence of a Franklin Roosevelt or a Dwight Eisenhower . . . or the fiery cockiness of Harry Truman. He lacks John Kennedy's wit, and you don't detect a sense of humor.[54]

---

46. "Ford's New Start," *Newsweek*, May 17, 1976, 26.

47. "More Blood in the G.O.P.'s Donnybrook," *Time*, May 24, 1976, 6.

48. "Republican Rumble," *Time*, May 17, 1976, 12.

49. David Broder, "How Did He Get Into Such a Predicament?" *Washington Post*, May 16, 1976, C7.

50. Dennis Farney, "Republican Rumble: Reagan's Missouri Win Gives Him a Boost, Shows Ford's Problems," *Wall Street Journal*, June 14, 1976, 1.

51. "Ford's Defense," *Wall Street Journal*, May 4, 1976, 22.

52. James Reston, "The Best and the Worst," *New York Times*, October 15, 1976, A31.

53. "A President in Jeopardy," *Newsweek*, May 17, 1976, 23.

54. Vermont Royster, "The Transformation of Gerald Ford," *Wall Street Journal*, April 21, 1976, 22.

Philip Shabecoff said that Ford presided "over what appears to be the least potent Presidency since the Eisenhower Administration." Shabecoff added that

> Mr. Ford's own bland public personality, as well as his social philosophy, which leans toward a passive role for the Federal Government in domestic affairs, have undoubtedly reduced the power of the executive branch. These limitations would continue only if Mr. Ford were re-elected [*sic*].[55]

After four weeks of both Republican candidates arm-twisting uncommitted and wavering delegates, Ford came to the national party convention in Kansas City on August 15, claiming enough delegates for a first-ballot victory. Reagan disputed Ford's claim and kept challenging. Ford won on the first ballot, 1,187 to 1,070 delegates.[56] When it appeared that Ford would indeed control the convention, Joseph Kraft quipped: "The Reagan forces have been reduced to scattering banana peels around the place in the hope that Mr. Ford will take one of his well-known pratfalls."[57] After the balloting, James M. Naughton concluded that "Mr. Reagan was more alluring as a candidate—more exciting, more telegenic. . . . But Mr. Ford was already President [and he] move[d] steadily to the right philosophically" to counter Reagan.[58] Several weeks before the convention, *Time* favorably compared Ford to Reagan.

> Ford is more stolid and less articulate, but nobody can question his depth of experience. For all his widely publicized flaws and stumbles, he has been a better president than he has been given credit for. His moderate-growth policies have helped lift the nation out of recession and curb inflation. With Henry Kissinger, he has handled foreign affairs capably, and he has restored a measure of trust and faith in the White House.[59]

Despite the perception of Ford as inarticulate, or perhaps because of it, *Time* declared the president's nomination acceptance speech "the best . . . Jerry Ford ever made. He seemed transformed—vigorous, authoritative."[60]

---

55. Philip Shabecoff, "Presidency Is Found Weaker Under Ford," *New York Times*, March 28, 1976, 1, 44.

56. Ford, *Time to Heal*, 397–99.

57. Joseph Kraft, "Political Pratfalls, and Banana Peels," *Washington Post*, August 12, 1976, A15.

58. James M. Naughton, "Incumbency was the Key," *New York Times*, August 19, 1976, 27.

59. "Who Would Lose Less to Carter?" *Time*, June 28, 1976, 11.

60. "Coming Out Swinging," *Time*, August 30, 1976, 6.

Ford spoke "with unaccustomed fervor and a punchy delivery."[61] Nonetheless, *Time* thought that Ford had a tall order ahead of him to beat Democratic nominee Jimmy Carter.

> Among his other problems, the President is burdened by Watergate; memories of Ford's pardon of Richard Nixon will surface again in the next ten weeks.[62]

> The best thing Ford has going for him seems to be, well, Jimmy Carter. The Georgian is still an enigma to much of the public, including many of his own supporters.[63]

Ford received some press criticism for his selection of Senator Robert Dole (Kansas) as the vice presidential candidate. Many journalists viewed the selection of Dole, a staunch conservative, as another Ford capitulation to the Republican Right. The *Washington Post* thought that "sooner or later [Ford] must stop looking over his shoulder at Ronald Reagan." The *Post* continued:

> Governor Reagan may have lost the balloting on [August 18], but he has already won a great deal from Mr. Ford in a policy way, and in a sense, Sen. Dole is his gift to the party ticket as well as Mr. Ford's. . . .Gerald Ford will have to cease reacting to a challenge from the right, if he hopes to attract the support of moderate Republicans, independents and disaffected Democrats.[64]

Time magazine also provided critical commentary.

> Dole is a crony of Ford's, a fellow Midwesterner with an almost identical ideology. By picking him, Ford appeared to be looking inward instead of reaching out as the G.O.P. must do.[65]

Dole had a reputation in the Washington community not only as a staunch conservative, but also as a fierce partisan with a sharp tongue. The early criticisms of Ford's vice presidential choice did not compare to the severity of press criticisms levied at Dole during the 1976 general election campaign.

---

61. "Instant Replay: How Ford Won It," *Time*, August 30, 1976, 22.
62. "Coming Out Swinging," 7.
63. "A Tight Race Shapes Up," *Time*, September 6, 1976, 11.
64. "Dole?" *Washington Post*, August 20, 1976, A26.
65. "Coming Out Swinging," 7; see also "The Dole Decision," *Time*, August 30, 1976, 22–23.

Second Year Retrospectives

The same month as the Republican National Convention in Kansas City marked the two-year point of Ford's presidency, an opportunity for journalists to review the president's successes and failures. Once again, journalists generally credited Ford with having restored trust in the White House. *U.S. News* declared that "respect for the Presidency, badly shaken by the Watergate scandals, is largely restored."[66] Philip Shabecoff wrote that "there unquestionably is more public trust in the White House than there was during the Presidency of Richard M. Nixon."[67] Joseph Kraft said, "Sustained and undoubted progress toward peace, prosperity and moral regeneration. That claim can fairly be staked by President Ford as summing the two years since President Nixon resigned. . . . [T]he stink of Watergate has been clearly dispelled. Mr. Ford is a decent man."[68] And the *Wall Street Journal* maintained that "[Ford] has a credible record in his two years in the office, and a reassuring nice-guy personality."[69]

Leading journalists also noted that Ford either failed to convey these successes or that he had undermined some of the progress he had made in restoring public confidence. Philip Shabecoff asserted that "his early pardon of President Nixon probably dissipated some of this advantage."[70] *U.S. News* wrote that "while respect for Ford and the office he holds has increased, there remains widespread doubt over his abilities."[71] Joseph Kraft added, "But Mr. Ford is having a hard time making the claim [of restoring trust] stick. For he has been unable to manage the symbols of authority in ways persuasive to the country."[72] Lou Cannon assessed Ford's successes as "not widely perceived."

> His strategists say this is because his achievements "have not been effectively communicated," but this formulation disregards the fact that effective communication is an essential of presidential leadership, not just an afterthought.[73]

---

66. "The Ford Presidency: A Record of Gains and Losses," *U.S. News and World Report*, August 30, 1976, 28–29.

67. Philip Shabecoff, "Ford on His Second Anniversary: Still Battling for Nomination and Trailing Democratic Candidate in Polls," *New York Times*, August 10, 1976, 13.

68. Joseph Kraft, "A President Who Has Not Done Badly," *Washington Post*, August 10, 1976, A17.

69. "Mr. Ford's Opportunity," *Wall Street Journal*, August 20, 1976, 4.

70. Shabecoff, "Second Anniversary," 13.

71. "Ford Presidency," 28.

72. Kraft, "President Has Not Done Badly," A17.

73. Lou Cannon, "Jerry Ford: Modest, Persevering—and Lucky," *Washington Post*, August 19, 1976, A16.

According to the press, Ford's failures included not just poor communication, but also the inability to establish a commanding presence and a method of leadership different than that of a House Minority Leader. Philip Shabecoff contended that Ford had "not made any dramatic use of the Presidency to put his own indelible stamp on the office. . . . After two years in office, Mr. Ford is still in the position of having to prove that he is more than a caretaker."[74] David Broder maintained that Ford had failed to provide "a vision of where he is going and a strategy for achieving his goals. Mr. Ford works very hard, but he often seems to be running in place." In Broder's view,

Gerald Ford is a man of expansive personality, with a restricted vision of the future. He is a man inclined to take negative actions for positive reasons. He is a gregarious soul, who is frustrated and hobbled by his inability to communicate more than generalized good will. He is at once the "safest" recent President America has had, in constitutional terms, and the "sorriest" in the exercise of leadership skills. . . . There has been no framework of policy, no articulated philosophy, that has given shape or coherence to the President's deeds.[75]

Lou Cannon thought that Ford did not understand "how to rouse people, a quality he does not deem especially important," and that the president lacked a big ego, "a quality useful in the Speaker of the House . . . but perilous in a President." Cannon explained that

Gerald R. Ford, President by inheritance, is a genial and expansive man accustomed to the horsetrading and camaraderie of the House. . . . Mr. Ford comes to solutions in the congressional manner, "roundtabling" options with a variety of sources and making decisions that are reactions to events.[76]

The most negative press assessment of Ford's two years in office came from Anthony Lewis. The *New York Times* columnist both disputed the view that Ford had restored decency to the White House and revived the issue of the pardon of Richard M. Nixon, which Lewis characterized as "utter insensitivity to the need for . . . a reaffirmed commitment to law. . . . Mr. Ford did not understand the lessons of Watergate and Vietnam." Clearly, Lewis believed that Ford had failed the "decency" standard because the administration

---

74. Shabecoff, "Second Anniversary," 13.
75. David Broder, "Mr. Ford: A Man of Contradictions," *Washington Post*, August 18, 1976, A19.
76. Cannon, "Jerry Ford," A1, 16.

did not go along with the domestic policy agenda of the political left. Lewis described Ford as

> a President who had an extraordinary opportunity to restore the failing of political legitimacy in this country, has failed to inspire the confidence of country or party. . . . We used to speak of his decency, but that is an inappropriate word for someone so insensitive to human suffering.[77]

U.S. News offered perhaps the most positive assessment of Ford's two years in office. The news weekly agreed that Ford had a difficult time leading Congress, but attributed this difficulty to the inevitable policy clashes that transpire among leaders of different parties. *U.S. News* credited Ford with improving the economy and enhancing relations with international allies and rivals.

> Taken as a whole, the record of the last two years would practically guarantee another term for most Presidents. But Ford . . . now starts out as a clear underdog to Democrat Jimmy Carter. Why? . . . Ford still is perceived by many as an accidental, unelected President and not as an effective leader.[78]

The General Election Campaign

The 1976 presidential election campaign pitted Ford against former Governor of Georgia Jimmy Carter. Ford came out of the Republican National Convention in Kansas City trailing Carter massively in the national public opinion polls. With a combination of a still troubled economy, lingering memories of Watergate and the unpopular pardon of Richard M. Nixon, and Ford's unexceptional leadership repute, most observers gave the Republican nominee little chance of winning the election. Despite these seemingly insurmountable deficits, *Time* reported that "Ford does have the considerable advantage of incumbency. . . . And Ford—a hearty, unaffected man, a kind of prototypical Midwesterner—has clearly restored both dignity and informality to the White House." *Time* added that

> Ford's go easy tactics of letting the economy largely right itself are so far working out fairly well. No American boys are fighting overseas; none are even being drafted. There is a growing sense of well-being in the country.[79]

---

77. Anthony Lewis, "The Search for Legitimacy," *New York Times*, August 16, 1976, 31.

78. "Ford Presidency," 29.

79. "Campaign Kickoff," *Time*, September 13, 1976, 12–13.

Perhaps the economy had improved, the nation remained at peace, and Ford could take advantage of his incumbency. The president still suffered from a serious image problem—in fact, a potentially devastating image problem in a national campaign where intense media scrutiny and highly visible political events provide ample opportunities for a misstep or misstatement. Journalists said that Ford "stumbled" too often and that his mishaps symbolized his failure to get a grip on the nation's problems. No candidate goes through a presidential campaign without the occasional mishap. Given his well-established image, the press undoubtedly would magnify any of Ford's mishaps. Journalists also said that Ford had failed to project a strong "presidential" image. It is especially difficult to project such an image in an election campaign. Presidential decisions and activities would be characterized by the press as either (1) motivated by political expediency, not merit, or (2) cleverly concocted to look "presidential," an explicit attempt to use incumbency for electoral gain.

Ford's incumbency also posed a political problem in 1976: as president, Ford led the national government "establishment" in a time of anti-Washington public sentiment. As Evans and Novak attested,

> In a time of pervasive public hostility toward Washington, Mr. Ford is running . . . as the Washington candidate. He is tied, for better or worse, to the OMB mentality, Henry Kissinger's mission to Africa and the overriding political image of the federal government.[80]

Throughout the general election campaign, journalists assessed Ford's leadership. Clearly, his presidential activities and campaign appearances did little to change the negative press image. In viewing the 1976 campaign, William V. Shannon noted that voters had to choose between "a pleasing personality and a leader in the White House." Shannon clearly preferred Carter to Ford.

> If the people are content with a pleasing personality, Gerald Ford will do very well. He is financially honest, about as candid as most political men, and is a likable person. But he is not a leader. He lacks the intellectual gifts, the imagination, and the inner force, that leaders have. . . . Mr. Ford offers four more years of drift, bluff, and fumble. Historically, it is the choice between the possibility of another Roosevelt and the certainty of another Coolidge.[81]

---

80. Rowland Evans and Robert Novak, "Ford's Clinical 'Vision for America,'" *Washington Post*, September 18, 1976, A19.

81. William V. Shannon, "In Search of Leadership," *New York Times*, September 26, 1976, 15.

The *New York Times* similarly criticized Ford for a "lack of discernible evidence of any vision that might be turned into reality." The editorial concluded that "trustworthiness, though crucial, is not enough. Personal integrity is more than ever the indispensable starting point; but it is no substitute for a candidate's obligation to spell out a program in pursuit of credible goals."[82] The *Wall Street Journal* agreed.

> From the first, Mr. Ford's failing as President has been an inability to articulate what he would like to do with the office, where he would like to take the nation. He remains the Congressman, merely resolving the forces acting on him, one day this way, another day that way as the wind blows.[83]

In terms of harshly negative press commentary on Ford's leadership, probably nothing could match an invective-ridden column in late September by Anthony Lewis. Once again, Lewis went beyond his colleagues' criticisms of Ford for not asserting bold leadership and characterized the president as lacking basic compassion and caring.

> The record of Gerald Ford should be the central issue in this campaign. It is the narrow conservative record of a narrow conservative man. It ought to please voters who have no interest in human rights, who do not care about official obedience to the law, who believe in government secrecy, who are not willing to forgive or forget resistance to the Vietnam War. . . . It is indecent for those who care about sensitivity and humanity in politics to talk of the decency of Gerald Ford.[84]

Time magazine offered a generally favorable assessment of Ford's presidency in late September. The news weekly asserted that "he has grown in office. He is less narrowly partisan than he was. Exposure to national and international problems has broadened his perspective." *Time* viewed the contrast of Ford to his predecessors as an important basis for assessing his presidency.

> . . . the friendly man from Grand Rapids has not let the White House go to his head. He would never experiment as Richard Nixon briefly did— with dressing up the guards in comic-opera uniforms in the hope of

---

82. "Questions and a Yawn," *New York Times*, September 19, 1976, 14.

83. "None of the Above?" *Wall Street Journal*, October 14, 1976, 22.

84. Anthony Lewis, "Decent Is as Decent Does," *New York Times*, September 23, 1976, 41.

evoking grandeur. . . . He is unafraid to question his counselors. In contrast to Johnson and Nixon, Ford does not have a psychological need to seek reassurance from subordinates.[85]

Yet the same issue of *Time* featured an article assessing the first national debate between Ford and Carter. By most accounts, Ford carried the debate. Opinion polls reflected the perception of a Ford "win." Even in apparent victory, Ford received a humiliating review from one of the nation's leading news magazines. A *Time* news story quoted the West Coast Bureau chief's "counterklutzical theory" as an explanation for the debate outcome. The seemingly gratuitous commentary about Ford's debate "strategy" is worth noting as representative of an image problem that just would not go away.

> First you walk into your chopper door. Then you fall down the ramp of *Air Force One*. Before you even take office you arrange for the last Democratic President to suggest your inability to chew gum and do much of anything else. Then, when your opponent is all set up, you show up for a campaign debate, leaving your college football helmet at home, and play 90 minutes of *What's My Line?* without falling on your fanny. Viewers are impressed. You aren't an utter boob after all.[86]

By October, Ford seemed to be gaining campaign momentum. The opinion polls reflected a significantly narrowed Carter lead, and many voters had started to express concern about the Democratic nominee's relative national political inexperience. But two events in the first several days of October slowed the Republican campaign momentum. The first, a racial slur by Secretary of Agriculture Earl Butz, the second, a misstatement by Ford in the second presidential candidates' debate. Each event had serious repercussions for the presidential campaign. Most important here, journalists assessed each event as a reflection on Ford's leadership ability.

On an airplane returning from the Kansas City Republican National Convention, Secretary Butz confided a tasteless racial "joke" to former Nixon White House counsel John Dean. The former Nixon White House counsel wore a new hat after breaking open the Watergate scandals—political correspondent for *Rolling Stone* magazine. Butz's slur, once reported, created a firestorm of protest and demands for his firing.

President Ford did not fire Butz or demand the secretary's resignation. Ford reprimanded Butz and demanded a public apology. Butz apologized for the offensive remark. The criticism did not subside. Many journalists pro-

---

85. "The Team Player Makes Good," *Time*, October 4, 1976, 22, 27.
86. "When Their Power Failed," *Time*, October 4, 1976, 16.

claimed that Ford had failed a major leadership test by not immediately firing Butz. The *Washington Post* led the criticism of Ford.

> It is not enough for President Ford to have reprimanded Mr. Butz or for Mr. Butz to have expressed his regret. . . . He should be fired. Earl Butz is a man who has revealed a cast of mind so benighted and cruel as to render him unfit for public office. That President Ford did not perceive as much at once, says a great deal about his vaunted claim to "leadership."[87]

Butz resigned his position on October 4, but the press continued to lambaste the president for not having initiated the secretary's removal from public office. The *Washington Post* continued its criticism of the president.

> What we find hard to comprehend, however, is the way the President's "decision" was made, and therein, we think lies the real—and lasting— significance of the Butz affair. . . . [Butz's] resignation was never demanded, merely accepted. That is to say, *the decision was left entirely up to him.* . . . That Mr. Butz has now departed his agriculture post . . . cannot take away the fact that there was a severe test of the President's leadership in the Butz affair—and that Mr. Ford failed that test.[88]

Joseph Kraft argued that the Butz controversy offered Ford an opportunity to look "decisive" and in command. "Instead, Mr. Ford took his time."

> The fact is that Mr. Ford lacks leadership qualities. He does not come on as a decisive man, sure of himself on essential policy matters and capable of lining up subordinate officials around his views. . . . Certainly, it was not a case of heroic leadership. Nobody can rate aces high for reacting with force and rapidity to a glaring act of vulgar insensitivity.[89]

Two days after Butz resigned, the League of Women Voters sponsored the second presidential candidates' debate in San Francisco. The debate offered Ford an important opportunity to shift the campaign momentum and move beyond the Butz controversy. Ford performed well enough in the first debate for *Newsweek* to declare that he "shucked his bumbler's image, proved

---

87. "Butz," *Washington Post*, October 3, 1976, C6.

88. "The Butz Test," *Washington Post*, October 6, 1976, A14.

89. Joseph Kraft, "The Butz Episode: No Political Gain," *Washington Post*, October 7, 1976, A25; see also "The Butz Affair: 'He Had to Pay the Price,'" *U.S. News and World Report*, October 18, 1976, 18; "Butz: A Tongue Out of Order," *Newsweek*, October 11, 1976, 27.

himself articulate and not such a nice guy that he couldn't zing an opponent."[90]

Unfortunately for Ford, no such favorable assessment followed the second debate. In the debate, Ford committed what Vermont Royster called "that inexplicable gaffe . . . about Soviet domination, or lack of it, behind the Iron Curtain."[91] In response to a reporter's question, Ford boldly declared that "there is no Soviet domination of Eastern Europe, and there never will be under a Ford Administration."[92] Ford's declaration caused a political uproar made only worse by his initial refusal to explain the comment and then by his explanations that only appeared to show that he did not comprehend the magnitude of the misstatement. *Time* carried an article entitled "The Blooper Heard Round the World" that made the following comment.

> Gerald Ford made what could well be the most damaging statement of his career. For any politician, calling Eastern Europe free would be an amazing gaffe. For a President, especially one who is running partly on a campaign theme of experience in foreign policy, the mistake reawakened many voters' suspicions that Ford is a bumbler.[93]

Evans and Novak asserted that "Mr. Ford's Polish blooper" had "resurrected the old image of fumbler and stumbler he had very nearly shaken off."[94] A *Wall Street Journal* news column reported that "[Ford] bumbled in the second debate with Carter. He risks ridicule by claiming the Soviets don't dominate Eastern Europe."[95] Ellen Goodman proclaimed: "It isn't a question of Ford's policy toward Eastern Europe—he isn't going to 'liberate' Poland— but of his grasp of policy at all."[96] *Time* magazine declared that "Ford's grasp of foreign policy and even his mere competence were called into question during his debate with Carter when he insisted that the Soviet Union does not dominate Eastern Europe."[97] Other journalists offered similar commentaries.

Nicholas von Hoffman: What Debate II showed us is that Jerry Ford is a bad Polish joke. The President, who has spent an adult lifetime listening

---

90. "The Race: Stay Tuned," *Newsweek*, October 4, 1976, 22.

91. Vermont Royster, "The Squabble," *Wall Street Journal*, October 13, 1976, 20.

92. Ford, *Time to Heal*, 422.

93. "The Blooper Heard Round the World," *Time*, October 18, 1976, 13.

94. Rowland Evans and Robert Novak, "The Real Jerry Ford?" *Washington Post*, October 9, 1976, A17.

95. "Washington Wire," *Wall Street Journal*, October 8, 1976, 1.

96. Ellen Goodman, "The Character Campaign: In Search of the Psyche," *Washington Post*, October 9, 1976, A19.

97. "Ford's Toughest Week," *Time*, October 18, 1976, 10.

to members of his own party accuse Roosevelt of selling out Eastern Europe at Yalta, knows perfectly well that Poland is a Russian satellite.[98]

George F. Will: It would be understandable if Ford twice spoke absurd nonsense because he had just been awakened from a deep slumber at 3 A.M. by someone shouting "Helsinki" in his ear. But Ford had known for more than a year that the Helsinki agreement, and hence the U.S. attitude toward Soviet domination of Eastern Europe, would be a campaign issue. . . . Henry Kissinger has custody of Ford's mind in foreign policy matters.[99]

Wall Street Journal: President Ford's Eastern European blunder stems from the same conceptual inability that has hampered his presidency; the remark simply did not fit his own policies. The thrust of the Ford presidency has come from his advisers, with a Kissinger foreign policy and a Simon-Greenspan economic policy.[100]

Mr. Ford might have won handily if he had not made [that] one bonehead play.[101]

Of all the leading press commentary on Ford's debate performance, only the *Washington Post* downplayed the significance of the Eastern Europe statement to official policy. The *Post* acknowledged that Ford's comment could "cost him dearly in political terms. . . . But it is important to note that it was much more a fault of articulation than a reflection of a real flaw in the Ford administration's policy with respect to Eastern Europe."[102] *Newsweek* added the following observation.

Ford's stumbles in the debate accomplished one thing; they overshadowed his other problems of the week. The embarrassing Earl Butz affair almost seemed ancient history.[103]

---

98. Nicholas von Hoffman, "Weighing Flubb vs. Fluff," *Washington Post*, October 18, 1976, D1.

99. George F. Will, "Tiresome Little Men Clawing for Lincoln's Chair," *Washington Post*, October 14, 1976, A19.

100. "In Defense of Debates," *Wall Street Journal*, October 22, 1976, 14; see also "Ford Drops a Brick," *Newsweek*, October 18, 1976, 24.

101. "Carter 110, Ford 108," *Wall Street Journal*, October 8, 1976, 8.

102. "Round Two," *Washington Post*, October 8, 1976, A24.

103. "Round Two to Carter," *Newsweek*, October 18, 1976, 23.

The Issues

Because of the election season, journalists placed considerably less emphasis on substantive policy issues throughout 1976 than during the earlier stages of Ford's term. Oftentimes journalists discussed and assessed the issues within the context of the presidential campaign.

In the foreign affairs realm, journalists generally portrayed Secretary of State Henry Kissinger, not President Ford, as the nation's leading force. Implying that Ford did not direct his own foreign policies, *U.S. News* thought that, if elected in 1976, "Ford would try to make his own mark in world affairs. . . . In the foreign policy field, Ford would be anxious to show historians that he is more than merely a willing student of Secretary of State Henry Kissinger on maintaining America's global leadership."[104] *Time* magazine agreed.

> Major foreign policy initiatives . . . have been articulated by Secretary of State Henry Kissinger, further contributing to Ford's bystander image even though Ford, of course, approved the policies.[105]

Newsweek featured a news report in October entitled "Abroad: Who's In Charge?" The report inquired, "Does Gerald Ford have a foreign policy of his own? . . . And without the awesome energy, creativity and expertise of Kissinger, is Ford up to handling the problems that a second term will bring?" *Newsweek* also evaluated Ford's foreign affairs leadership.

> He came to office inexperienced, untested and widely suspect as inadequate, especially in the perilous arena of foreign policy. . . . At the beginning, Kissinger all but played the role of Svengali, with Ford as his dutiful student. . . . By endorsing Kissinger's tactics and accepting his strategy, the President has made Kissinger's foreign policy his. That policy has most often been one of reacting to events rather than offering new and imaginative programs. And there's reason to argue that the times did not demand innovation.[106]

The press viewed some of Ford's foreign policy decisions as blatantly calculated for political gain, an inevitable accusation of an incumbent

---

104. "Changes to Look for If Ford is Elected," *U.S. News and World Report*, August 30, 1976, 22–23.

105. "Where Has All the Power Gone?" *Time*, May 24, 1976, 9.

106. "Abroad: Who's In Charge?" *Newsweek*, October 18, 1976, 52, 55.

officeholder seeking election. When Ford rejected a proposal to normalize
U.S. relations with Vietnam, the *Washington Post* portrayed the decision as an
attempt to pander to political conservatives. By reacting to conservative criticism of his foreign policy, according to the *Post*, Ford had lost "all balance
and restraint."[107] When Ford decided to sell military equipment to Israel, the
Post responded that he had made that decision only to suit "domestic politics."[108]

> The way the campaign is going, October could turn out to be a very
> expensive month. The other day Mr. Ford approved the new sales of
> ultra-sophisticated weapons of war to Israel; on Wednesday he raised
> price supports for wheat and other grains. . . . Both decisions . . . were
> blatantly transparently political. They were intended to please crucial
> blocs of voters.[109]

Time magazine added that

> in blatantly political appeals for the votes of farmers and Jews, the
> President used the muscle of his office last week. Just before a weekend
> trip to the farm belt, he ordered grain price supports boosted. . . . Ford
> also agreed to the sale of previously prohibited compression bombs and
> other sophisticated weaponry to Israel.[110]

Ford received generally better grades from the press in 1976 than in
earlier years for his handling of the domestic economy. Many journalists
thought that Ford did not fashion any bold or innovative economic policies.
He received much criticism throughout his term for not offering large-scale
government policies to turn around the economy. In January 1976, Joseph
Kraft asserted that "a 19th century economic philosophy restrains the President from actions which could bring down both inflation and unemployment
far more rapidly than presently planned. . . . Mr. Ford, true to his free enterprise bias, rejects various novel proposals for government action to arrest
inflation."[111] But in 1976, as the economy improved somewhat, Ford's policies began to receive some favorable press comment. A week before the
election, *Time* evaluated the presidential candidates' economic policy
positions.

---

107. "Mr. Ford's Vietnam Policy," *Washington Post*, September 15, 1976, A20.
108. "Arms and the Election," *Washington Post*, October 13, 1976, A20.
109. "Vote Buying," *Washington Post*, October 17, 1976, C6.
110. "Bitter, Not Better, Down the Stretch," *Time*, October 25, 1976, 12.
111. Joseph Kraft, "The Politics of the Budget," *Washington Post*, January 26, 1976, A15.

In describing the present situation Gerald Ford is more accurate than Carter, and he is correct that . . . the recovery has run into only a temporary slowdown. . . . Ever since he became President, Ford has erred on the side of caution. . . . Of course, he deserves much credit for bringing down inflation.[112]

Time praised Ford for refusing to provide an increased federal government fiscal stimulus, "a refreshing departure from the usual tendency of Presidents to pump up the economy during election years."[113] *Time* also predicted the likely economic policies of a second-term Ford administration.

Ford would try to cut red tape, consolidate existing programs, reduce Government regulation of business and farming, and eliminate bureaucratic overlap. But there would be no bold, new social programs to grapple with the problems of the disadvantaged.[114]

U.S. News predicted that, if Ford won the 1976 election,

at home, that would mean a strong drive to hold back on federal spending and new government programs. The aim would be to reduce sharply Washington's control over people's lives and entrust more responsibility to states and local officials.[115]

Newsweek portrayed Ford as a president who developed an understanding of economic policy by necessity. In a preelection review of Ford's policies, the news magazine reported that "no President since Franklin D. Roosevelt had entered office with so many economic troubles facing the nation." With a faltering economy "nobody knew exactly what to do—least of all an accidental President with little knowledge of economics."

Ford's policies are profoundly Calvinistic in their willingness to accept the suffering of unemployment to tame inflation. . . . Ford has gone through a rather painful, sometimes embarrassing, crash course in economics. . . . Ford now has a solid, if unimaginative, grasp of economics. He works hard at mastering detail, and last year he knew the budget numbers so well that be became the first President since Harry Truman to brief the press on the subject personally.[116]

---

112. "The Pocketbook Election," *Time*, November 1, 1976, 18–19, 22.
113. "Pocketbook Election," 19.
114. "The Shape of the Next Four Years: A Ford Administration," *Time*, November 8, 1976, 23.
115. "Changes to Look For," 22.
116. "The Economy: Hard Choices," *Newsweek*, October 18, 1976, 56–57.

Preelection Reviews

Within a few weeks of election day, a number of retrospective analyses of Ford's presidency appeared in the press. These analyses show that Ford's basic image had not changed: journalists still perceived him as a simple, unpretentious man who restored integrity to the White House yet failed to provide visionary leadership. *Newsweek* described Ford as "the quintessential commoner President—a man distinguished . . . for the very plainness of his mind and bearing. . . . [Ford is] a Main Street Republican of square tastes, decent heart, homely speech, modest vision, great industry, and most of the Boy Scout virtues from trustworthiness to reverence." The news story said that Ford lacked "brilliance" and had a cast of mind belonging "to the meat-and-potatoes school—dogged, common-sensical and geared to solving particular problems." *Newsweek* praised Ford for having cleansed the White House of "Caesarism and scandal," but added that he lacked "vision," "inspiration," and "innovative leadership."[117]

> Ford has yet to specify his domestic goals in clear terms—or catchwords. He has offered no New Frontier, no Great Society or even the Lift of a Driving Dream.[118]

David Broder described the "dilemma" voters confronted in the 1976 election. "With Ford there is little risk of abuse of power, but also little expectation of leadership." Broder believed that Ford would not abuse presidential powers and "neither will he exercise those powers to lead the nation, as did Presidents admired by history."

> If the Lord of Chanty had seen fit to rescue this nation from being engulfed by the evils of the imperial presidency, he would have sent us, not an ark, but a Gerald Ford. . . . No one could have invented a better cure for the excesses of the neurotic, vision-driven and fear-haunted men who paced the Oval Office from 1966 to 1974 than the exceptionally ordinary man who inhabits it now. . . . It's a damn shame he doesn't know what to do with the presidency, since he has it. How anyone could occupy the White House for two years without grasping its potential for leadership is almost inexplicable.[119]

---

117. "How Good a President?" *Newsweek*, October 18, 1976, 30, 35.

118. "At Home: Can We Afford It?" *Newsweek*, October 18, 1976, 58.

119. David Broder, "The Incumbent: 'Exceptionally Ordinary,'" *Washington Post*, October 24, 1976, B7.

Time magazine offered a similar assessment.

> Ford is likable, unpretentious, undevious. . . . While he is certainly a bright man, his image as a bumbler nevertheless is not totally unfair; he is also a man who can forget three times in a day which town he is in. . . . Far from an inspirational leader, Ford has a limited let's-not-rock-the-boat perspective of the presidency. He offers a prospect of predictability that may reassure many—assuming no imaginative initiatives may be needed over the next four years.[120]

The *New York Times* maintained that Ford had failed to provide "vigorous, detailed, attentive leadership." According to the *Times*, Ford failed a major test of "executive leadership"—the ability to attract a top-quality White House staff. The *Times* concluded that "on the whole it has been a tired and undistinguished Administration and one likely to become more tired and passive if confirmed in office for what would be a lame-duck term."[121]

Anthony Lewis described Ford as a person who had "lived in a corporate cocoon . . . oblivious to the realities of poverty and discrimination for millions of Americans." Lewis again reminded readers of Ford's earlier links to Nixon. "He backed Richard Nixon to the end, and kept Nixon people around him afterward. . . . The worst recent blow to Americans' belief in equal justice was his sudden and premature pardon of Richard Nixon."[122]

Vermont Royster offered the following preelection review of Ford's presidency and prospective assessment of a possible second Ford term in office.

> President Ford has hardly been an inspiring leader, often a vacillating one. . . . No man has come to the presidency with so little ambition for it, so little warning. . . . That he floundered in the beginning is hardly surprising. That he succeeded in restoring the integrity of the office, in calming the turmoil, is something he can be proud of. . . . His two years have seen the recession eased, inflation diminished and our taxes reduced. His foreign policy is largely a continuation of his predecessor's, which makes it controversial, but it has brought the country no major crises. . . . So about all we're left with is the feeling that if it's Mr. Ford we can expect pretty much what we've had, which may not be good but isn't too bad.[123]

120. "D-Day, And Only One Poll Matters," *Time*, November 8, 1976, 14.
121. "The 'Big Government' Issue," *New York Times*, October 28, 1976, 42.
122. Anthony Lewis, "The Real Mr. Ford," *New York Times*, October 25, 1976, 29.
123. Vermont Royster, "Choosing," *Wall Street Journal*, October 27, 1976, 22.

Ford lost the extremely close presidential election to Jimmy Carter on November 2, 1976. In fact, a switch of just several thousand votes in two states would have given Ford the victory in the electoral college. Despite the pardon of Richard M. Nixon, the "bumbler" image, the uncertain economy, the Eastern Europe gaffe, and the press insistence that the president lacked "vision," Ford nearly overcame Carter's earlier very substantial lead in the national opinion polls. Ford's near comeback could be attributed, in part, to a well-run campaign, public and media concern about Carter's presidential qualifications, and the traditional Republican benefit from the electoral college system.

The postelection environment provided an important time for journalists to present their retrospective assessments of Ford's presidency. Journalists offered additional reviews of Ford's leadership at the end of his term in January 1977. These press reviews are presented in the following summary of journalists' assessments of the Ford legacy.

The Ford Legacy

Lou Cannon called Ford's narrow defeat, after having trailed Carter by thirty points in some public opinion polls, "the most remarkable comeback in the history of American presidential politics." Cannon echoed the widespread sentiment that Ford's vice presidential selection could have cost the Republican ticket the election. "It is conceivable that if Ford had been more selective in his own pick of a running mate that Carter might not have been able to make it."[124] *Time* magazine underscored this point in a postelection analysis. "Having presented a bad-mouth image and fared poorly in the polls during the campaign, [Dole] may well receive blame for the party's defeat and stands little chance of being nominated again for the G.O.P. ticket."[125]

As Ford prepared to leave office, journalists assessed not only why he lost the election but also the legacy he would leave to the nation. Though presented in a more favorable, sometimes sentimental, tone than earlier analyses, these commentaries repeated the major themes of the press assessments of Ford's leadership. According to *Time*, "he restored trust and integrity to the presidency,"[126] yet did not, in Evans' and Novaks' description, rally the nation with "inspirational leadership."[127] As James M. Naughton wrote,

124. Lou Cannon, "A Political Comeback That Just Missed," *Washington Post*, November 4, 1976, A16.

125. "There's Life in the Old Party Yet," *Time*, November 15, 1976, 36.

126. "Goodbye to Jerry," *Time*, November 15, 1976, 37.

127. Rowland Evans and Robert Novak, "GOP Post-Mortem," *Washington Post*, November 12, 1976, A27.

The Ford legacy, measured not so much in deed as in tone, is apt to be that of a revival of will. . . . [Ford] appeared likely to be judged as a President who achieved stability after chaos; who served, in Hoover's terminology, as the link between the self doubt and trauma that marked the end of Richard M. Nixon's Presidency and the uncertainty and hope that characterized the beginning of Jimmy Carter's. . . . If Mr. Ford was seldom inspirational and never visionary . . . he was at least steady, at a time when steadiness may have counted for much.[128]

A number of other journalists presented similar analyses in their postelection commentaries on the Ford legacy.

Dennis Farney: He was open, all-of-a-piece, a splendid human being. . . . Although level-headed in times of crisis, Gerald Ford never seemed to have a clear idea of just what he wanted to do with the vast powers he inherited. . . . Jerry Ford, the man, had a theme, but his presidency did not. In the end, "decency" was not enough. . . . What he did do, in his steady, unassuming manner, was to stabilize the nation at a time of national turmoil.[129]

Washington Post: Mr. Ford did not need continually to ask people to trust him. By and large they *did* trust him. They did not see a vast difference between the public man and the private man. Conveying this trustworthiness has been Mr. Ford's principal contribution to the public welfare since he has been in office. When you recall the circumstances under which he came to the presidency and the political turmoil of the time, the magnitude of his contribution becomes plain.[130]

Hugh Sidey: In history Ford may figure as little more than a short, interim chapter, an expanded footnote. . . . Ford's call for a pause was characteristic of the man but was not in the tradition of change that is at the center of American life. . . . Surely there will be a place someday down in the White House foyer for the portrait of the man who pulled the country out of its worst political scandal.[131]

---

128. James M. Naughton, "The Unique and Necessary Presidency of Gerald Ford," *New York Times*, November 14, 1976, IV, 5.

129. Dennis Farney, "In the End, Decency Wasn't Enough," *Wall Street Journal*, November 4, 1976, 20.

130. "The Election," *Washington Post*, November 4, 1976, A26.

131. Hugh Sidey, "Closing Out an Interim Chapter," *Time*, November 15, 1976, 28.

At the end of 1976, with indications of an improving economy, the *Wall Street Journal* wrote that Ford's policies had thereby received "vindication." The *Journal* maintained that Ford's refusal to open the floodgates of public spending "may rank alongside putting Watergate behind us as Mr. Ford's two greatest contributions to the nation."[132]

Within several days of the Carter inauguration, a number of press commentaries addressed the question of Ford's legacy. The *Wall Street Journal* asserted that "the nation is in better shape today than when he came to power in 1974. . . . The fact that Mr. Ford could report that the state of the Union is good owes very little to Congress."[133] The *Journal* also reported that "Ford leaves office with bipartisan esteem for his integrity, moves to restore faith in government, cooperation with the Carter transition."[134] *Journal* reporter Vermont Royster thought that "Ford served us well. He was the right man for the times. . . . What the country needed this time was a healer, and that is what it got in Gerald Ford. . . . [H]is calmness, his civility, his obvious integrity have restored to the people their trust in the Presidency." Yet Royster added that Ford would not be ranked as a "great" president.

> One reason is that he lacks the strong ego, the personal drive and sense of overwhelming self-confidence, that makes great leaders, like Roosevelt or Churchill, and makes them want to seize the times and shake them. He proved too much the man of the legislature, conditioned by training and experience to await events rather than shape them with his own vision.[135]

Joseph Kraft identified Ford's major presidential accomplishments as "the recovery of national morale. . . . He personally exemplified truth, openness and affection for other Americans." Kraft described Ford as uniquely qualified to "have played the role he played. . . . All Americans are in his debt." Kraft attributed an improved national political condition to "the innate goodness of Jerry Ford."[136]

When President Nixon chose Gerald Ford to replace Spiro T. Agnew as vice president, the *Washington Post*, among others, blasted Nixon's choice as a narrow, ideologically minded, petty partisan one. In its January 16, 1977, editorial, "The Ford Years," the *Post* confessed that "we were wrong" about Ford.

---

132. "A Moment of Optimism," *Wall Street Journal*, December 31, 1976, 4.

133. "The President's Goodbye," *Wall Street Journal*, January 14, 1977, 10.

134. "Washington Wire," *Wall Street Journal*, January 14, 1977, 1.

135. Vermont Royster, "Gerald Ford," *Wall Street Journal*, January 19, 1977, 16.

136. Joseph Kraft, "Ford Looks to the GOP Future," *Washington Post*, January 16, 1977, B6.

[Ford] brought precisely the needed temperament, character and virtues to the high offices he has temporarily held. . . . Gerald Ford brought to the White House an open, unsinister and—yes—decent style of doing things that altered the life of the city and ultimately of the country. . . . We think it is enough to point out that Gerald Ford had an all but impossible assignment—and that he did a hell of a job.[137]

Thomas M. DeFrank had covered Ford for *Newsweek* since late 1973 and presented a retrospective assessment of Ford's performance as president. DeFrank contended that without the new set of leadership standards created after Watergate, Ford would not have been judged much more than "an ordinary President." The *Newsweek* reporter believed that Ford lacked John F. Kennedy's "grace" and Lyndon B. Johnson's "political acumen," and, unlike Harry S Truman, "he failed to grow significantly in his job."

His stumbles and his oratorical bumbles were a source of gallows humor among even his loyal aides. But Gerald Ford brought a sense of common decency to his office. . . . Ford quietly restored the Presidency to human proportions, an achievement for which history may give him more points than his countrymen did last November.[138]

Two additional reviews of Ford's presidency deserve to be quoted at length. The *New York Times*, so critical of Ford's policies while he served as president, praised him for having "renewed public faith in the integrity of the Presidency" and for having "restored a sense of calm and dignity to the entire public scene."

His personality was Mr. Ford's main asset in the task of healing and renewal. He is naturally a candid, friendly, forthright man with admirable emotional balance. . . . Not since Mr. Truman has there been a President who so nearly embodied and expressed what Americans think of their typical virtues. . . . He never persuaded the public that he was firmly in charge or keenly determined to lead the nation toward specific objectives.[139]

David Broder, despite his earlier assessment that Ford had no idea what to do with the powers of the presidency, concluded that "Gerald Ford can

---

137. "The Ford Years . . . ," *Washington Post*, January 16, 1977, B6.
138. Thomas M. DeFrank, "Suited to a Tee," *Newsweek*, January 31, 1977, 30.
139. "The Ford Years," *New York Times*, January 13, 1977, 34.

leave office with some confidence that history will record that he was, in truth, the President the country needed at this time and knew that it wanted, even by another name."

> After a decade of presidential excess, they wanted a man of modesty, good character, honesty and openness. They wanted a President who was humane and prudent, peaceable but firm. Especially, they wanted one uncorrupted by the cynicism and lust for power that they had come to associate with Washington politicians. . . . [Ford was] exactly the kind of personality they prayed to find in the presidency.[140]

Conclusion

By the end of its term in office, the Ford administration never fundamentally turned around the negative aspects of the president's press image. Even in praising Ford for restoring faith in government, journalists criticized him for not being a more commanding, activist, visionary president. The basic elements of Ford's press image during his final year in office can be summarized as follows.

Timing

Election year politics significantly influenced the nature of press reporting on the presidency in 1976. Journalists often assessed Ford's actions within the context of the primary and general elections. They characterized most of his actions as politically motivated and, hence, not always "presidential." When Ford did not move to negotiate a Panama Canal agreement, when he opposed efforts to normalize relations with Vietnam, when he advocated cutbacks in domestic spending programs, journalists attributed the events to the president's political motives. Ford had a difficult time getting the press to judge his decisions more on their merits than on his motives.

During this late stage of Ford's brief term, the press expected the president to have established a clearly focused, effectively articulated agenda for the future. Journalists believed that Ford had succeeded in the first of his presidential duties—reestablishing public confidence in the integrity of public leaders and institutions. They thought that he did not succeed in moving on to the next step—consolidating and vigorously exercising presidential powers.

---

140. David Broder, "The President the Country Needed," *Washington Post*, January 16, 1977, B6.

Symbolism and Rhetoric

In the press's view, during his last year in office, Ford did not project a more effective use of presidential symbols and rhetoric than he did earlier in the term. Journalists said that he lacked an organizing theme or catchphrase to convey to the public what the Ford administration stood for. Ford not only failed to make effective use of symbols, but he also did not successfully employ the "bully pulpit" of the presidency to his advantage. According to the press, Ford did not convey a strong leadership image and he did not rouse the public with his speeches.

Undoubtedly, Ronald Reagan's presence in the Republican presidential nomination campaign drew more attention than otherwise to what journalists considered an important Ford weakness—his public speaking skills. And given the unfortunate "bumbler" image, journalists amplified each presidential misstatement and seized on it as further evidence of an "accident prone" and "accidental" president.

Agenda

Because of the national elections, the press gave less attention than usual to substantive policy issues. In general, journalists viewed Ford's domestic policy agenda as too cautious, status quo oriented, not "bold" enough to deal with the social and economic needs of the times. Oftentimes, journalists compared Ford to such former presidents as Herbert Hoover and Calvin Coolidge because he endorsed market-oriented economic policies. According to the press, Ford lacked the imagination and foresight to embark upon the kinds of far-reaching, innovative policies proposed by former presidents Franklin D. Roosevelt and Lyndon B. Johnson.

Ford fared somewhat better in the press treatment of his foreign policy agenda. His pursuit of détente with the Soviets generated favorable press comment, although some journalists said that Ford, fearing a conservative backlash, did not pursue the policy vigorously enough. The press mostly criticized Ford for allegedly not fashioning his own foreign policy, for relying too heavily on the advice of Secretary of State Henry Kissinger.

Policy Development

Journalists saw Ford playing a "negative" role in the policy process. That is, rather than establishing a wide-ranging policy agenda to deal with public problems and a strategy to enact that agenda, he devoted his energies to stopping the Democratic Congress from controlling national policy-making.

In this sense, according to many journalists, Ford did not "lead" but, instead, "reacted." The press did credit Ford with playing that role very effectively. Nonetheless, journalists tended to define "leadership" as policy activism, taking the initiative and controlling the agenda.

Staff

Press esteem for the quality of Ford's staff did not improve in 1976. David Broder's assessment reflected a common press perception. "His White House staff is a reflection of the man—limited, parochial and pleasant."[141] *Time* magazine maintained that "many of Ford's difficulties can be traced to his White House staff, which is disorganized and at least temporarily dispirited."[142] Somewhat less tactfully, Nicholas von Hoffman declared that "Ford is trying to run the government with Richard Nixon's third team, the guys Haldeman and Ehrlichman had for bench warmers."[143]

Clearly, the Ford administration suffered a press image problem, one that hampered its efforts to lead the nation and secure a full term in office. Conscious of the magnitude of this problem, the Ford White House had to try to overcome or to change the prevailing press perceptions. In the next chapter, I turn to the important matter of the Ford White House press strategy and what the efforts of Ford staff members reveal about what a White House can and cannot do to manage press relations.

---

141. Broder, "The Incumbent," 137.

142. "More Blood in the G.O.P.'s Donnybrook," 8.

143. Nicholas von Hoffman, "You Mustn't Say Those things About (an Incumbent) President," *Washington Post*, October 4, 1976, D1.

CHAPTER 7

Ford's Press Strategy: Retrospective Assessments by the Press Office Staff

This chapter looks inside the Ford White House to better understand how the president and his communications advisers developed their press relationship. Every White House in the modern era understands the important role that the press plays in creating and sustaining a presidential image. Yet not every White House attaches the same importance to press relations. Given the extraordinary number of activities in which presidents engage, some chief executives (e.g., Carter) have downplayed the role of press relations, whereas others (e.g., Reagan) have given exceptional attention to that presidential role. It is all a matter of presidential priorities, and, no doubt, it can be argued that Jimmy Carter undermined his leadership image by not emphasizing press relations and that Ronald Reagan neglected important presidential duties by spending so much time on imagery. But no president has discovered the ideal mixture of presidential duties—including the point at which public relations have gone too far.

Understanding the Ford White House press relations apparatus—its successes and failures—can contribute significantly to our knowledge of modern press-presidency relations. Gerald Ford was the first president to be tested by the press in the post-Watergate environment. That environment brought about some significant changes in the nature and tone of modern presidential press relations, and Ford's presidency laid the groundwork for much of what would later develop in this area. For future presidents, there are important lessons to be derived from the experiences of the Ford White House with the press.

In this chapter, I identify and assess the Ford White House press strategy: How much emphasis did the White House place on its press relations? Did the White House employ a conscious strategy to manage its press relations? What were the major elements of its strategy? Which aspects of the press strategy succeeded? Which ones failed? How did the White House deal with press problems as they arose? What lessons can be learned about modern presidential press relations from the Ford White House's experiences?

To address these questions I rely primarily on a series of interviews that I conducted with Ford White House staffers who were involved in press relations. These interviews took place between December 13, 1989, and November 27, 1990. I interviewed the following people:

> Gerald R. Ford, president of the United States, December 13, 1989
> Robert Hartmann, counselor to President Ford, December 15, 1989
> William Greener, deputy press secretary, January 23, 1990
> Larry Speakes, assistant press secretary, February 6, 1990
> Gerald Warren, deputy press secretary, March 15, 1990
> John Carlson, assistant press secretary, May 2, 1990
> John Hushen, deputy press secretary, May 14, 1990
> Margita White, assistant press secretary and then director of White House Office of Communications, June 7, 1990
> Jerald terHorst, first press secretary, June 27, 1990
> Ronald H. Nessen, second press secretary, July 5, 1990
> Louis M. Thompson, Jr., assistant press secretary, November 20, 1990
> J. William Roberts, assistant press secretary, November 27, 1990

I also consulted a number of White House documents at the Gerald R. Ford Presidential Library in Ann Arbor, Michigan. In particular, I reviewed the files of the press secretaries, Jerald terHorst and Ron Nessen, and of Gerald Warren, David Gergen, and Margita White, among others. My third set of sources includes the memoirs of Ford White House staffers and other published records of their recollections of the Ford years.

The Early Press Strategy

Becoming president under such unusual circumstances provided Ford with both pitfalls and opportunities to exploit in his press relations. To believe many of the journalistic accounts, to succeed with the press, Ford did not initially need to do much more than not be Nixon. To be sure, the national euphoria that accompanied Nixon's departure and Ford's ascendancy to the White House at first benefited the new president's press relations. But the sudden change in the nation's leadership denied the Ford White House an opportunity to plan a coherent press relations strategy. Jerald F. terHorst, the press secretary during Ford's first month in office, said that "we never sat down and consciously devised what is called a 'media strategy' or a 'P.R. strategy.' There wasn't time for it, for one thing. We had to walk in there and hit the ground running." Terhorst described his "transition" to office in this way.

> I had twenty minutes of briefing from [Nixon press secretary] Ron Ziegler. Which was really, "here's the office, the men's room is around

the corner, the safe is under my desk, here's the combination, if you need me give me a call in California—they're calling me to the helicopter now." That was the extent of the transition from one administration to another, as far as the press secretary was concerned.[1]

Deputy Press Secretary John W. Hushen and Assistant Press Secretary Larry Speakes also emphasized that the lack of a transition period made formulating a press strategy difficult.

> *Hushen*: One of the great complications for the Ford presidency was the fact that there was no regular transition period. Jerry Ford literally went from being vice president of the United States to president of the United States overnight. So there was not time to give a lot of thought initially to press strategy.[2]

> *Speakes*: Ford being thrust into the presidency as he was, there was not the usual time available to sit down and to plan a strategy. I think that was largely responsible for Ford's inability to get a good press for his initiatives. The first thirty days in the White House press office in 1974 are often compared to standing by a railroad track and watching a freight train go by while trying to read the words on the boxcars. . . . There was no structure. Usually, in other White Houses, there had been an office of communications or somebody, a chief of staff for example, who had an interest in looking at long-term strategy. We just didn't have that luxury in the Ford White House.[3]

Speakes contrasted his experiences dealing with press relations in the Ford and Reagan White Houses. In 1981, the Reagan White House had a "100-days" plan for setting the agenda that had been mapped out months before the transition period. The Ford White House had to work out its agenda and means of communication on a day-to-day basis.[4]

But even without a blueprint for press relations, members of the Ford White House had ideas about how to get off to a favorable start dealing with the press. In the early days of Ford's presidency, the White House capitalized on the president's reputation for honesty and integrity—a major public relations asset that did not need any slick packaging. To the extent that the White House had a press "strategy" early in the term, that included (1) the need to

---

1. Author interview with Jerald F. terHorst, Washington, D.C., June 27, 1990.
2. Author interview with John W. Hushen, Washington, D.C., May 14, 1990.
3. Author telephone interview with Larry Speakes, February 6, 1990.
4. Speakes interview.

emphasize the change taking place in the nation's leadership, and (2) the attempts to project the "open" presidency theme. President Ford explained that his administration was "not too concerned about conveying a rigid line or a specific message. We wanted to create the impression of an open administration in contrast to that of my predecessor."[5] Each Ford White House staffer interviewed for this study also emphasized these aspects of Ford's press "strategy." For example:

> *Greener*: Generally speaking, the strategy was to be open and above-board, and to answer [reporters'] questions as much as possible. And to make people available.[6]

> *Warren*: If the Ford administration had any strategy at all it was to impress upon the press corps that this was a different administration. That this was not the Nixon administration. It was an administration under which things would be different. . . . And there was a press strategy to try to humanize the presidency. You may remember the president fixing his own breakfast and other such activities designed to humanize the presidency. . . . The other strategy . . . was to try to be as forthcoming as possible on all questions raised by journalists.[7]

> *TerHorst*: We wanted to convey that this administration would be an open place in a democratic, American fashion. It was important to make people once again proud of their president and proud of the White House. . . . [Ford] understood the need for what we were trying to do. . . . He did want to establish himself as a change from Richard Nixon. He may not have stated that publicly, but that was his personal view of the situation.[8]

TerHorst noted a number of symbolic and substantive actions adopted early by the Ford White House to convey the themes of change and openness. Having been deprived for so long of a presidential press conference, members of the media clamored for an early Ford press conference. Ford agreed and, at terHorst's suggestion, the president entered the East Room press conference by walking down a long, open hallway to the simple podium that stood before the press corps.

---

5. Gerald R. Ford, quoted in John Anthony Maltese, *Spin Control: The White House Office of Communications and the Management of Presidential News* (Chapel Hill: University of North Carolina Press, 1992), 118.

6. Author telephone interview with William Greener, January 23, 1990.

7. Author telephone interview with Gerald Warren, March 15, 1990.

8. TerHorst interview.

I did *not* want Jerry Ford standing behind a huge, bulletproof podium with his back to the wall and that blue curtain, as Richard Nixon and Lyndon Johnson did. That set-up made them look like men surrounded by cameras and reporters, with the press in a feeding frenzy, almost like sharks. Jerry Ford agreed to let me fashion something that would be different, more open. . . . And it did indeed look open! The press liked it. It worked. It was cosmetic, but it also was symbolic. It reinforced Ford's promise to be an open, accessible president.[9]

TerHorst also emphasized his accessibility to the president, another change from the practices of the Nixon White House. The press secretary wanted the press to be confident that, when he announced a presidential directive or comment, the words actually came from Ford, not some senior staffer speaking on behalf of the president.

One of Ron Ziegler's constant press problems was, "Ron, have you seen the president? When was the last time you saw him? Or are you just talking with General Haig?" Which was often the case. . . . One of the first things I had to do to demonstrate that I did have direct access to the president whenever I needed it so that questions could get answered. . . . We wanted to demonstrate that this president at least talked to his press secretary and the press secretary knew what he was saying. There was both an open door for the media through me, and an open door for me within the environs of the administration.[10]

---

9. TerHorst interview. These symbolic innovations evidently struck a responsive chord with the news media. Consider the following letter that NBC-TV's John Chancellor wrote to terHorst on August 20, 1974, just after Ford announced his vice presidential selection of Nelson Rockefeller.

This is a letter you can put aside for a rainy day (if you guys ever have one, after your *splendid* beginning). . . .

It was *informal* television. No Royal Family stuff. No holding a picture of the regal seal; no shots designed to keep the President smack in the middle of the picture, all the time. I liked it very much. . . .

Since Kennedy, I suppose, television directors and producers on the White House staff have worked very hard to show the boss in shots and angles which are not only flattering, but which tended, in the end, to be so damned *monarchical*. And I think those kinds of shots create a void between a President and the other people in the room with him.

What I saw today was the Administration, the leaders—the government, of which Mr. Ford was a part. There were some shots which didn't show the President at all. How long has it been since we saw that? Today's ceremony had a fine, plain, honest look about it. (Letter from John Chancellor to Jerald terHorst, August 20, 1974, Folder: "Subject File-General," Box 3, terHorst Papers, Gerald R. Ford Library).

10. TerHorst interview. Assistant Press Secretary Louis M. Thompson, Jr., provided an

TerHorst explained that the president directed him "to straighten out the press office." That meant taking off the payroll a number of people from the Nixon White House who really did not work for the press secretary. It also meant cleaning out of the press office such people as Father John McLaughlin, whom the press strongly associated with the Nixon public relations apparatus.

I had firm instructions from the president that there was no room for him. We didn't have on my staff any room for such things as an "attack force" and a "defense force." I surely didn't need any of those offices. And I certainly didn't need those sorts of people. . . . The guard had changed.[11]

interesting insight into the problems Ford had to deal with because of what had transpired during Nixon's term.

One of the issues that we kept having to deal with from time to time because it was one that came up frequently in the Nixon administration, particularly toward the end, was "when you say you speak for the president are you speaking for the President? Is the President even aware of this?" Jerry Warren told me a story one time where he had to handle the press briefing, and this was basically after the press secretary [Ron] Ziegler was taken off the briefings, and Ziegler was sitting up in his office listening to the squawk-box, the briefing, and Jerry was addressing a particular question. Well, a reporter said to Jerry, "Well, if you're speaking for the President, have you talked to the President? Have you seen the President today?" Initially Jerry kind of tried to waffle around it a little bit, but ultimately he had to say, "No, I did not see the President this morning." And after the briefing was over, Ziegler takes Warren by the arm, walks him over to the Oval Office, opens the door and says, "Now today you've seen the President." Then he shut the door. So we had to deal with the press suspicion from time to time as a result of that (Author interview with Louis M. Thompson, Jr., Washington, D.C., November 20, 1990).

11. TerHorst interview. TerHorst noted that the press unrealistically expected the Ford White House to be cleansed of every Nixon Republican. From 1952 to 1972, recall, Nixon had been on the Republican ticket as either the vice presidential or presidential candidate in every election except 1964. Few prominent Republicans could claim no Nixon association. However, some Nixon loyalists who posed serious problems for Ford did not immediately leave. McLaughlin hung on long enough for terHorst's successor, Ron Nessen, to write in a September 30, 1974, memo: "He is the major holdover problem from a public relations standpoint. There is absolutely no place for him in my operation and he must go as soon as possible" (Memo from Ron Nessen to Donald Rumsfeld, September 30, 1974, Folder: "Press Office-Administrative Matters," Box 23, Nessen Papers, Gerald R. Ford Library). Louis M. Thompson, Jr., joined the Ford team as an assistant press secretary on November 13, 1974. The second press secretary, Ron Nessen, gave Thompson a mandate to organize the White House press office. Thompson explained to me:

In terms of an organizational philosophy one of the things we did was we felt those people who were closely identified in the Nixon administration with the apologist's role or the role of explaining Watergate—the guys like John McLaughlin, Pat Buchanan, Ken Clawson, et cetera—that those folks had to go. Because clearly we were aware of the fact that we were dealing with a post-Watergate situation where press relations had become extremely bitter and it was just a snakepit environment (Thompson interview).

As noted previously, Ford adopted other symbolic changes to convey the theme of an open, unpretentious White House. These included replacing "Hail to the Chief" with the "The Victors" (the University of Michigan fight song), referring to the White House as the residence, and renaming the presidential airplane *Air Force One* (not the *Spirit of '76*). Ford also initially dropped the name from the White House Office of Communications, Margita White noted, "largely because there was still a great deal of sensitivity to the impression of that office left by the Nixon White House. That office took on a very political role under Ken Clawson during the last days of Watergate."[12] Eventually, the name White House Office of Communications resurfaced, but the initial dropping of that name again signified Ford's intention to convey that his presidency differed from Nixon's.

Despite the lack of a normal transition period and of a well-developed press strategy, Ford received a most favorable press his first month in office. White House press office staffers attributed this favorable press to Nixon's departure and, more important, to Ford just being himself. Commenting on Ford's thirty days of good press relations, terHorst said that "I don't think that I had a lot to do with it. I think the best press secretary at that point was Jerry Ford himself. He made life very easy for me."[13] Larry Speakes commented that "it was Ford's personality—from toasting his own English muffins to this good-guy, boy scout, eagle scout image—that carried him for the first thirty days. And, of course, there was the end to turmoil and the calmness of his demeanor."[14] Speakes also commented that "during those first days, President Ford pushed all the right buttons. . . . The stage was set to create a favorable public image."[15]

The Pardon and terHorst Resignation

The set on Ford's public image stage underwent a major change after he pardoned Richard M. Nixon and Press Secretary Jerald F. terHorst resigned. Not surprisingly, each Ford staffer pointed to these two events as the crucial turning point in Ford's press relations. From a press relations standpoint, did the Ford White House handle these events properly? Was the negative press reaction to the pardon inevitable, or could the president have turned that decision into a public relations plus? On these questions, Ford's press people offer valuable insights.

---

12. Author telephone interview with Margita White, June 7, 1990.
13. TerHorst interview.
14. Speakes interview.
15. "Remarks by Larry Speakes: The Ford Image," Seventh Presidential Conference, Hofstra University, Hempstead, New York, April 8, 1989.

For the most part the staffers agree that, from a public relations stand-point, Ford did not handle the pardon effectively. Robert Hartmann attributed the president's national press image problems in large part to "the surprise that Ford sprung on the press with the pardon, because it wasn't Ford's nature to do things by surprise, to keep little secrets. That particularly applies to the beltway press." Hartmann added:

> The honeymoon, the feeling of openness, was sharply constricted by the pardon. Not entirely because the pardon itself was unpopular with the press, but because, in his last press conference before the pardon, he seemingly had said that he was not going to do that [pardon Nixon], at least for a while. He seemed to say in the press conference . . . that while he was not going to rule out pardoning Nixon that this was some-thing a long way off and nobody should expect it next week, when in fact it was the next week. They felt that they were had on this because they were unprepared for it, and, of course, they didn't like it. They felt about Nixon the way many people now feel about Mrs. Helmsley—they wanted to knock him down, stomp on him, kick him, and then bury him alive. . . . So when Ford did this he lost some of the rapport he always had [with the press].[16]

John W. Hushen stated more bluntly that "we delivered it [the pardon] to the country like Pearl Harbor." Hushen elaborated:

> The White House press corps, which prides itself on knowing everything that's going on, was caught completely flat-footed and went up in smoke. They were apoplectic that this "villain," as far as they were concerned, had been let off the hook and they took it out on Ford. The reporters were particularly angered by the surprise because they like to foster the belief that they know everything that's going on. And then the columnists picked up the hue and cry.[17]

The terHorst resignation placed Hushen in a most difficult position. As the acting press secretary, Hushen had to meet the press and try to explain the president's pardon. The trouble was, Ford kept his own press office out of the loop on the decision, and neither the president nor Hartmann provided any direction to the press office about how to communicate the White House's position. Hushen described the situation as "chaotic" and certainly not con-ducive to articulating a defense of the president's surprise action that would

---

16. Author interview with Robert Hartmann, Bethesda, Maryland, December 15, 1989.
17. Hushen interview.

lay the groundwork for dissipating the severely negative press and public reaction.

> One of the complicating factors was that the president said at a press conference in August that he would not inject himself into the judicial process until it had run its course. So we had the public leaning one way, and then out of the clear-blue sky, or so it seemed, Ford issued the pardon. . . . The Press Office was kept in the dark about the planning going on regarding the pardon and that was a mistake. When the president decided that he wanted his general counsel, Phil Buchen, to explore the legality of a preconviction pardon, there were only four people who knew that the president wanted the option explored. . . . And nobody thought to say, "Well you ought to at least bring Jerry terHorst into this." It was an unfortunate oversight.[18]

Buchen held a background press briefing on the day of the pardon announcement and, in response to a reporter's question, contended that no pardon considerations would be given to any other Watergate defendants. Buchen clearly wanted to end press speculation that Ford might consider pardoning other Watergate defendants. Unfortunately, Buchen's comments had placed the other Watergate defendants in a separate legal category—one in which they would not be accorded a basic procedural right available to all convicted felons: the right to petition for a presidential pardon and to receive due consideration.

The press did not view the pardon in such technical or legalistic terms. Reporters looked for any evidence that Ford might pardon such Watergate figures as H. R. Haldeman and John Ehrlichman. Acting Press Secretary Hushen held the first full press briefing two days after the pardon announcement and explained that the Watergate defendants deserved to have the same procedural rights as any other person. Unfortunately, reporters—their suspicious natures tweaked by Ford's surprise pardon decision—leaped to the conclusion that the president must have been planning to issue pardons to the Watergate defendants.

> I went to great lengths to say that there were no pardon requests on the president's desk, that there were no pardon requests on the way to the president, and that no applications had even been filed. All we were doing was looking at the question and trying to make sure that the Watergate defendants received the same treatment as anyone else.[19]

---

18. Hushen interview.
19. Hushen interview.

The rumor that Ford was planning to pardon the Watergate defendants spread in typical Washington fashion during a big news event. After the briefing, reporters rushed to their offices to call in their stories, and the assignment desks then called Capitol Hill correspondents to push for congressional reactions. Responding to reporters' questions about Ford's alleged plan to issue more pardons, political leaders expressed shock and dismay. Phone calls protesting the idea of more presidential pardons inundated the White House. The Republican leadership held an emergency meeting in the Cabinet Room of the White House the next morning and a White House clarification was then issued. For the most part, the clarification put the controversy to rest. But the controversy was evidence of the enormous press sensitivity at that time to potential underlying motives or hidden plots behind official White House statements. Journalists thought that they had uncovered a big story and acted on certain assumptions that proved to be incorrect.

Hushen explained that all of this "turmoil" exacerbated the angry press and public reactions to Ford's decision. In his words, "it was a bumpy period which did not sit well with the media. The press corps expects the White House to run very efficiently. Despite their dislike of Richard Nixon, at least the trains appeared to run on time."[20]

Robert Hartmann's comments indicate that the president and the close circle of advisers who guarded the decision to consider a pardon had more pressing concerns than press strategy or public relations.

> TerHorst . . . was perfectly entitled to resign if he didn't like the pardon and if he felt hurt, as he should have, by being excluded in advance from this news so that, in effect, he had been made to lie. That was a mistake of the president's and I didn't bear down on it at the time, and neither did anyone else, because the decision was being so tightly held. And it was tightly held not to deceive the press but to keep Nixon from pulling a trick. What would have happened if Nixon had said, "thank you, but I don't accept your pardon"? If Ford had announced earlier the pardon decision, and Nixon refused, then Ford would look dumb, especially since he had been running around for a good deal of time saying that Nixon wasn't guilty. . . . In retrospect, Ford should have earlier taken terHorst into his confidence. A press secretary had to have that. Ford's theory was that, knowing that terHorst couldn't lie, it would cause a major dilemma for him if journalists asked if Ford planned to issue a pardon.[21]

---

20. Hushen interview.
21. Hartmann interview.

Meanwhile, Ford had secretly dispatched attorney Benton Becker to San Clemente, California, to negotiate a pardon acceptance statement from Richard M. Nixon. Preferably, a statement of contrition that would, no doubt, help to mitigate the effects of any negative reaction to the pardon. Former Press Secretary Ronald Ziegler steamed "contrition is bullshit" and proceeded to offer statement after watered-down statement on behalf of Nixon accepting the pardon, but refusing to be contrite. The Nixon statement that Ford finally accepted failed to mention any wrongdoing or regret, except that the former president had not managed the Watergate crisis more effectively. As some of Ford's press office staffers commented, the Nixon statement added fuel to the fire over the pardon.

> *Hushen*: President Ford's only condition in giving Nixon a full pardon was that Nixon accept it. There were no other strings. Nixon didn't have to make a statement, didn't have to say anything, in fact. He did issue a brief statement, but it didn't do anything to help our situation. . . . We got no help from Nixon. No statement of contrition.[22]

> *TerHorst*: We had not even prepared Richard Nixon for accepting the pardon. It was only much, much later that he finally got around to saying "thank you," in effect. How do you pardon somebody who is not even contrite or asking forgiveness? . . . President Ford wasn't getting any of that from [Nixon at] San Clemente.[23]

TerHorst's assessment of Ford's handling of the pardon from a public relations standpoint is worth quoting at length. As the presidential press secretary who chose to resign rather than explain a decision he could not accept and as a long-time White House press corps member, terHorst offers important insights on this controversy.

> I think the one failing—and it was a serious one—that President Ford made, in terms of the press and the presidency, was that he did not consider the public relations aspects of granting the pardon. They were considered from a legal basis and from a political basis, but not from the standpoint of convincing the American public that it was the right thing to do at that time. . . . [T]here was this glaring omission of any constructive work about "how do we convince the American public that Richard Nixon deserves to be pardoned?" That was not done. A brief

---

22. Hushen interview.
23. TerHorst interview.

speech on a Sunday morning, when people are going to church—the whole thing had so many downsides to it that it was no surprise to me that the country reacted as though someone had just torn the scab off of Watergate. That put us right back into the mess again. To this day, people suspect that there was a deal.[24]

Ford's press officers identified the pardon as the crucial turning point in the president's press relations. But, as Gerald Warren noted, the negative press atmosphere already existed. Warren commented that "there is no question that relations between the press and the presidency had deteriorated severely during the Nixon administration. And there was a lack of civility in the White House press group that is now just starting to come back [to a more congenial relationship]." Warren added:

Then the negativity was enhanced, immeasurably perhaps, by the pardon of Richard Nixon. That really had an impact on how the press viewed President Ford. And especially as regards the terHorst resignation. And whether or not there was a deal struck between Haig and Ford before the resignation. That really added a lot to the negative atmosphere.[25]

The terHorst resignation added significantly to that "negative atmosphere." Several Ford staffers identified this event as a major contributing factor to Ford's difficulties in handling the severely negative reaction to the pardon. Robert Hartmann explained to me the importance of terHorst's resignation.

So, by quitting on the same day that the pardon was announced, so that this became the second line in every story about the pardon—"President Ford today issued a full and unequivocal pardon of former president Richard Nixon, and Jerry terHorst, one of Ford's closest aides, resigned in protest." That set the tone for the rest of the press corps, from whom terHorst had not withdrawn completely.[26]

Gerald Warren reflected on the resignation in the following way.

I think the resignation of Jerry terHorst really hurt Mr. Ford. Especially coming at the time that it did. . . . And I wish it hadn't happened. I told Jerry later that it was a good time to go to the White House staff and say,

---

24. TerHorst interview.
25. Warren interview.
26. Hartmann interview.

"look, we have a real problem here. One of you told me that no one was working on a pardon. And I went out, faithfully reported it to the press corps and it turned out to be inaccurate. Now the president has authorized me to tell you that if that happens again somebody is going to be in serious trouble, and it's not going to be me." I think he could have done that. . . . And the White House would have been better for it. Then if Jerry still felt that the pardon was a mistake, he could have picked a more decent time to resign. Resigning at that time because of the pardon and blaming the pardon for the resignation I think really hurt his president. I think it was a big mistake.[27]

J. William Roberts added that

a month [after Ford's inauguration] came the pardon and it's back to Nixon. Even though we were different, from the press standpoint there was some kind of deal and they just didn't like it. Boy, did we have a brutal time. And the terHorst resignation really compounded the problem. If he had stayed on it might have turned around. But for a long, long while the suspicion was there and you could really feel it in the questions that came and the attitude of cynicism and distrust. It was very painful for me because I knew that we weren't operating that way. It hurt.[28]

According to Larry Speakes, terHorst hurt the president significantly in two ways: (1) by resigning at such a difficult time, and (2) by later trumpeting the incident in the news media.

I think what he did was wrong. Ford had picked him to be a press secretary because he was a friend. And now, in Ford's most difficult moment, terHorst was abandoning him and making a public show of his disagreement with Ford's decision to pardon Nixon. Moreover, terHorst said he wasn't going to give any interviews, but he quickly turned up on the morning talk shows, and he granted interviews to a number of reporters. I always felt that Jerry let Ford down . . . by going out and talking about [the pardon]. My feeling was if you felt you had been done terribly wrong, you kept your mouth shut and left in your own good time, but you never torpedoed the President.[29]

---

27. Warren interview.

28. Author interview with J. William Roberts, Falls Church, Virginia, November 29, 1990.

29. Larry Speakes, *Speaking Out* (New York: Avon Books, 1989), 67. Speakes contends that terHorst wanted to leave the position of press secretary for reasons other than the pardon and

Hushen agreed that "terHorst's resignation made the whole thing so much more difficult. Jerry showed me his letter that day. . . . I said, 'Jerry, you can't do this.' But he did and I thought, 'now I know how Truman felt when he said the weight of the world had fallen on him when Roosevelt died.' With terHorst out . . . I was the one going to be chewed out for this."

If he had stayed, we would have weathered the storm much easier. The fact that the president's press secretary quit over the pardon had a major impact on the story. There was a lot of suspicion that there was some kind of deal between Nixon and Ford, and when the public heard that the press secretary resigned in protest, it convinced many of those people that there really was something questionable about it. It was a real setback for the Ford White House.[30]

---

just used Ford's controversial decision as "a convenient excuse" and then "present[ed] himself as a martyr" (299). Deputy Press Secretary William Greener offered the following observation.

I do think that Jerry terHorst could have become the most powerful press secretary ever if he went into the Oval Office after the pardon and said "if anything like this ever happens again, I'm going to blow the lid off it." But instead he quit. And frankly I think he quit more because he, as a columnist, had no idea that [being press secretary] was twenty hours a day, seven days a week. It was a great shock to him. It was harder than he wanted to work (Greener interview).

A number of terHorst's colleagues from the press office not only expressed regret over his resignation but said that he was not completely forthcoming about the reasons underlying that decision. Recall that terHorst said that he had to resign because he disagreed with the pardon and could not in good conscience defend it or speak for it publicly. Echoing Speakes's and Greener's explanations for terHorst's resignation, several press officers commented that the former press secretary also had other, personal reasons for leaving the White House. One explanation given is that the pardon was the "last straw" for the press secretary who had become frustrated by White House secrecy and being left out of administration deliberations over policy. A staffer commented that terHorst's former press corps colleagues "started to get to him. They kept telling him that 'they're [the White House] doing the same thing to you that they did to [Ronald] Ziegler and [Herb] Klein.'" In other words, keeping him in the dark about White House decision making and telling him only what they wanted the press secretary, and hence the public, to know. Another explanation given was that terHorst quit over a combination of factors: White House secrecy, disagreement with the pardon, and family pressures (his wife, a partisan Democrat, and grown children allegedly implored him to quit because of the pardon). Of course, only terHorst knows his own reasons for resigning.

What became clear from the comments of terHorst's former colleagues is just how strongly they believed that he had done the wrong thing by resigning and how instrumental that decision was to undermining Ford's press and public reputation. The most common criticism of terHorst by his former colleagues was that "he didn't understand the job of press secretary." One staffer said he told terHorst that "nobody cares what you think. People want to know what the president thinks. You're just a mouthpiece." That is, the press secretary need not agree with policy decisions. He is not personally associated with those decisions. He merely speaks for the president and it is the president, not the press secretary, who is held personally responsible for White House policy.

30. Hushen interview.

Hushen recalled that the press office devised a strategy to try to minimize the impact of terHorst's resignation. The plan called for Hushen to travel with the president on Monday while terHorst quietly cleaned out his office. On the return trip, the resignation would be announced and then followed by a press briefing. Hushen and Assistant Press Secretary Tom DeCair met with terHorst at 2:00 P.M. the day of Ford's announcement.

I said, "Now Jerry, are you sure you haven't spoken to anyone in the media." Earlier he told me he had not. Again he said no, except for Tom DeFrank of *Newsweek*. I said, "What did you tell him?" Jerry said, "I told him that I had submitted my resignation." Jerry thought it didn't matter because *Newsweek* didn't come out until Tuesday. I said, "Well, now we have three hours and 55 minutes to come up with something before *Newsweek*'s story is filed with a 6:00 P.M. dateline." . . . So the problem that we faced is that we just didn't have the luxury to plan this all out. We were just flying by the seat of our pants.[31]

Even if the press office had the time, "the luxury," to plan out a public relations strategy, would that have made a significant difference to the press and public reaction to the pardon of Richard M. Nixon? On this question, press office staffers differ in their assessments. Some staffers articulated the view that Ford actually could have emerged from the pardon with an improved public image—a proper public relations strategy, in other words, would have led to Ford being viewed as courageous and assertive rather than devious and incompetent. Larry Speakes asked, "Why was the pardon of Richard Nixon, a bold step taken so that the nation could bind up its wounds, not depicted as an act of political courage worthy of a chapter on some future *Profiles in Courage*?" Speakes maintained that

a basic rule in the formation of public opinion is that bold, decisive, unexpected actions must be preceded by careful preparation of the landscape of the public mind before the seed is planted and nurtured—let alone reaping the harvest of favorable public reaction. The more unexpected these actions are, the more preparation must take place.[32]

In Speakes's view, the Ford White House failed properly to prime the press for the pardon, and he attributed the negative reaction to the pardon to that apparent failure.

---

31. Hushen interview.
32. "Remarks by Larry Speakes."

The Nixon pardon, too, was sprung on the public, and of course it had to be, but terHorst was left out of it and he resigned. And that left Jack Hushen and myself as the sole press people and we had no way of understanding Ford's thought process going into it.

Had he issued that pardon at 11:00 A.M. on Sunday, and then sat down with reporters from the wire services, the *Post* and the *Times*, and the networks and said "look, the president was devoting half of his time to Nixon matters and every time he looked up someone said, 'what about this, what about that,' the best that he could do for his job was to get rid of the Nixon thing and put it behind us." That probably would have been a good explanation had it gotten into that first wave of stories on a background basis, or whatever.

We could have sat down with a Hugh Sidey, or someone like that, and get the piece in *Time* that would have been quoted and repeated in the press. Instead, it was just out there, the country was reeling from it and so was the press. There was all this press antagonism—"the big shots get off and the little guys have to pay."

It was really an act of political courage, and he never got credit for that. It was pictured entirely wrongly. . . . If a press story gets off on the wrong foot, it's hard to turn it around. It's so important to lay the groundwork and proceed carefully.[33]

Jerald terHorst agreed with Speakes's assessment that Ford could have emerged from the controversy looking like a strong leader—in short, looking "presidential." In response to an inquiry about how Ford could have avoided the severely negative reaction to the pardon, terHorst said:

Well, he could have done it by asking questions. For example, if he had been candid in his press conferences rather than trying to avoid the problem. He could have said, "One of these days, folks, I have to address this question: if the former president is indicted should we proceed with the prosecution? Is that in the national interest? Do you think that's proper? What about the other issues that have to be addressed? This is taking up too much of my time, and I can't do what I want to do, and the national interest is not being served as long as this cloud is hanging over us. How can we remove the cloud? Should we pardon him? Should we not?"

In other words, get the public thinking along with you about your problem. I think he might have generated a lot of understanding—if not agreement, at least some understanding. He might then have created a

---

33. Speakes interview.

climate in which the opinion polls and the government could say, "This is what the American people want. They want Richard Nixon pardoned so the country can move forward."

He could have looked really presidential. And that would have been in character for him too. He was not the kind of man who liked to drop surprises. That was not his political forte—going around surprising his constituents. It would have been very much in his character to have followed that procedure.[34]

J. William Roberts thought that the pardon decision should have been handled differently.

The pardon was the turning point on everything. I think the election hinged on that, everything. The whole problem to me was that if President Ford had just done a little more exploratory work, floating a few balloons, consulting with more people, instead of keeping it so secret, he could have come out of it better. . . . But to just spring it at that time and that way, everything was just wrong about it from a public relations standpoint.[35]

Some press office staffers disagreed with this assessment. In their view, no amount of planning and preparation of the press could have changed the press corps reaction to the pardon decision. Margita White expressed one contrary view.

I know that some people will disagree with me. I remember some people in the Ford administration wanted to "blueprint" everything that was to be done. To a certain extent it is very helpful to outline what you want to do before taking action. But if you think that it's going to come out exactly as you planned it, then you're going to be surprised or disappointed. I don't doubt that the impact of an event such as the pardon could have been softened. But no matter what P.R. strategy was em-

---

34. TerHorst interview. Richard Cheney, who later became the Ford White House chief of staff, also assessed retrospectively that the president handled the pardon poorly.

The pardon was also handled poorly in terms of notifying other players. We could have gone to Capitol Hill and to other prominent Americans and talked about the Nixon pardon before it was done. That way, we might have built some support and understanding for it around the country. When we totally surprised everybody, it generated the kind of reaction that obviously created big problems for us (Richard Cheney, "Forming and Managing an Administration," in *The Ford Presidency: Twenty-Two Intimate Perspectives of Gerald R. Ford*, ed. Kenneth W. Thompson [Lanham, Md.: University Press of America, 1988], 72).

35. Roberts interview.

ployed, we weren't going to change the negative press reaction to that decision.[36]

Even though he believed that the president and the few White House advisers aware of Ford's decision to consider a pardon for Nixon erred by not including the press office in the process and by surprising the White House press corps, John Hushen acknowledged that the negative reaction to the pardon was probably inevitable.

> Looking back, I don't know if there was any better way to handle it than simply drop it on an unsuspecting public like an atom bomb. If there had been any leaks about what the president was considering, or if the White House tried to send up a trial balloon, the objections from the media and the Nixon-haters would have been so loud that the president might have decided not to do it.
>
> How can you prepare them for a decision like that? . . . Calling the press in earlier would not have changed anything. In their minds, we were letting this villain off the hook. There was no way that they were going to be appeased. There was no way that we could have gotten the columnists and editorial writers to be sympathetic.[37]

The press officers agreed, nonetheless, that the pardon of Richard M. Nixon set the negative tone for Ford's press relations throughout the term. Ford's press image never fully recovered from the effects of that controversial decision. As Gerald Warren stated, "I don't think after the pardon there was much that the White House could have done to fundamentally change the nature of its press relations. I think the venom had to run out of the system."[38]

To be sure, Ford did not fare well with the Washington beltway press corps throughout his term and his generally negative press could be attributed not only to the pardon, but to other factors as well (e.g., press cynicism, lack of a campaign or a regular transition, "stumbling" image). But the timing of the pardon, so soon after Ford had started to build a favorable press image, severely damaged the president's efforts to move beyond the climate of press cynicism toward public leaders. The White House, in a sense, had to embark upon a public image rebuilding effort, a most difficult task given the reaction to the pardon of Richard M. Nixon.

In the next section, I identify and assess the Ford White House press strategy, focusing on the various policies and decisions adopted to try to

---

36. White interview.
37. Hushen interview.
38. Warren interview.

enhance the president's press image. I then examine the underlying reasons press officers pointed to for Ford's difficulties managing his press relations.

Ford's Press Relations Strategy

Ford White House staffers clearly recognized the difficulties they faced dealing with a White House press corps that had such a combative relationship with former president Nixon. Ford's people knew that they had to make important overtures to the press to convince reporters that this administration wanted a different kind of relationship with members of the fourth estate. As noted earlier, Ford initially embarked upon a public relations strategy to demonstrate his intention to be an open, accessible president.

It is no coincidence, too, that Ford chose both of his press secretaries from within the press corps. Before becoming press secretary, Jerald terHorst worked as the White House correspondent for the *Detroit News*. TerHorst's replacement, Ron Nessen, covered Vice President Ford for NBC-TV news. For Ford, having a press secretary drawn from the press corps symbolized the White House's trust of, and respect for, political journalists. This administration, in other words, wanted to put an end to the "us versus them" mentality that pervaded the Nixon White House–press corps relationship. Ford felt comfortable enough with the press to make some of its members leading players on his White House team.

White House Press Office

Ron Nessen succeeded Jerald terHorst as press secretary on September 30, 1974. Nessen wrote that "terHorst's successor would have a tough act to follow. In fact, two acts to follow. The new man would have to live down Ziegler and live up to terHorst."[39]

The White House press office under Nessen initially had a staff of forty-five, including two deputy press secretaries—John Hushen and Gerald Warren—and eight assistant press secretaries. This staffing arrangement differed from the Nixon White House Press Office, which had fifty-eight people, but fewer with the deputy or assistant press secretary title. Initially, Nessen had responsibility for the activities of the other divisions within the press office, including the Office of Press Advance, Office of Television Advisors, Office of the White House Photographer, and the Office of Communications.

The major duty of the press officer, of course, was to respond to questions from members of the news media. Other responsibilities included hold-

---

39. Ron Nessen, *It Sure Looks Different From the Inside* (New York: Playboy Press, 1978), 10.

ing daily press briefings, holding special press briefings to announce new programs, preparing press releases on the president's activities, and making arrangements for members of the news media.[40]

Nessen maintained that President Ford made a number of important overtures to the press to establish a favorable relationship between the White House and reporters. For example, Ford restored the custom of inviting reporters to White House social events, a practice shunned by the Nixon administration. At terHorst's suggestion, Ford allowed follow-up questions by reporters in news conferences. In his twenty-nine months in office, Ford held thirty-nine news conferences, granted some 200 media interviews, and had 133 other media contacts.[41] Ford also adopted an innovative policy of allowing local reporters to ask questions along with members of the White House press corps during the out-of-town news conferences. And the president allowed one news writer, John Hersey, to spend a week at the White House as an observer. Hersey produced a lengthy *New York Times Magazine* story and later a book about this experience. Nessen noted that "although Hersey disagreed with [Ford's] politics strongly, we agreed to do this, again a gesture of openness toward the press." Nessen elaborated:

> One of the first things I asked Ford was how much time did he want to devote every week to dealing with the press. He said about two hours. So we used the two hours every week sometimes divided up between interviews, news conferences, other press activities, and out of town conferences. Sometimes he would do interviews over the telephone and so forth.[42]

During most of his first year in office, Ford's press contacts tended to be with reporters for major newspapers, magazines, and television stations. As late as May 22, 1975, Nessen wrote to presidential staff secretary James Connor that the president wanted to start meeting informally with columnists because these opinion leaders had "been ignored" by the White House. The White House adopted a series of "conversations with the president" in which five or six columnists at a time met with the president in the White House for about one hour.[43] These gatherings subsequently generated some favorable opinion columns by the people invited to the White House.

---

40. "Introduction to the Series Descriptions of David R. Gergen Files," 4, Gerald R. Ford Library.

41. Nessen, *It Sure Looks Different*, 349–50.

42. Ron Nessen, "The Ford Presidency and the Press," in *The Ford Presidency: Twenty-Two Intimate Perspectives of Gerald R. Ford*, ed., Kenneth W. Thompson (Lanham, Md.: University Press of America, 1988), 184.

43. Memo from Ron Nessen to Jim Connor, May 22, 1975, Folder: "Press Office—Philosophy/Policy," Box 24, Nessen Papers, Gerald R. Ford Library.

The White House Press Office experienced a number of difficulties, subsequently discussed in more detail, effectively communicating the president's goals and decisions. In short, Nessen had a combative relationship with the White House press corps and members of the various press offices had serious difficulties coordinating their activities. Staff infighting became a most discouraging problem for the press office people.

To address these and other problems, the press secretary, twelve staff members, and their spouses retreated to Camp David for the weekend of June 28, 1975. Margita White described the importance of the weekend retreat.

> One of the things we did to develop press strategy was to take a weekend away from the "pressure cooker" and went to Camp David to talk about what we were doing. You have to get away from the pressure-filled environment once in a while. It's good to just reflect on what your role is, how you can best help the president. It was a combination strategy session and getting to know each other better. It was a retreat, of sorts. It helped us to assess how well we were doing and to think about what we could do better.[44]

Out of the meeting came proposals for a number of substantive changes in press office procedures and a better rapport among the press office staffers. The substantive changes included the decision to hold daily press briefings at 11:30 A.M., whereas previously the briefings had not been held at a fixed time—a practice that angered press corps members. The press office agreed to post the president's activities in the press office at 10:30 A.M. and again at 3:30 P.M. The office followed up with an end-of-the-day news summary, listing that day's presidential actions and announcements.

The press officers proposed instituting these changes, in part, to be responsive to press criticism that Nessen's operation had not provided a timely and reliable flow of information. Press officers recognized, too, that this problem hurt the White House's ability to generate adequate news coverage of its activities.

The strategy sessions involved candid comments by press officers about what had been done wrong in the past and which areas of press relations needed improvement. The outgoing deputy press secretary, Gerald Warren, spoke at length about the needs to be responsive to reasonable press requests, not to be defensive in responding to difficult inquiries, and not to dignify grandstanding reporters with angry retorts. He urged that a professional demeanor would serve best to deal with press cynicism and present the president in a favorable light. Warren and other staffers urged more effective communications among the various press office divisions. Press office staffers also

---

44. White interview.

urged efforts to better coordinate communications between their office and the senior White House staff.[45]

Ron Nessen thought that these sessions provided enough positive feedback and good ideas to justify holding more such meetings. Nessen held another press office improvement meeting, this time at the Executive Office Building, on October 18, 1975. He called that session "a combination of group therapy, brain storming, management planning." The press office compiled a list of suggestions from its previous sessions and of actions taken on those suggestions. A similar list of suggestions for improving press operations came out of the October 18 meeting. Departing assistant press secretary Tom DeCair addressed the group on how to improve press relations, particularly on how to overcome the press perception of the president as lacking "a grand plan" or vision. Press officers discussed the need to coordinate press office operations with other White House offices. They pointed to the National Security Council, particularly Kissinger's penchant for internal secrecy, as a most bothersome problem. Again, press officers discussed ways to end "the game playing between offices in the White House" and how to "work more closely together."[46]

The press office divisions held a third media strategy session on August 7, 1976. This meeting focused much more on getting out the president's message to help his election campaign. This meeting occurred after the press office staff changes that resulted in David Gergen assuming the post of communications division director and being placed on equal standing with Nessen in the White House staff structure. Gergen largely led the discussions, which emphasized such concerns as how to better orchestrate White House events for the purpose of good media coverage.[47]

White House Office of Communications

Margita White first served the Ford administration as an assistant press secretary. She became director of the White House Office of Communications once Gerald Warren vacated that post in June 1975 to return to his earlier employer,

---

45. This summary of the Camp David Press Officers' retreat is derived from two documents: Press Office Staff Meeting, June 28, 1975, 10:15 A.M.–12:35 P.M., Folder: "Press Office Improvement Meeting (1)," Box 23, Nessen Papers, Gerald R. Ford Library; Press Office Staff Meeting (Afternoon), June 28, 1975, 3:15–5:45 P.M., Folder: "Press Office Improvement Meeting (2)," Box 23, Nessen Papers, Gerald R. Ford Library.

46. Press Office Improvement Meeting, October 18, 1975, Folder: "Press Office Improvement Meeting (2)," Box 23, Nessen Papers, Gerald R. Ford Library.

47. Communications, Advocates, News Summary and Research Staff Meeting, August 7, 1976, Folder: "Press Office Improvement Sessions—August 6–7, 1976," Box 24, Nessen Papers, Gerald R. Ford Library.

the *San Diego Union*. White had worked in the Office of Communications in the Nixon White House, serving the director, Herbert G. Klein.

Under Klein, the Office of Communications had a number of important functions, including providing editors and broadcasters outside the Washington community with copies of speeches, press releases, and other information; coordinating administration public relations campaigns; acting as the White House contact for radio stations, television networks, and independent stations; supervising public affairs activities in various federal agencies; and setting up interviews between correspondents and public officials.

Late in Nixon's term, Kenneth Clawson directed the Office of Communications. Under his direction, that office took on an increasingly political role and became a central resource in the Nixon White House's public relations response to Watergate.

When Ford became president, members of the White House staff debated whether or not to disband the office entirely because of the notorious reputation that it had gained during Watergate. The Ford White House abandoned the name Office of Communications and made that operation a part of Ron Nessen's press office, with down-scaled responsibilities and fewer employees. Gerald Warren assumed the title Deputy Press Secretary for Information Liaison.[48] The name Office of Communications did eventually reappear, but as White noted,

> . . . we didn't name it the Office of Communications until after Jerry [Warren] left, largely because there was still a great deal of sensitivity to the impression of that office left by the Nixon White House. . . . In my incarnation, the Communications Office technically came under the press secretary, which had not been the case under Herb Klein. So they were more coordinated in their efforts at devising a press strategy. I attended the morning press office staff meetings prior to attending the senior staff meetings.[49]

The office's downscaled responsibilities included mailing White House information to newspapers, arranging speeches before groups by administration officials, and compiling a daily news summary for the president as well as his briefing book for encounters with the media.[50] When asked to elaborate on the public relations strategy employed under this office, White replied as follows.

---

48. "Introduction to the Series Descriptions of David R. Gergen Files," 4, Gerald R. Ford Library.

49. White interview.

50. "Introduction to the Series Descriptions of David R. Gergen Files," 4, Gerald R. Ford Library.

This reminds me, ironically, of the statement Herb Klein had made that "truth will be the hallmark of the Nixon presidency." Of course, Watergate showed that wasn't always so. I think . . . we were especially sensitive to bending over backwards on behalf of openness, integrity, and restoring credibility.

To give an example, in my meetings with the public affairs officers I remember saying how important it was that departmental public affairs officers speak out when mistakes were found, rather than sweeping the dirt under the carpet that would only build up anyway for all to see. So there was a tremendous stress on getting the word out and making sure that credibility was maintained, regardless of personal reasons, efforts to embarrass, whatever.[51]

White explained that her office focused on communicating the president's messages to the outside-the-beltway media. Her office, for example, arranged for the president to hold breakfast or lunch meetings with newspaper editors, broadcasters, and other prominent media people from the region in which Ford was traveling. The office gave news briefings to local media and stayed in contact with the outside-the-beltway media through frequent mailings. In conjunction with Ron Nessen's operation, the Office of Communications met frequently to plan presidential announcements for the best public relations effect.

White recalled that the Ford White House had a generally positive relationship with the outside-the-beltway media, a significant contrast to how other press officers viewed Ford's relationship with the elite press. Indeed, the Ford White House employed a conscious strategy of directly reaching regional news media sources from around the country, believing that those sources, as well as the elite media, influenced public perceptions. The White House also understood that local news media—so grateful just to have access to the president—were more likely to produce stories favorable to Ford. In an interview with John Maltese, President Ford commented that "I can assure you that those regional meetings with local press were very productive. . . . They developed a good rapport that, in my opinion, paid off."[52] Robert Hartmann made the following comments.

What also was useful was having the president travel around the country articulating his message. The beltway press would get bored and complain "We've heard all this before, it's old·news." But when the president

---

51. White interview.
52. Maltese, *Spin Control*, 126–27.

took his message outside the beltway that same message was treated as big news.

That was important because presidents tend to gauge how they stand with the press by looking at what's said in the *Washington Post*. And that doesn't give a complete or accurate picture.

The press outside the beltway would be more accepting of the president's message therefore. And he used this technique effectively in order to promote his legislative agenda. . . . Ford recognized the importance of getting his message out beyond metropolitan Washington. I think he used this technique more than any of his predecessors and probably more than his successors.[53]

Ford not only traveled to make contact with local news media, but the Office of Communications also scheduled meetings at the White House with groups of regional media people. An April 23, 1975, White House memorandum from White to the president summarized the highly favorable editorial and column reactions of participants in some of these meetings. She singled out the following quotation from a *Detroit News* column as indicative of the benefits of this media strategy.

Afterwards the spokesman for the regional media feel they've been given a deeper look into affairs of state. And if you think this feeling won't be translated at some later time into a fairer break for the administration, you just don't understand human nature.[54]

Another public relations strategy that White encouraged involved placing Opposite-Editorial columns by cabinet heads in newspapers around the country. White looked upon this strategy as "an excellent way to provide the reading public with information about the administration's programs and to set the record straight."[55] Secretaries Earl Butz (Agriculture), Rogers Morton (Interior), and Frank Zarb (Federal Energy Administration), among others, placed Opposite-Editorial columns in large city newspapers explaining and trumpeting the administration's programs.[56]

From April 1975 until August 1976, James B. Shuman held the position

53. Hartmann interview.

54. Memo from Margita White to President Ford, April 23, 1975, Folder: "White, Margita—Reaction to President's Meeting With Media Executives," Box 145, Nessen Papers, Gerald R. Ford Library.

55. Memo from Margita White to Jim Cavanaugh, May 3, 1976, Folder: "White, Margita—Cabinet Op-Ed Articles," Box 143, Nessen Papers, Gerald R. Ford Library.

56. Memo from White to Cavanaugh.

of associate director of communications. Aided by four or five staffers, Shuman edited the president's news media briefing books, a responsibility carried out in the Ford administration by Philip Warden until April 1975. Specifically, Shuman's office edited Associated Press and United Press International stories, monitored and summarized television news broadcasts, and excerpted articles from magazines and forty newspapers read daily and another sixty newspapers that the staffers scanned.

In July 1976, during the election campaign, the Office of Communications underwent another set of changes. Ford nominated White to the Federal Communications Commission and David R. Gergen, the former Nixon speech writer, took over as the communications director. Gergen brought in William F. Ratican to be the deputy director. Rather then serve under Nessen, as did White, Gergen reported to Chief of Staff Richard B. Cheney and held coequal status with the press secretary in the White House organizational chart. Agnes Waldron took over the position of associate director of communications and Shuman went to work on press matters for Gergen and Nessen. A substantial increase in the communications office staff accompanied these changes.

In part, the Ford White House initiated these changes because of the perception that the president's achievements had not been effectively communicated to the public. During the election year, such a problem took on additional significance to the president. After Gergen took over, this office became much more involved in such areas as developing campaign themes and responding to partisan attacks. The communications office developed a better link to the President Ford Committee and coordinated the White House's activities with the needs of the campaign. The office, downplayed earlier in Ford's term, had become a White House focal point for the 1976 campaign, a highly politicized operation. David Gergen defended the use of the Office of Communications in that fashion. "I think it's part of how you run a decent White House. There are some people who think it's too political. But I think if you've got a president who's running for office, you've got to do it. It doesn't bother me in the least." And the chief of staff, Richard Cheney, added that once the Ford White House had entered the "campaign mode," changes needed to be made. "We *had* to do better than we had done. We had to have a more disciplined system" for getting out the president's message.[57]

Speech-Writing Department

President Ford placed considerable emphasis on speech writing. Presidential speech writers often complain that they do not have enough contact with the president and, thereby, cannot do a very good job at understanding and con-

---

57. Maltese, *Spin Control*, 137, 130.

veying his beliefs and emotions.[58] Ford's director of the speech-writing department, Robert Orben, offered a more favorable view of the relationship between the speech writers and President Ford.

> We had, in retrospect, and in talking to other presidential speech writers, amazing access to the President. . . . On average we met twice a week for roughly one hour a meeting. One hour would be devoted to going over the schedule of events coming up in which the President would have to speak. Before I took over, Paul Theis, who was the executive editor and head of the speech writers, would bring in three options for every speech. These represented the speech writers' observations on what might be said in the speech. But it was always the President who made the key decisions. He either went with one of the options or told us "No, I don't want to do that. This is the area we should cover." So we left this one-hour session, knowing where we were going on every major speech.[59]

Orben explained that the head of the speech-writing department then would assign the speech to a writer. The writer then composed the speech and worked either with the editor or the director of the speech-writing department on improving the product. The director finally approved the speech and the document then went to presidential counselor Robert Hartmann, who had to approve the speech before it went to the president.

Later in the week, the speech writer, director, and Hartmann met with Ford for another hour to go over the speech. Orben explained:

> So the speech writer always had the option of knowing what was right, what was wrong, and had a chance to fight for his or her words, and that's an extreme rarity. At any rate, the President went over every line of the speech, and if he didn't like something it would be changed on the spot, or if it called for a major rewrite, it would be redone. But essentially the President gave the speech that he wanted to give.[60]

---

58. See the many comments of President Jimmy Carter's speech writers in Mark J. Rozell, "President Carter and the Press: Perspectives of White House Communications Advisers," *Political Science Quarterly* 105, no. 3 (Fall, 1990): 419–34.

John J. Casserly served as a speech writer to President Ford for fifteen months and resigned in frustration over staff disunity and the speech-writing staff's lack of "consistent counsel and direction." See Casserly's book, *The Ford White House: The Diary of a Speechwriter* (Boulder, Colo.: Colorado Associated University Press, 1977), 254.

59. Robert Orben, "Speeches, Humor and the Public," in Thompson, *Ford Presidency*, 235.

60. Orben, "Speeches," 236.

Orben did believe that the speech-writing staff needed to be larger to do the job properly. The department had six speech writers, four researchers, and three secretaries. In his twenty-nine months in office, Ford presented approximately twelve hundred speeches and prepared remarks. As Orben commented, "We did better than a speech a day. The average amount of time we were given to write a speech was usually too little. We were understaffed for the amount of work that we had to do."[61]

One study counts 9,969 public speeches by presidents in the over forty-year period of April 16, 1945, until December 31, 1985. Postwar presidents averaged 20.3 such speeches per month. Ford averaged 36.5 speeches per month in office.[62] The prolific extent of Ford's public speaking is all the more remarkable when we consider too that the earlier postwar presidents could not rely on television as an effective medium to reach most citizens. Frequent presidential travels and speech making often served the function for which modern presidents rely upon television: reaching large numbers of people in an effort to persuade public opinion. Ford understood that he projected a favorable image of sincerity and trustworthiness in person, qualities that did not always carry as well on the television screen. Though not an inspiring stump speaker, Ford chose to place considerable emphasis on direct contact with the public through frequent travels and speeches.

Ford assigned enough importance to speech writing to provide a "door knock privilege" to the head of the speech-writing department. Essentially, that gave the department head the privilege of meeting with Ford, without an appointment, for a few moments between presidential appointments. Ford always brought a speech writer with him on *Air Force One* when traveling to some event.

The official speech writers did not always write the president's speeches. Oftentimes, Robert Hartmann did. Ford formally organized the speech-writing division under Hartmann's authority. Hartmann, no doubt, had a knack for capturing President Ford's feelings and beliefs in words, and composed such memorable phrases as "our long national nightmare is over." As a result, Hartmann did much more than organize the speech-writing operation. He also wrote many of the president's speeches and engaged in turf battles with colleagues to exercise control over Ford's utterances. Officially, Hartmann lost control over approving all presidential speeches in the July 1976 press office staff shake-up.

Hartmann instituted one speech-writing process innovation for the president's bicentennial addresses. To the horror of some speech writers, Hartmann established a "multiple track" system of composing Ford's addresses. In

---

61. Orben, "Speeches," 238.
62. Roderick P. Hart, *The Sound of Leadership* (Chicago: University of Chicago Press, 1987), xix, 8.

short, the system consisted of a speech form presented to the writers who would each compose a speech. By committee, Hartmann and the writers chose the best sections of the separately written speeches and then, with scissors and paste, constructed one speech. Orben initially fought Hartmann's idea, but conceded in retrospect that

> it proved to be a marvelous idea. . . . [W]e took the best thinking of everybody and as a result the Bicentennial speeches were exceptionally good. . . . In fact, the acceptance speech of the nomination was put together in this form, and it got something like 65 rounds of applause because we had so many good punch lines that would activate and excite an audience.[63]

Ron Nessen noted that the speech-writing unit suffered a number of problems, from turf battles and infighting to the inability to produce good speeches in a timely manner. The White House recruited staffers from other divisions to write speeches when these problems arose, expanding the number of persons actually involved in the process of composing the president's addresses well beyond the six official speech writers.[64]

Other Divisions/Tactics

In their retrospective comments, Ford's press office staffers pointed to some other public relations strategies employed by the White House. Gerald Warren referred to one strategy as "to get [Ford] on top of the issues." Warren explained that, in light of the pardon, the White House could not do very much to overcome Ford's "image problem." So the White House tried to shift national attention to substantive issues—particularly the economy and energy—and "to let the American people see that what he was doing was in the best interest of the country. They thought perhaps this problem would go away if Mr. Ford showed himself to be a master of the substance of the issues."

> Now I felt that he really did that, in terms of economic and energy issues. . . . We were, in late 1974 and early 1975, putting on regional briefings around the country on those two issues. I felt they were pretty successful, both with the regional press and with the people out in the regions. Those briefings were discontinued. . . . I thought that was a shame.[65]

---

63. Orben, "Speeches," 236–37.
64. Nessen, *It Sure Looks Different*, 85.
65. Warren interview.

Chief of Staff Richard Cheney noted that, on another occasion, the White House purposefully presented the president in a fashion to appear on top of the issues. In January 1976, Ford briefed the press on his administration's budget, a task not usually assumed by the president. Cheney said that the White House set this event up to try to get rid of Ford's press image as not very intelligent. The briefing showcased the president as the expert on his own budget, and some favorable press comments followed.

> It was just a masterful piece. It wasn't the country at large so much as it was directed directly to the Washington press corps. At that point it totally put to rest the whole question we then were faced with politically which is the bungler, stumbler, hit-your-head-on-the-helicopter type thing. We did it very deliberately.[66]

Assistant Press Secretary J. William Roberts also singled out as noteworthy Ford's performance in briefing the press on the budget.

> He did it all himself and he really did well. He showed that he was a nuts-and-bolts kind of guy and that he had a lot of knowledge of budgeting. . . . The briefing didn't get a lot of exposure—not an exciting topic. But it showed people that Ford knew his stuff.[67]

Assistant Press Secretary John G. Carlson said that the Ford White House did try, at times, to plan events around news coverage. Carlson pointed out that Ford "didn't devise his day-to-day operations around the press."

> But, on the other hand, we would put out a calendar for the next month and try to program what was going to happen and what were going to be the major stories, as much as possible.
> For example, if we knew that, at the end of May, the president was to leave for an international economic summit in Puerto Rico, the week before we would plan to display the president in various ways preparing for the meeting. And maybe the week before that we would plan some domestic activities so that not everything looked foreign. So we would look at a map a month ahead of time and try to plot in whatever we could.

---

66. Quoted in *The Ford White House: A Miller Center Conference Chaired by Herbert J. Storing* (Lanham, Md.: University Press of America, 1986), 80. Although Ford did give an impressive performance briefing the press on the details of his administration's budget, the tactic did not change the president's press image. Journalists generally are uncomfortable with such issues as budgeting and do not judge a president's performance on the basis of his command of the budgetary process.

67. Roberts interview.

But, let's say, on a Thursday, we would try to plot events more specifically for the next week. And then every morning we would try to refine that day's or the next day's activities. We would start the day at the White House at 6:15 A.M., go through the news summaries, then watch the morning news shows, and then, at 7:30 A.M., we had a staff meeting of all the key senior staff people in the White House. When it came to be my turn to address the staff I might say, "here, this looks like the top story of the day," or "this is going to be what we push today," or "today we're announcing a new $6 billion transportation bill that's going to the Hill, we're holding a briefing at the White House today, we'll be summarizing it, and then secretary so-and-so will elaborate on it for the transportation policy writers."

So we planned generally a month in advance, then we planned in more detail a week in advance, and then a day in advance we would nail everything down—that is, what we wanted to be the lead story on the news shows that evening and in the newspapers.[68]

For press conferences, the Office of Communications prepared briefing books for the president. The press secretary tallied the number of questions asked of him in the daily press briefings to gauge what journalists were thinking about the most and which issues likely would be addressed in presidential news conferences. Robert Hartmann identified another form of presidential press conference preparation.

Another thing we did was to have skull sessions with the president where we would ask him the damndest questions. Staffers would present embarrassing questions to the president to see how well he could handle those questions "off the cuff." We did this with Ford quite regularly. . . . Sometimes we would ask him the tough questions in the dirtiest manner possible. We would even try to get him mad! . . . These sessions were good preparation for the president in that they helped him to confront and prepare for the most difficult questions he could face in the press conferences.[69]

The Office of Public Liaison, headed by William J. Baroody, Jr., also assisted the White House's public relations agenda. Though not directly involved with the press, Baroody's office worked on improving Ford's public standing through contacts with various interest groups and civic organizations nationwide. Indirectly, such efforts influenced White House–press relations because many interest and civic group leaders are consulted by the media for

---

68. Author telephone interview with John G. Carlson, May 2, 1990.
69. Hartmann interview.

comments about the president's performance. By reaching out to these groups, the White House could better convey its message and goals as well as maintain a positive relationship with influential organizations.

Despite many efforts at enhancing its public and press relations, the Ford White House had serious difficulties generating a favorable presidential image. No doubt, a major reason for much of the negative press commentary is that Ford's leadership approach did not conform to many journalists' expectations of activist, visionary leadership. In their retrospective assessments of Ford's press relations, press office staffers also stated other important reasons for some of the negative press image problems that Ford confronted.

Negative Press Image—Causes

Press Cynicism

Ford's press officers stressed the important role that the events surrounding Watergate and the Vietnam War played in setting the tone of White House–press relations. Although the excesses of Nixon's White House made a Ford presidency possible, those same activities made Ford's efforts to overcome press cynicism toward public officials and institutions most difficult. As Ron Nessen explained,

> The specter of Richard Nixon haunted the Ford White House from the first day to the last. The White House press corps, particularly, remained obsessed with Nixon. It was difficult for many journalists to come down from the high of Watergate. They were addicted. Lies! Tapes! Exposures! Drama! Officials caught, disgraced, jailed! A President driven from office! A valiant press vindicated! Its wicked accusers discredited! Who could be happy again covering mundane matters like budgets, energy and legislative proposals?[70]

Jerald terHorst also emphasized the press attitudes at that time.

> Nearly every question reflected a White House suspicion of a ploy or game. You couldn't talk about policy and the need for continuity without someone questioning whether there was a devious plot behind it all. The press had been feeding on Watergate and Vietnam for so long that it was hard for them to shift gears. Hard for them to ask new and different questions. . . . Many in the media had become Vietnam and Watergate junkies, who needed their daily fix, almost like addicts.[71]

---

70. Nessen, *It Sure Looks Different*, 29.
71. TerHorst interview.

A number of other press officers cited similar problems that plagued Ford's press coverage.

Hushen: There was a great deal of suspicion within the press corps because of Watergate. They felt they couldn't trust what any government official said. That certainly influenced the events of the Ford presidency. The media viewed everything with a skeptical eye. That's why the pardon was so damaging. Many journalists seemed determined to show that there must have been a deal between Nixon and Ford. . . . Everything was viewed in relationship to the Nixon problem.[72]

Speakes: You really were dealing with certain givens. You were dealing with a press corps that had changed slowly through Vietnam and dramatically through Watergate. They felt they had been misled. They knew they had been scooped in Watergate by two guys who had never stepped inside the White House. And from that point on the press corps made an assumption that the government was lying. It colored the entire atmosphere. By the time Ford got there, no matter what you said, the question was raised, "now wait a minute, did you tell us everything?"[73]

Greener: Clearly the Watergate and Vietnam era was there, then everyone wanted to have the success of Bernstein and Woodward. So every reporter, if not overtly jealous, was covertly jealous of their monetary success. They had all discovered investigating reporting. And they thought that they could do investigating reporting from the White House press room. Well, the fact is, that's not where it's done. But they wanted to make sure that they weren't being duped by the government, or by each other. And that attitude carries on to this day. "We're not being taken in by government, we're not going to have the wool pulled over our eyes and let some reporters who don't even cover the White House get the big story."[74]

Carlson: It was a very, very difficult time after Nixon. And then you had Vietnam and Watergate. And I think what happened a lot to cause much of this was the reporting of Woodward and Bernstein. They got the story of what was going on in the White House. . . . [They] were able to get a lot more information than the people who were there every day. This embarrassed a lot of the White House press corps. So they started trying to be more aggressive. When they had a chance to see the press secretary

---

72. Hushen interview.
73. Speakes interview.
74. Greener interview.

or the president they thought they had to be more aggressive to get the story.[75]

Thompson: What we were going through at that time was one of the strangest periods between the White House and the press, having come off of Watergate and Vietnam. There was extreme doubt about the veracity of official statements. And an attitude due to the way the Nixon people had treated the press. We were really caught in the aftermath of that.[76]

President Ford: We inherited a very bad rapport between the White House press corps and the presidency as a result of Watergate and the Vietnam War. It was difficult to quickly change that negative attitude of the White House press corps.[77]

After leaving office, Press Secretary Ron Nessen wrote a bitter book about his experiences with the White House press corps in which he examined a number of reasons for the administration's press image problems. Nessen emphasized the nature of the times and noted that "Ford's role in history was to clean up other people's messes." That is, public and press cynicism caused by Watergate, the end of the war in Vietnam, a troubled economy, and intelligence agency scandals. Nessen added that "as press secretary I had my own legacy from the past to deal with: the attitude of cynicism and self-righteousness held by the White House press corps."[78] Nessen continued:

Feeling that they had not been suspicious enough of Nixon (and Ziegler) early enough, they became doubly suspicious of Ford (and Nessen) from the beginning. Like generals who always make the mistake of fighting the previous war, White House correspondents made the mistake, during the Ford years, of covering the previous president.[79]

Nessen cited incident after incident in which he believed press corps cynicism got in the way of accurate and fair reporting of news events concerning the Ford presidency. But nothing angered Nessen more than another factor in Ford's press image problems: the "bumbler" image. And other press officers from the Ford White House articulated similar beliefs about that aspect

---

75. Carlson interview.
76. Thompson interview.
77. Author telephone interview with President Gerald R. Ford, December 13, 1989.
78. Nessen, *It Sure Looks Different*, xiv.
79. Nessen, *It Sure Looks Different*, 32–33.

of the president's news coverage. As John Carlson commented, "After Watergate, Vietnam, big headlines, Ford comes in. And what kind of news can you write? 'Ford bumps his head on the helicopter'? That's the kind of stuff they based their news on."[80]

The "Bumbler" Image

You know, all these reporters who are reporting how clumsy I am on the ski slopes get most of their exercise sitting on bar stools. [President Ford to Ron Nessen][81]

Ford's press officers and other staffers expressed frustration at the persisting press image of the president as clumsy. Larry Speakes asked, "Why was the All-American football player, the most athletic president ever, not portrayed as a robust Teddy Roosevelt?" As Speakes pointed out, the news commentaries on presidential clumsiness reinforced the more troublesome image of Ford as not in control of the presidency.[82] John Hushen agreed with Speakes's comments.

The "stumbling-bumbling president" image didn't help Ford either. When he went skiing, the only thing the press wanted was pictures of the president falling. I think the public associated his physical missteps with a man who was not fully in control of his office.[83]

Speakes also said that Ford's public presentational style reinforced the "image as not-too-bright, played too many games without his helmet." Speakes added:

Ford's manner of speaking was halting—he wasn't a great orator. Although he came across as a very sincere person. But [Ford's speeches] contributed to the image problem, as well as the fall [in Austria and] bumping his head. In reality, he was a fine athlete, a war hero, a fellow who had a good academic record. Yet that never came across.[84]

---

80. Carlson interview.
81. Nessen, "Ford Presidency," 187.
82. "Remarks by Larry Speakes."
83. Hushen interview.
84. Speakes interview. Richard Cheney corroborated Speakes's assessment.

I would . . . give him high marks for his very wide knowledge of government. Oftentimes, I don't think this quality came through to the public, because he was not a man who was especially articulate. There were times when President Ford did not speak effectively enough to convey his impressive ideas (Cheney, "Forming and Managing," 73–74).

Presidential Counselor Robert Hartmann said that the clumsy image became reinforced by the pictorial media and the entertainment industry. As for the television and nightclub comics, "The idea of a president who falls down or stumbles, even if he was the most athletic president in many years, was good for them and they wouldn't let go of it." Hartmann explained:

> But this all goes back to the egg laid by Lyndon Johnson who said that "there's nothing wrong with Jerry Ford except he played football too long without a helmet." Now that was a work of art. It meant not that Ford was dumb but that he was a "comer" in the opposition party. Lyndon Johnson was very adept at recognizing [a rising talent] and conferred recognition by appointing Ford to the Warren Commission. The idea that a stumblebum equals a dimwit was therefore planted early.[85]

Chief of Staff Richard Cheney offered similar observations.

> The image was a problem, and I must say that Lyndon Johnson had contributed to its being rather negative. . . . That false image was strong enough so that when Ford came on board, it was something we had to deal with on a regular basis. I think it was accentuated by the President's speaking style. On occasion his remarks may have sounded less than articulate and I think that contributed to his problem. . . . He was very active athletically. . . . Nonetheless, the press oftentimes—and this is more aggravating than anything else—would get a shot of him falling down in the snow. . . . It was a rap from Lyndon Johnson, and occasional policy problems that led to this notion of a bungling, stumbling Jerry Ford. Of course, Chevy Chase on "Saturday Night Live" didn't help either. Once you get to the point at which something becomes a stock gag on Johnny Carson's "Tonight Show" or one of those kinds of TV shows, that label sticks and you can't get rid of it.[86]

The sometimes defensive comments of Ford's press officers confirm not only the existence of Ford's press image problem but the perception from inside the administration that this image problem contributed to the president's difficulties articulating a positive governing philosophy.

White: There was the unfortunate image of the president as a bumbler— always hit his head getting off *Marine One*, and all that. He was probably the greatest athlete ever to occupy the presidency. It bothered me a lot

---

85. Hartmann interview.
86. Cheney, "Forming and Managing," 76–77.

because we had worked so hard to restore a positive, credible image not just to the presidency but to government in general. Here was this wonderful president who did so much to restore confidence in government and in the White House and he was made out to be a buffoon. I thought that was a national tragedy.[87]

Greener: I think that the press harped on the slips, the bumping the head, et cetera, to the extent that they created the thought that Ford was the kind of guy who couldn't chew gum and walk in a straight line at the same time. I think it was unfair. He was the most athletic president in the history of the country. He graduated from Yale Law School quite well.[88]

Carlson: "Ford bumbling" and "Ford stumbling." Until Bush there has never been a more athletic president than Gerald Ford. . . . When the guy skis great you don't get a good picture. So you wait for a fall, show him tumbling. To suggest that he was clumsy, or unorthodox was just sad.[89]

Orben: That really irritated me, this question of his being called clumsy or inept. Here's the most athletic president we have had in this century. The man was captain of the University of Michigan football team; he was offered two spots on professional football teams; he played in the East-West Shrine game.[90]

TerHorst: Was this man awkward and disjointed? Not really. He was an All-American football player. He was the first president who publicly skied in front of the cameras.[91]

It still puzzles me that it persisted for so long. Maybe they were trying to find some dent in his armor, I don't know. It was so ironic because he was certainly the most athletic president we've had. . . . And then to be pictured as a stumblebum just didn't make sense.[92]

Ford could not understand how these news stories of presidential clumsiness persisted. Ford noted that Nessen asked him what to do about the lingering "stumbler" image. Thinking the stories eventually would end, that jour-

---

87. White interview.
88. Greener interview.
89. Carlson interview.
90. Orben, "Speeches," 249.
91. Jerald terHorst, "President Ford and the Media," in Thompson, *Ford Presidency*, 222.
92. TerHorst interview.

nalists would recognize Ford's athleticism, the president told Nessen not to be concerned about such trivial coverage. Ford admitted, "I was wrong. From that moment [of the fall in Salzburg] on, every time I stumbled or bumped my head or fell in the snow, reporters zeroed in on that to the exclusion of almost everything else." Ford recalled that he often found the comic routines of presidential impersonators funny, but did not find amusing the "stumbler" image that developed out of such routines and the "harmful" news coverage.[93]

Ron Nessen had a more difficult time accepting this kind of news coverage. He pointed out that Ford graduated in the top third of a Yale Law School class "which produced two Supreme Court justices, a secretary of state, a governor of Pennsylvania, mayor of Philadelphia, a senator, et cetera." Nessen complained:

> Gerald Ford's biggest continuing problem in the White House . . . was the portrayal of him in the media as a bumbler. . . . Alleged physical clumsiness was subtly translated into suggestions of mental ineptitude. Such ridicule in the press and on television undermined public respect for Ford as a leader. . . . It was a sorry and mindless performance by the press. The idea that Ford was a not-very-bright klutz was just plain wrong, a false image spread by herd journalism at its worst.[94]

Nessen reacted very defensively to the press's reporting of the bumbling president stories and, in so doing, he only made matters worse. At one point Nessen lectured journalists during a news conference about Ford's athletic prowess, resulting only in more press ridicule. Toward the end of the 1976 campaign, Nessen tried to block reporters from watching Ford enter the presidential helicopter, apparently fearing that a press photographer might get a picture of the president bumping his head upon entering.[95] A Nessen speech to the National Press Club lambasted the fourth estate for trivializing coverage of the presidency. Again, he certainly did not endear himself to the reporters covering Ford. From a public relations standpoint, the fact that Nessen offered accurate and justified criticism of the press did not matter. He challenged the press in a battle that no press secretary can win.

Press Office/Staff Problems

Though defensive about some aspects of Ford's negative press coverage, press officers and other White House staffers offered a good deal of self-

---

93. Gerald R. Ford, *A Time to Heal* (Norwalk, Conn.: Easton Press, 1987), 289.

94. Nessen, *It Sure Looks Different*, 163.

95. Thompson interview.

criticism for the nature of Ford's press relations. They identified such problems as inexperienced press secretaries, a difficult relationship between Press Secretary Ron Nessen and the media, and a chaotic staffing system that often undermined White House efforts to portray Ford favorably.

Ford's press secretaries, Jerald terHorst and Ron Nessen, had extensive journalistic backgrounds before working at the White House. In that sense, they had vast experience. But neither press secretary had worked previously as a government information officer. Did such a lack of government background make any difference to their performances and, hence, Ford's press relations? Robert Hartmann thought this was the case.

> Another factor [in Ford's press relationship]—and perhaps here I am guilty to some degree—both of Ford's press secretaries, Nessen and terHorst, whom I had approved (and in the case of Nessen had actively recruited), went directly from the White House press room to the White House press office. They had absolutely no experience in government, let alone a White House press office. They had no instincts that had in any way been conditioned to the differences between a press officer and a member of the press. It was difficult for them to establish where their allegiances were and whom they were supposed to please and serve.
>
> The press officer had to know who he's working for; not to please the press, he's supposed to do everything for the press that he can within the limits of his duties. He's supposed to be sympathetic to their needs, demands, and even their more unreasonable ones. He is a lightning rod for the president.
>
> Both of Ford's press secretaries contributed to the mistakes we made by not being themselves familiar enough with the process. We had a novice president working with a novice press secretary. His press secretaries did not have experience as "go-betweens" between a president and the press.[96]

John Hushen agreed that the lack of government background was a disadvantage for Ford's press secretaries.

> [When] I learned that Jerry terHorst was on the list . . . I said to [Robert] Griffin: "he's the guy for the job." The best press secretaries are the ones who have had a long association with the man in the Oval Office. But I was concerned then, and my theory has subsequently been proven, I think, that unexpected problems develop when a press secretary is drawn directly out of the media without some kind of interim position. The

---

96. Hartmann interview.

transition of responsibilities is very difficult. A media person goes from being a free and independent spirit to that of a captive spokesman for a particular point of view. A realization quickly comes about that you have given up a great deal of independence and that can be quite depressing.

. . . you just don't know what it's like if you've never been a government information officer. As a media person, you're trained to ask the tough questions, but answer none of them. Then you get out on the other side of the fence and you suddenly realize that unless you've thought about your response beforehand, you're not prepared to answer questions for the president.[97]

Nessen, in particular, had a difficult relationship with the White House press corps. TerHorst had not served long enough to develop either a favorable or troubled press relationship. Deputy Press Secretary William Greener said that Nessen disliked the press and carried that dislike openly: "Ron was a hard-working press secretary. But Ron didn't like the press corps even when he was a part of it. So he carried that antipathy over in some ways. He was never really part of the [press] gang."[98] Hushen noted that "Ron . . . would sometimes make fun of a newsman during a briefing, just ridicule him. Not a good way to develop a rapport with the media. They'll get you back one way or another."[99]

They did, and Nessen acknowledged that "I think, in terms of faulting myself for my own performance in the White House, I didn't have enough of a sense of humor. I think my skin was too thin. I took things too personally and I was too defensive of Ford."[100] Robert Orben, the former comedy-show writer turned presidential speech writer, argued for the use of more White House humor to deflect press criticisms, because he perceived getting mad as an "unproductive" response. Orben said he usually lost those battles in the White House.[101]

Nessen's difficulties with the White House press corps began as soon as he met the president to accept the position of press secretary. After leaving this meeting with Ford, several prominent newsmen, including Tom Brokaw and Phil Jones, saw Nessen and asked if the president had just offered him the job of press secretary. Nessen said "no" to avoid letting the news out before the official announcement. Hushen recalled the subsequent press reaction as follows.

---

97. Hushen interview.
98. Greener interview.
99. Hushen interview.
100. Author telephone interview with Ron Nessen, July 5, 1990.
101. Orben, "Speeches," 249.

Well, a few days later when we announced it he stands up in front of
the White House press corps, says "I will never knowingly lie to you,"
and all these snickers could be heard. So Ron got off to a real rocky
start.[102]

The problems with the press office operation did not end with Nessen's
troubled relationship with the White House press corps. Some members of the
press office feuded with one another, making it difficult for the White House
to coordinate a press relations strategy and to present a consistent image.
Nessen had problematic relationships with his two deputies, Greener and
Hushen. Greener left the deputy press secretary position in January 1976 and
Hushen resigned his post one month later. Left without his deputies, Nessen
looked outside the administration for replacements and, after experiencing
some difficulty in the job search, offered the position to a British subject
who declined saying, "Ron, don't you have to be an American to do this
job?"[103]

The lack of effective communication within the press office and between
that operation and the rest of the White House staff proved to be an important
obstacle to developing good press relations. In the October 18, 1975, press
office improvement meeting, Ron Nessen told other staffers that the perception of the press office becomes the image of the White House. The press
corps sees the White House through the press office, and if that operation "is
inefficient and sloppy, it does the President harm." At that meeting, Assistant
Press Secretary Tom DeCair expressed this concern.

There is a growing view that we don't see which is affecting us—that the
Administration is without direction, fumbling without a game plan, that
it has no goal. There is a feeling afoot that we don't know what we're
doing.

This affects us in the Press Office. In 1972 the press didn't like Nixon
and didn't feel any affection for McGovern. But because of the lack of
professionalism in the McGovern operation—it swayed them toward
Nixon. They thought that if McGovern's group couldn't run a campaign,
they most likely could not run the nation.

We need to get the image conveyed that we look like we know what
we're doing. We need to handle things in a professional manner. There
has been a tendency over the last year that too many or too few people
are focusing on an area. Areas of defined responsibility are important.
Important that one person speaks on an issue publicly to reporters, so

102. Hushen interview.
103. Background interview with Ford White House staffer.

they can identify the person doing it. If four people are quoted, reporters will go to everyone until they get the answers they want.[104]

Prior to the first series of press office improvement meetings in June 1975, Hushen wrote a memo to Nessen regarding possible topics for group discussions. The memo identified a number of problems with the press office. Hushen wrote that "our operation seems to have hit a flat spot in our relations with the press corps. This is due to a variety of factors, to which both sides have contributed, but a summer offensive might serve to convince the newsmen that we really are trying to assist them." Hushen continued:

Reporters are never sure just when the briefing will start even when we tell them in the morning. And when it slips past noon, they really get irritated because their time is being eroded by what they think is an inconsiderate Press Secretary—and they don't like it.

Late briefings reduce coverage of Administration positions because afternoon papers do not make over like they used to and second day stories are usually very abbreviated because of the play given by evening TV news shows and morning papers.

Our image as an open administration has been fading, partially due to the strong impression that the President's communicator would rather not communicate, given a half-way legitimate excuse to cancel a briefing. The press's image of you as their lever to the Presidency and the White House is under attack and needs shoring up.[105]

Hushen cited the need for the press office to "improve information liaison" with key spokesmen in other departments and also to communicate better within the press office divisions.[106]

But even as late as the August 7, 1976, press office "retreat," staffers noted the problems of poor internal communications, inefficient communications between the press office and other White House staffers, and the failure to time events for maximum press coverage. Two years into Ford's tenure Assistant Press Secretary J. William Roberts said:

I wanted to talk a minute about the problem of putting things out late in the afternoon. We have been getting the President's statements and ad-

104. Press Office Improvement Meeting, October 18, 1975, Folder: "Press Office Improvement Meeting (2)," Box 23, Nessen Papers, Gerald R. Ford Library.

105. Memo from Jack Hushen to Ron Nessen, June 26, 1975, Folder: "Press Office Improvement Meeting (1)," Box 23, Nessen Papers, Gerald R. Ford Library.

106. Memo from Hushen to Nessen.

ministration statements in the Press Office for 2 years 90% of the time coming in between 5 and 7 P.M. We would get the word in the morning something would be coming, but it drags around. We get it so late in the evening it gets no play anywhere.[107]

Assistant Press Secretary Larry Speakes responded.

A lot of people don't understand how the wires work during the course of the day. At 12:30 or 1:00 P.M. the schedule of major stories runs. At about 2:00 P.M. they are moving the night leads. If we don't put out a statement until 5:00 P.M. it will move only as an insert into the story. At 5:00 P.M. the statement never catches up with the story.[108]

Office of Communications Director David Gergen offered additional observations.

The hope is that I can get separated out to do things like statements. I would like to think everyday we can focus on the event for that day and the next day that we want to have on TV. I care about what happens on TV and in the newspaper headlines. . . . A major problem is the lines of authority are not clear-cut. We never do the same thing the same way twice. You never know who is responsible. The only way you run an organization of this size is to make sure everyone knows who is doing what. . . . Information is not widely shared on the staff. In order to have a confidence level in ourselves we have to trust in each other. We have to have lines of responsibility.[109]

Chief of Staff Richard Cheney recalled that the Ford White House did not adequately coordinate speech writing and policy making. "[W]e often felt we made excellent policy but we were unable to get it across because somehow the communications system broke down. . . . [O]ne of the problems we always had, frankly, was trying to integrate the speech-writing process with the policy process. And with the political process."[110]

Speech writer John Casserly left the Ford White House after only fifteen months, complaining of the speech-writing staff's lack of "consistent counsel

---

107. Communications, Advocates, News Summary and Research Staff Meeting, August 7, 1976, Folder: "Press Office Improvement Sessions," Box 24, Nessen Papers, Gerald R. Ford Library.

108. Staff Meeting, August 7, 1976.

109. Staff Meeting, August 7, 1976.

110. Richard Cheney, quoted in *Ford White House*, 77–78.

and direction." In late 1975, Casserly wrote in his diary of events: "The real difficulties are . . . that so many people are editing the President's speeches and the entire speech-writing operation is being mismanaged."[111] Ron Nessen noted that "the writing operation was so unreliable that other staff members were quietly recruited to produce presidential speeches and statements."[112]

Nessen identified as especially noteworthy the process of drafting the president's 1975 "fireside chat" and State of the Union address. The process of drafting the latter speech proved so divisive and chaotic that Ford did not approve a final version until 4:00 A.M. on the day of the speech, only nine hours before its scheduled delivery.

> Obviously, the long, bitter struggles required to produce a fireside chat and a State of the Union address were not the way to write presidential speeches. It was a wasteful and divisive process. It exposed serious weaknesses in the Ford organization. More distressingly, it exposed Ford's unwillingness to get tough with his staff, to demand a better speech-writing operation and less infighting.[113]

The divisive speech-writing process underlied the White House's staffing problems that, according to Nessen, hurt the president's public and press image.

> I am appalled by the amount of time Ford's men devoted to fighting with, plotting against and leaking bad stories about each other. . . . The staff fighting made Ford look like a President who could not select and inspire a united team.[114]

---

111. Casserly, *Diary*, 254, 224.

112. Nessen, *It Sure Looks Different*, 232–33.

113. Nessen, *It Sure Looks Different*, 85; see also Ford, *Time to Heal*, 232–33.

114. Nessen, *It Sure Looks Different*, 148. According to some of the press office staffers interviewed for this study, Nessen shares a good deal of the blame for the "staff fighting" that "appalled" him. By these accounts, he was not above the infighting and scheming that was very well known to have existed in the Ford White House. One of the better-known staff controversies occurred in April 1975 over Henry Kissinger's dual role as Secretary of State and chairman of the National Security Council (NSC). Ford and his closest advisers retreated for several days to Palm Springs, California, to discuss a presidential run the next year. "It was there the idea was hatched that Ford would run for president and therefore he would have to be in charge of foreign policy. Kissinger's role would have to be put down in some way so that Ford's in charge," said Louis M. Thompson, Jr. Nessen later announced to his staff that Kissinger would be possibly losing the NSC position and that the president would be controlling administration foreign policy. The story leaked to the press, the plan to demote Kissinger was scuttled, and Thompson lost his White House post—blamed by Nessen for the leak. CBS newsman Bob Schieffer was the recipient of the news leak and publicly declared that Thompson was not the source. Numerous news reports later identified Nessen as the source of the leak (Thompson interview; background interviews; news reports).

A number of press office staffers noted that the unprecedented way that Ford became president—without a campaign and transition—made any efforts to put together a united, collegial White House staff extremely difficult. For example:

Casserly: From the beginning, the President and his principal advisors failed to exercise the political power available to them because the Ford White House "team" lacked unity and internal discipline. Unlike the staffs of elected presidents, Mr. Ford's staff had not been forged in the heat of a lengthy campaign, where team strengths are solidified and weaker members winnowed out. The Ford staff was primarily, and remained, a "team" of individual players.[115]

Nessen: Honestly speaking, we brought a lot of our troubles on ourselves in the Ford White House because of constant feuding among members of the White House staff. The primary reason for this was the manner in which Ford came to the White House. He came practically overnight. Most candidates get to the White House after a long period of campaigning in which they get to know staff members, and staff members learn to work together. The good ones are put in the proper slots, and the bad ones are dumped overboard. But Ford didn't have that opportunity.[116]

The assistant to the president and later secretary of defense, Donald Rumsfeld, stated bluntly that when Ford became president there existed "no structure, no people, no organization, no nothing."[117] The chief of staff, Richard Cheney, made the following assessment.

Early in the Ford administration we had problems with staffing and the decision-making process, partly because we had come to power in an unusual way. The vice president and President had both resigned under scandal within the year before Ford came to power. He had never run a nation-wide campaign. He had been a vice president with a small staff and a congressman with an even smaller staff before that. His own personal style was not at all related to the role of a strong executive and it was in those early days much more the style of a congressman. . . . The worst conflicts in terms of personal relationships were inside the White House. There is no question about it. We had conflicts between the old

---

115. Casserly, *Diary*, 297.

116. Nessen, "Ford Presidency," 189. Nessen described Ford's staff as a collection of four diverse groups: Nixon administration holdovers, the "Michigan Mafia," holdovers from Ford's congressional and vice presidential staffs, and people with no previous connection to Ford (see Nessen, *It Sure Looks Different*, 151).

117. Maltese, *Spin Control*, 134.

Nixon carryovers, and the new Ford staffers. . . . We had to meld those two groups together and it wasn't very easy to do.[118]

Other Causes

Press office staffers cited other reasons for the president's press image problems. TerHorst pointed out that the lack of a campaign for president not only hurt White House efforts to unify the staff, it also resulted in a press corps lacking a "sense of loyalty" to Ford.

> There was a never a Ford coterie within the press, as there is with most new presidents, because Ford had never mounted a campaign for the office. There was no editor saying, "O.K., you covered the winning candidate's campaign so you will become our White House correspondent." When reporters cover a candidate's campaign they get to know the man's style, the key players. They aren't a rooting section, but they know that covering the White House—which is a prestigious job—depends in large measure on the success of the man in the White House. That doesn't mean that they are sycophants or fans. But through their coverage and understanding of what he's talking about—the ambiance of all this creates a sense of familiarity within the White House press.
>
> Ford had none of that going in. He was a creature of Richard Nixon. So the whole effort had to be staff driven because we didn't have any news media coalition out there. As a result, it was difficult to devise a [press] strategy that would hold up over time.[119]

President Ford wrote that he came to the White House "with a set of unique disadvantages." These included the lack of a transition period, an abbreviated term in office that hurt his efforts to lay the political groundwork to build support for policies, and "I'd been a Congressman for a long time. The White House press corps doesn't take members of Congress very seriously. To many of those reporters, my Vice Presidency had seemed disorganized, so they harbored a natural skepticism about my talents and skills."[120]

According to terHorst, the inability to make a clean break with the policies of the Nixon administration hurt Ford's press image.

> Another problem, from the press standpoint, was that Ford was upholding many of the policies of the Nixon administration, especially in for-

---

118. Cheney, "Forming and Managing," 63, 71.
119. TerHorst interview.
120. Ford, *Time to Heal*, 125–26.

eign affairs. He didn't sweep out the Nixon staffers and he didn't change the whole course of public policy. . . . So reporters were asking hostile, cynical questions.[121]

Richard Cheney confirmed that Ford's image suffered from the expectations of others that most aspects of the presidency, but not all, would change with the new administration.

> On the one hand, there was a great need after the strife and turmoil of the Watergate years to reassure everyone, especially our allies and adversaries overseas, that we were going to emphasize continuity. On the other hand, after all of the scandal and turmoil of Watergate, domestically it was very important to emphasize change and the fact that the old crowd was out, that we had a house cleaning at the White House and that the people who had been responsible for the Watergate scandals were no longer in power.
>
> We lived with these conflicting objectives. We had to emphasize continuity, on one hand, and change, on the other.[122]

Larry Speakes attributed much of the White House's image problems to a failure, first, to prepare the press for major policy initiatives and, second, to present a clear, consistent message of what the president sought to accomplish.

> The major administration initiatives—the summit conference on the economy, the Vietnam Veterans' thing, the amnesty business, and the pardon—all showed up on the press screen suddenly and without warning. So we had no way to deal with it. Essentially, they showed up without warning and we just had to roll with the punches. . . . [W]e really had those events with Ford that should have been major positive things for his image and yet they were not fully explained to the press and the public.
>
> Whereas in the Reagan administration and the Nixon administration a press communications plan was written that included our appearances on the morning talk shows and meetings with Congress to prebrief them and sessions with the anchor people. These were all major initiatives. But it was just a luxury that we didn't have. It wasn't anyone's fault, except for the times and the way that Ford became president.
>
> It was first the conference on the economy. It just didn't get anywhere. Two days of meetings with businessmen and it didn't make any impres-

---

121. TerHorst interview.
122. Cheney, "Forming and Managing," 59.

sion since there was no follow-through to it. And then the Vietnam Veterans' thing and the amnesty was highly controversial because there was no preparation of the press or the public to show what Ford was trying to do. It should have been portrayed as an act of political courage—that and the pardon—but it wasn't seen that way.[123]

Conclusion

This chapter looked inside the Ford White House to develop a better understanding of the administration's press strategy, degree of emphasis on press relations, public relations successes and failures, and causes of the president's press image problems. The comments of Ford White House press office staffers make clear that the administration neither dismissed the importance of public relations nor was consumed by imagery.

These comments also convey the belief that Ford came to the presidency with too many disadvantages to be able effectively to "manage" press relations: lack of a campaign to unify the staff and build a rapport with journalists, lack of an ordinary transition period to plan press strategy, press cynicism due to Watergate, press expectations that could not be met such as the need to eliminate all Nixon "holdovers" and public policies, a divisive staff and press secretaries who did not have previous experience as government information officers, and the "bumbler" image that, once formed, became unchangeable. Major events during Ford's term, such as the pardon of Richard M. Nixon and Press Secretary terHorst's resignation, exacerbated press cynicism and made the creation of a favorable presidential image even more difficult.

Despite all of these difficulties, Ford's press office staffers worked hard at trying to get the president's initiatives portrayed in a favorable fashion. As some of these staffers recalled, after the pardon of Richard M. Nixon, the president's communicators had a tall order in front of them. And, no doubt, despite such efforts, the negative elements of Ford's press image persisted, excepting the area of presidential trustworthiness, where Ford's positive press image eventually returned to the prepardon view of him as decent and ethical.

The most important questions still must be addressed. What lessons about presidential-press relations can be learned from the Ford White House's public and press relations efforts? Can the modern White House, armed with an impressive public relations strategy, "manage" its own news? Do journalists operate with certain preconceived notions of presidential leadership that no amount of imagery can change? What is the Ford White House's legacy to the modern press-presidency relationship and to our understanding of that relationship?

---

123. Speakes interview.

CHAPTER 8

Evaluating Presidents and "Managing" the Press

Though regarded favorably by journalists for his integrity and commitment to ethics, Ford had difficulty effecting a similarly positive press reputation for presidential leadership. The "ridicule problem" certainly had much to do with this difficulty. Ford's leadership approach also did not conform to the press's expectations. The political environment—post-Vietnam, post-Watergate— framed the conditions under which the press judged Ford's leadership.

How did journalists frame their judgments of Ford's presidency? Which evaluative criteria did they most often employ when assessing the president's leadership? What major lessons can be derived from the press evaluations of the Ford presidency? What major lessons can be derived from Ford White House efforts to manage its press relations? What is the legacy of the Ford-press relationship to the modern presidency? I now turn to these questions in my concluding assessments of the press and the Ford presidency.

Journalistic Evaluations

I previously identified two sets of expectations employed by journalists evaluating a president's performance: (1) *general expectations of presidential leadership*, and (2) *specific expectations of the president*.

Expectations of presidential leadership generally are stable, applied from one presidency to the next. These expectations are derived from popular and even ideal notions of presidential leadership. Regardless of the partisanship or ideology of the incumbent, journalists view as "successful" those presidents who articulate a leadership "vision" and a set of broad-ranging government policies to achieve the public good. The press view of presidential leadership entails an activist policy agenda framed by the White House. The president is expected to use the White House "bully pulpit" to "sell" his proposals to the public and Congress.

The ability to exercise forceful and effective leadership of Congress is a most important ingredient of the press's general expectations of the presidency. Frequently, journalists refer to the legislative savvy of such former presidents as Franklin D. Roosevelt and Lyndon B. Johnson as a basis for assessing an incumbent's congressional leadership. Ever since FDR's early massive legislative output, journalists compare every incumbent's legislative agenda at the hundred-days stage of the term to Roosevelt's accomplishments. Clearly the notions of presidential policy activism and aggressive leadership of Congress are strongly ingrained in the press's view of executive leadership. The idea of presidential "greatness" as a standard of evaluation also is prevalent in modern journalism. *Washington Post* reporter Edward Walsh wrote that "it is only against the accomplishments of the few giants who have held the office that we can measure the deeds of others."[1]

Ford did not look upon the presidency as a vehicle for effecting large-scale social and economic policies. He did not seek to effect fundamental changes in the country's domestic and foreign policy direction. He did not seek to conform to a leadership model undoubtedly more suited to politically progressive presidents during times of profound economic or social disruption. Ford inherited the presidency from a philosophically like-minded chief executive, and he perceived a need for policy continuity in a number of areas, particularly foreign affairs. As a generally conservative chief executive, he was disinclined to advocate large-scale spending programs to deal with domestic economic problems.

Ford viewed the presidency one way and journalists viewed it in another. This disjunction in perspectives of presidential leadership explains, in large part, the press perception of Ford as not a particularly effective leader. Journalists did not evaluate what Ford was trying to do on his own terms. Instead, they evaluated him against the backdrop of an activist, "visionary" leadership model to which he never sought to conform. Journalists do not alter their basic evaluative criteria because of any change in the political context or in national leadership. A president has little control over this reality.

Although a president cannot change the basic notions of leadership held by political journalists, he can influence their assessments of himself. Doing so has much to do with a president's overall image and leads to the second category of press evaluations: specific expectations of the incumbent president.

In the case of Ford, these expectations pertained to what journalists thought the president should and could do in office. Journalists based these expectations on their understanding of the man and on the nature of the times.

After the conclusion of the Nixon presidency, journalists harbored somewhat high expectations for the new president, Gerald R. Ford. They defined his job as, first, overcoming the rancor and divisiveness of the Nixon years and restoring trust and integrity in political Washington. Second, they

---

1. Edward Walsh, "A Flawed Presidency of Good Intentions," *Washington Post*, January 18, 1977, C4.

expected Ford to then consolidate his power and exercise a new kind of leadership devoid of the practices, personnel, and policies of the Nixon presidency. Third, journalists viewed Ford primarily as a man of Congress and, therefore, most capable of effecting positive and fruitful relations with the legislative branch.

Ford, no doubt, fared very well in the press assessments of the man—his honesty, integrity, and success at restoring faith in government and its leaders. Ford's reputation in political Washington and the press corps for such positive traits enabled him to get off to a fine start with the press and to weather some of the more difficult times of his presidency. To be sure, the pardon of Richard M. Nixon resulted in many journalists calling into question Ford's basic decency and honesty. But most journalists eventually returned to their earlier, basic assessments of Ford as decent and trustworthy.

Ford could not possibly meet the press expectation for a complete break from the Nixon administration. Ford recognized the necessity of portraying himself as different than his predecessor. On basic public policy issues, Ford did not fundamentally differ with Nixon. Some of his priorities, particularly in domestic affairs, diverged from Nixon's. Yet Ford never sought a fundamental break in the public policy direction of the Nixon administration. Ford did display, especially in the area of press relations, a desire to conduct his White House in ways quite the opposite to those of Nixon White House practices. Yet Ford refused to accept the press expectation that all "Nixon Republicans" be purged from the government. He believed that many of these people did not deserve the taint of Watergate, having had nothing to do with that scandal. Ford, it seemed, willingly opened himself up to press criticism rather than accept the press's definition of his responsibility.

As I have noted, journalists expect all presidents to exercise effective leadership of Congress. For Ford, journalists expected even more because of his long career as a member of Congress. Numerous press commentaries pointed out that Ford had an important leadership advantage, having served in Congress and become acquainted with the legislative leadership and membership. This press expectation ignored the partisan equation—Republican president, huge Democratic majorities in Congress, and fundamental differences over the public policy agenda. It also ignored one other factor that Larry Speakes identified.

> This familiarity that Ford enjoyed probably hurt. Congressmen could respond when Ford hit Congress on something "oh that's just good ole' Jerry, and he won't mind if I oppose him. He'll understand that being a member of Congress I have to do this for my district."[2]

---

2. Author telephone interview with Larry Speakes, February 6, 1990.

In the end, Ford did not fare especially well with the press, in large part because of journalists' high expectations of presidential leadership and of the man. Robert M. Entman wisely advises that presidents use their "honeymoon" periods to lower, rather than to raise, expectations, as a way "to inject caution and realism into public (and journalistic) consciousness."[3] Yet Ford posed a very special case because he lacked an electoral mandate and needed to use the "honeymoon" period to establish his legitimacy before the public. Hence, Ford could not ignore the need to establish himself as a change from his predecessors—open, candid, trustworthy, willing to work constructively with Congress, the press, and his critics. He could not, in other words, avoid raising expectations.

Ford's Press Evaluations: Lessons

The press is in the business of both informing the public and selling good copy. Oftentimes these duties are in conflict with each other. What intrigues or interests people, including journalists, is not usually the most informative, relevant information. Even among the prominent "inner ring" publications, the emphasis on interesting and entertaining news is very strong. Press coverage of the presidency focuses on such matters as presidential successes and failures, presidential style and image, White House battles with Congress, leadership personalities, and trivial events and peculiarities that nonetheless interest people.

A major difficulty that the press faces in covering the presidency is the limitations of time and space. Short deadlines leave little time for reflection and deep thought. Limited space means that some events are covered and others are not. The dilemma is put well by David Broder's perception of the *New York Times*'s slogan: "All the News That's Fit to Print."

> It is a great slogan, but it's also a fraud. Neither the *Times* nor the *Washington Post* nor any other newspaper . . . has space or time to deal with all the actions taken and the words uttered in the city of Washington with significance for some of its readers. . . . [S]electing what the reader reads involves not just objective facts but subjective judgments, personal values and, yes, prejudices.[4]

---

3. Robert M. Entman, "The Imperial Media," in *Analyzing the Presidency*, 2d ed., ed. Robert E. DiClerico (Guilford, Conn.: Dushkin, 1990), 163.

4. David Broder, *Behind the Front Page: A Candid Look at How the News Is Made* (New York: Simon and Schuster, 1987), 14; see also Broder's, "Politicians and Biased Political Information," in *Politics and the Press*, ed. Richard W. Lee (Washington, D.C.: Acropolis Books, 1970), 61–62; Walter Lippmann, *Public Opinion* (New York: Free Press, 1965).

Every newspaper when it reaches the reader is the result of a whole series of selections as to

The determination of "newsworthy" material, therefore, is not based on objective professional standards but on the values of journalists, editors, and readers. The press evaluations of Ford's presidency confirm the assessment that journalists are more interested in, and feel more confident writing about, personalities, peculiarities, successes, and failures, than substantive issues, institutions, and processes. This assessment is articulated by a number of leading scholars of the presidency and the press. Stephen Hess explains that journalists "are often ill at ease with abstractions." They are more at ease with anecdotal information "based on personal experience" than with theory or ideas.[5] Lewis W. Wolfson writes that "many reporters are not really curious about what government processes involve. They are not inherently interested in what's involved in developing policy or formulating a budget or administering a program."[6] Elmer E. Cornwell, Jr., correctly observes that

> journalists . . . know that personalities are more interesting to readers than events . . . and that leadership successes and failures are more interesting than the ebb and flow of policies. The press thus clearly recognizes, for its own part, the importance of public images, and has been known to create them when none is readily apparent.[7]

Leading journalists acknowledge these assessments. Lou Cannon explains that journalists are not "management minded."[8] David Broder admits that "most of us are a lot more comfortable thinking about and writing about individuals than about institutions."[9]

George C. Edwards notes that it is "not surprising" that journalists writing about the presidency focus on personalities instead of issues, because

what items shall be printed, in what position they shall be printed, how much space each shall occupy, what emphasis each shall have. There are no objective standards here. There are conventions. Take two newspapers published in the same city on the same morning. The headline of one reads: "Britain pledges aid to Berlin against French aggression; France openly backs Poles." The headline of the second is "Mrs. Stillman's Other Love." Which you prefer is a matter of taste, but not entirely a matter of the editor's taste. It is a matter of his judgement as to what will absorb the half hour's attention a certain set of readers will give to his newspaper (Lippmann, *Public Opinion*, 233).

5. Stephen Hess, *The Washington Reporters* (Washington, D.C.: Brookings Institution, 1981), 124.

6. Lewis W. Wolfson, *The Untapped Power of the Press* (New York: Praeger, 1985), 167.

7. Elmer E. Cornwell, Jr., "Role of the Press in Presidential Politics," in *Politics and the Press*, ed. Richard W. Lee (Washington, D.C.: Acropolis Books, 1970), 19. Cornwell also observes that "the press in quest of saleable news finds failures are more interesting than successes, corruption more exciting than dull virtue, backroom negotiations more fun than that which is in plain sight of all" (18).

8. Lou Cannon, quoted in Wolfson, *Untapped Power*, 167.

9. Broder, *Behind*, 215.

journalists have neither "special background" on the institution nor "policy expertise relevant to understanding the issues with which the president deals."[10] This assessment explains the nature of the press coverage of Ford's presidency well. Journalists placed an extraordinary amount of emphasis on Ford's leadership style, method of self-presentation, alleged clumsiness, and other themes that provided a fairly superficial perspective on his presidency and failed to reveal the substance behind what his administration was trying to achieve.

Worse yet, once journalists created certain themes in their coverage of Ford's presidency, they established, for the public, the "reality" of those themes through constant repetition. After journalists created the theme of "Ford the bumbler," they reinforced the image at every opportunity to the point of emphasizing any presidential behavior that fit their mold. Journalists failed to present a comprehensive picture of the man—his background and accomplishments—or of his presidency. What the public got instead was a broad-brush caricature that reduced a president, his administration, and policy goals to ridicule. That much has been acknowledged in retrospect by David Broder's observation of the risk behind "trying to sketch the character of a complex politician."

> But the greater risk is to repeat the conventional wisdom or the cliche of the moment. To my mind, the press treatment of President Gerald R. Ford was a prime example of falling into that trap. . . . An image had been fixed in the minds of reporters covering Ford and it was sustained by them with whatever material came to hand. . . . [T]he grip of the caricature we had created was so strong that we could not, or did not, revise it. In that respect, we were, if anything, less flexible than the best of the cartoonists.[11]

Broder explains that the job of journalism often is to select information, compress it to manageable dimensions, and, in the process, "we may exaggerate particular features of the people we are writing about, and in doing so, we create caricatures." The *Washington Post* columnist notes that journalists end up "reducing complex personalities to two-word labels," thereby distorting reality.[12] This point is confirmed by George C. Edwards's assessment that "Ford was typecast" by journalists who had established the "bumbler" theme and mindlessly repeated it.[13]

---

10. George C. Edwards, *The Public Presidency: The Pursuit of Popular Support* (New York: St. Martin's Press, 1983), 154.

11. Broder, *Behind*, 54, 62, 66.

12. Broder, *Behind*, 51.

13. Edwards, *Public Presidency*, 159.

The larger question becomes whether jou
dential image, reflect the reality of the man reas
Michael Baruch Grossman and Martha Joynt Kun.
study of the press-presidency relationship, believe th.
president generally represents reality.

> . . . what appears in the media does reflect who the Pres.
> he is doing. Although some stories may be unfair or ina
> large number present a fuzzy image, the picture that emerges
> tone and substance of the administration and the character of ,   .esi-
> dent. In particular, the impact of large numbers of stories has been to
> leave an impression of presidents' leadership that seems accurate in
> retrospect. What emerged was a portrait of . . . Ford as a good man who
> was not prepared for the job when he took office and who frequently
> stumbled as he learned the ropes.[14]

By maintaining that the not-ready-to-be-president, congenial-stumbler
image accurately reflected the reality of Gerald Ford, the authors fall into the
trap of accepting an interpretation of reality as it had been presented through
the press. One does not have to accept the words of Ford's White House press
officers who protested the press characterization of their boss. The comments
of David Broder also confirm that the image and reality of the thirty-eighth
president diverged. It is questionable whether press images of presidents can
ever be considered realistic given the press's propensity to reduce complexity
to simplification through the use of caricature and themes. The findings of my
study confirm, instead, the assessment of George C. Edwards that

> the press prefers to frame the news in themes, which both simplify
> complex events and provide continuity of persons, institutions, and is-
> sues. Once these themes are established, the press tends to maintain them
> in subsequent stories, even if they are inappropriate and therefore pro-
> vide a distorted view of the world. In other words, because the themes
> determine what information is most relevant to news coverage and the
> context in which it is presented, the theme becomes "reality" and may
> influence how people perceive whoever and whatever is in the news.[15]

Edwards explains that the press operates with a "structural bias." That is,
judgments are made about what stories to cover, how much coverage to give
them, which ones to ignore, and what to say about the events that are covered.

---

14. Michael Baruch Grossman and Martha Joynt Kumar, *Portraying the President: The White House and the News Media* (Baltimore: Johns Hopkins University Press, 1981), 324–25.

15. Edwards, *Public Presidency*, 159.

sts cannot cover everything. "Thus the news can never mirror
ality."[16]

In their coverage of the Ford presidency, journalists arrived at news judgments that colored their presentations and evaluations of the thirty-eighth president. Journalists chose to devote enormous time and print space to the "bumbler" image. They likewise chose to devote little effort to the budgetary process and the details of domestic economic programs, even during a deep recession. Journalists chose to focus often on presidential style, while not digging very deeply into the substance of Ford's agenda. The substance of diplomatic efforts and administration foreign policy objectives in pursuing international diplomacy received considerably less press commentary than such concerns as how the president conducted himself, whether he cut a strong image abroad, whether his efforts appeared as impressive or ground breaking as his predecessor's, and whether Henry Kissinger was winning the intriguing White House turf battles over directing foreign policy.

In many instances, the press fascination with the peculiar or interesting event obscured more serious matters clearly deserving of attention. Ford's November 1974 trip to the Far East, including the first presidential visit to Japan, resulted in numerous press commentaries about the president's pants being too short, the symbolic nature of the event, and the political controversy over a president going abroad during a time of economic troubles back home. Little press commentary addressed the substance of the diplomatic venture.

The best-known incident concerns the president's debate misstatement regarding Soviet domination of Eastern Europe. After the second 1976 presidential debate, the public initially told pollsters that Ford had outperformed Democrat Jimmy Carter. People had not even recognized, or attached much importance to, Ford's misstatement. A study by Frederick T. Steeper shows that the public began to attach importance to Ford's "error" only after the media made people aware of the misstatement. Subsequent polls overwhelmingly showed stronger debate ratings for Carter than for Ford. Steeper's data demonstrate the "power of the news media to 'penalize bloopers severely.'"[17] The press captured one trivial snippet of information—that the president had misspoken—and emphasized it to the exclusion of everything else said in the presidential debate. The incident reveals, as well, the enormous influence of the press on how people perceive and judge presidential performance.

Numerous other examples of press infatuation with presidential style,

---

16. Edwards, *Public Presidency*, 159.

17. Frederick T. Steeper, "Public Response to Gerald Ford's Statement on Eastern Europe in the Second Debate," in *The Presidential Debates: Media, Electoral, and Public Perspectives*, eds. George F. Bishop, Robert G. Meadow and Marilyn Jackson-Beeck (New York: Praeger, 1978), 82.

successes, failures, and interesting trivialities during the Ford years abound. The important point is that the public understood the Ford presidency as the press presented it—as error prone and lacking in "vision" and aggressive programs—and accepted the press assessments as "reality." And the Ford White House learned just how difficult it can be to try to turn around negative press coverage or to convince the public to accept a "reality" different from the national press's.

Lessons from White House Efforts to Manage the Press

All modern presidents recognize the need to give credence to their press portrayals. They understand that the success of a program often depends upon how it is presented in the press and, hence, received by the public. According to leading academic literature, in its battles with the press to have the president favorably portrayed, the White House has the upper hand. According to this perspective, presidents willingly can shape their own press coverage. Lewis W. Wolfson writes that

> presidents use the media to get elected and, once in office, have a free pass to reshape the terms of the debate over national policy. They can redefine the political mainstream and put themselves in the middle of it. Every day we get a rich diet of news showing them in command.[18]

Harvey G. Zeidenstein adds the following comments.

> . . . the president, his closest aides, and the White House press office are certainly in a position to create their own favorable news coverage. This can be accomplished by supervising what information is released, and the method or news medium through which key political interest groups and the public are informed. In short, the White House can influence—if not completely control—the *content, timing,* and *methods of publicizing* the news.[19]

Grossman and Kumar maintain that press coverage of modern presidents has been remarkably consistent, and favorable, following a predictable pattern of alliance, competition, and then detachment. They conclude that successive administrations, aware of the predictable patterns of press coverage, have

---

18. Wolfson, *Untapped Power*, 12.
19. Harvey G. Zeidenstein, "News Media Perceptions of White House News Management," *Presidential Studies Quarterly* 14, no. 3 (Summer, 1984): 391; italics in the original.

been able to develop their public relations strategies accordingly and with considerable success.[20]

Journalists often make similar points: that they are subjected to White House media manipulation and that presidents generally succeed at getting favorable coverage. David Broder contends that

> the President and his agents have clearly been winning the battle to control the way the most important official of our government is covered and reported most of the time. The White House has learned to keep the President from scrutiny, while projecting his voice and his views far more widely than any other politician's.[21]

Two explanations generally are provided for the alleged White House advantage over the press in presenting a presidential image. One is that journalists are passive agents who uncritically accept, and then pass on to the public, the official version of events. W. Lance Bennett decries the "emphasis given to official views in the news" and accuses the press of "dutifully reporting what officials dictate."[22] In Bennett's view, reporters sympathize with the people they cover, primarily because of direct contact with the "stressful conditions" under which leaders operate. A cozy relationship allegedly thereby develops between journalists and politicians.[23]

A similar point is made by Bill Moyers, the former Lyndon Johnson administration press secretary and now journalist. Moyers describes the White House press corps as "more stenographic than entrepreneurial in its approach to news gathering. Too many of them are sheep."[24]

The second explanation for alleged presidential control of press images is what Thomas Cronin calls the "disturbing" development of the "huge [White House] public relations apparatus."[25] Presidents have been described as "notorious for their attempts to 'manage' news."[26] Journalist James Deakin writes that it was during the Ford presidency that "the [White House] press office

---

20. Grossman and Kumar, *Portraying*, 253–98.

21. Broder, *Behind*, 194.

22. W. Lance Bennett, *News: The Politics of Illusion*, 2d ed. (New York: Longman, 1988), 105.

23. Bennett, *News*, 108. Bennett maintains that this cozy relationship breaks down for politicians such as Richard Nixon who antagonize the press.

24. Bill Moyers, quoted in David L. Paletz and Robert M. Entman, "Presidents, Power, and the Press," *Presidential Studies Quarterly* 10, no. 3 (Summer, 1980): 417.

25. Thomas E. Cronin, "The Presidency Public Relations Script," in *The Presidency Reappraised*, ed. Rexford G. Tugwell and Thomas E. Cronin (New York: Praeger, 1974), 168.

26. Harry Kranz, "The Presidency v. the Press: Who Is Right?" in *Perspectives on the Presidency*, ed. Aaron Wildavsky (Boston: Little, Brown, 1975), 208. See also Mark Hertsgaard, *On Bended Knee: The Press and the Reagan Presidency* (New York: Farrar, Strauss, Giroux, 1988).

blossomed into full imperialistic flower." According to Deakin, the Ford White House went to extraordinary lengths to emphasize public relations. Deakin cited as evidence for this view that Ford had, in addition to a press secretary, two deputy press secretaries, seven assistant press secretaries, and one of the assistant press secretaries was devoted exclusively to administration.[27]

Both the interviews with White House press officers and the journalistic commentary from the Ford years dispute the assessment that a president and his staff can deliberately manage an administration's press image. The data collected for this study thereby provide a strong case study exception to the widely held notion that the president and his staff generally prevail over the press in the battle to portray a presidential image. That is not to suggest that the White House cannot influence its press image. It can, and should, try to do so. But not every White House places the same emphasis on its press relations. *New York Times* reporter Hedrick Smith observes that such presidents as Richard Nixon and Ronald Reagan placed enormous emphasis on public relations, whereas such presidents as Gerald Ford and Jimmy Carter worked less diligently at "making the sale."[28] Ford said that he considered press relations important, but always secondary to policy considerations.

> My administration focused on the substance of our policies both domestic and foreign, but we recognized the desirability of having an affirmative press relationship. So we did have an aggressive, and I think sound strategy for dealing with the press. We tried to keep a good personal rapport between the White House press corps and myself, and Ron Nessen did his utmost to try to put an affirmative spin on what we were trying to do both domestically and internationally.[29]

Ron Nessen maintained that the ability of a modern presidential administration "to put an affirmative spin" on the news is limited by the historic context and the political environment. A major lesson that Nessen drew from his tenure as the press secretary is that, because of outside events,

> no White House can do much about a president's image. . . . I think the biggest mistake that any president, or any person in public life, can make is to base decisions on expectations or demands made by the media.[30]

---

27. James Deakin, *Straight Stuff: The Reporters, the White House, the Truth* (New York: William Morrow, 1984), 208–9. The assistant press secretary for administration was Louis M. Thompson, Jr., not Louis Johnson as reported by Deakin.

28. Hedrick Smith, *The Power Game: How Washington Works* (New York: Ballantine, 1989), 420.

29. Author telephone interview with President Gerald R. Ford, December 13, 1989.

30. Author telephone interview with Ron Nessen, July 5, 1990.

Nessen identified the post-Watergate environment of press cynicism as a factor that any president immediately after Nixon would have had to deal with and could not have controlled.

> And, of course, there was the end of the Vietnam War. . . . And there was a deep economic recession in 1974 and 1975—the deepest economic recession since the 1930s. So these outside events were a hundred times more important to influencing the public view and the media view of Ford than any kind of White House press manipulation or efforts at managing his image. . . . [T]he ability of the White House to manage the image of a president, to manipulate the press, is wildly exaggerated. The fact is that a president who is doing the right things in a substantive way and is popular because of what he is doing or for what he stands for is not going to have to worry about his image in the press. A president who is doing things that are unpopular, or the economy is bad, or his views are not fully accepted—he's going to have problems with the press. There's only a marginal, small impact that any sort of media management or image making can have on this relationship.[31]

Margita White agreed with Nessen's views.

> This whole idea that you can just stage your press relations is vastly overstated. Once events take place or events are initiated, they pretty much take on a life of their own. You just can't stage the presidency. Of course you want to put your best foot forward. But you can't just determine what your own news coverage is going to look like. Successes in the long run will affect press coverage more than anything else a White House may try to do.[32]

These comments are compatible with the view expressed earlier: that modern presidents cannot control their own press coverage. There are certain basic expectations of presidential leadership that carry over from one administration to another. Certain elements of the historic context and political environment also cannot be changed. But presidents can at least influence press coverage at the margins and sometimes—given the right set of circumstances—even more.

Ford and his press office staffers reflected on the kinds of measures that modern presidents need to adopt to at least put their "best foot forward" in

---

31. Nessen interview.
32. Author telephone interview with Margita White, June 7, 1990.

managing—but not controlling—press relations. For the most part, the president and his staffers agreed with the Nessen and White assessments that a White House cannot script its own news coverage. They also believed that modern presidents can learn a good deal from the Ford administration's experiences on how to improve the White House–press relationship. President Ford offered the following advice.

> First, an administration has to be as open as possible in responding to the legitimate questions of the press. Any attempt to be overly secretive or devious is a short-range, self-defeating approach to the press. Now that doesn't mean you have to *kowtow* to the press. And the press, or at least the responsible elements of the press, don't expect it. But by being as open and accessible as possible, that creates an environment whereby a future president can get a fair hearing from those who write about or discuss an administration's programs. You have to understand as a president that the press can be vitally influential in what a White House program needs to achieve. Therefore, you have to be aggressive, in a proper way, you have to be as open as possible, you have to be as accessible as possible and hope that those tactics will bear fruit.[33]

A number of Ford's press office staffers made similar assessments. For example:

> *John Carlson*: You don't want to *kowtow* to the press, to always give in to their demands. But you have to recognize that the press people have a job to do. You need to have frequent press conferences, and you need to be available and to bring the press in on things. . . . It's not healthy to have Sam Donaldson yelling over the helicopter to get a word from the president. A lot of times that goes on because they don't get to see the president for days. You need a regular press briefing by the president. If you wait too long, the journalists' list of questions grows longer. And no president can be up on every issue. No person can. But they expect him to be up on every issue. And when he's not, they think it's because he's not in command. . . . So don't *kowtow* to the press, but recognize that they have a job to do. Don't avoid them. Don't shut them out. . . . They can be very helpful in communicating your message.[34]

> *Ron Nessen*: The Ford approach and, I must say, the Bush approach too,

---

33. Ford interview.
34. Author telephone interview with John G. Carlson, May 2, 1990.

of frequent news conferences and frequent interviews, frequent contacts with the press, really drains a lot of the poison out of that relationship.[35]

Gerald Warren commented that Ford should have had even more press conferences to work better with the press corps. Warren also noted that Ford came across especially well in less formal contacts with selected journalists. He described Ford as "very comfortable" in such settings and said that the president could have done more of what President Bush is now doing: meeting frequently with small groups of reporters in the Oval Office.

> I think Bush has done a great job with the press. He's open, friendly, accessible. He's set some good ground rules and he's very firm about those rules. He doesn't shout over the sound of the rotor-blades of the helicopter. Most important: he is open, accessible, and unflustered by the press. . . . I think that the less tension that the White House puts into the relationship the better. When the tension rises, it's better to have a president who can laugh it off and not be too tense.[36]

Larry Speakes agreed that this press relations approach—openness, accessibility, frequent press contacts—worked well for Ford and now is well-suited to President Bush's style. Speakes too said that Ford would have fared better by meeting with "reporters more often one-on-one to 'see the man' in smaller, informal sessions." Speakes pointed to Bush's propensity to inundate the press with presidential contacts, to talk constantly with reporters without really saying very much. Hence, journalists can't complain of lack of access yet they're not getting much information either.[37]

These comments underscore the need for Ford to have devoted more attention to the kinds of activities that made him look good. The approach that a president takes to improving his press relationship should correspond to the personality of the man and the skills that he brings to the White House. None of the press office staffers said that Ford should have tried to stage events and go before the public frequently as Reagan later did. Clearly Ford and Reagan brought different sets of skills and personal inclinations to the White House, and what worked for one would not necessarily have worked for the other. Only Larry Speakes, who served both presidents, said that some of the things that Reagan did in the area of public relations could have helped Ford: focus the agenda, "simplify and focus the message," and "move quickly." But

35. Nessen interview.
36. Author telephone interview with Gerald Warren, March 15, 1990.
37. Speakes interview.

Speakes acknowledged that Ford's lack of a real transition detracted from the White House's ability to do those things.[38]

To take another example, Gerald Warren said that Ford did well when the White House emphasized the leading issues of the day: energy and the economy.

> I think when you have a bad press, and a problem to overcome such as the pardon, the best way to deal with it is to get on top of the issues. Even the *Mayaguez* provided only a momentary upward "blip" in the approval ratings. So I think the other issues were better for him. The closer the election came, the less he concentrated on those two issues, and I think that was a mistake.[39]

There is no evidence to suggest that any Reagan White House staffer convincingly advised the president to "get on top of the issues" as a way of managing press relations. If anyone did, there certainly is no evidence that the president took the advice. In contrast, President Carter stayed on top of the issues constantly. But who fared better with the press? Commanding the issues is a strategy that may suit some presidents' skills and not the skills of other presidents. And as Carter's press relations make clear, commanding the issues will not guarantee success in the area of press imagery.

Perhaps the best answer is that sound public policies and public relations go hand in hand. President Ford's two press secretaries explained the policy–public relations link differently, but essentially made the same point—that image needs substance and substance must be communicated.

> *Nessen*: Sometimes when I used to consult with corporations and associations after my time in the White House I used to tell them, "look, you can have the best media plan in the world, the best public relations plan in the world, but if you don't make the substantive corporate decisions that will allow you to depict your position as representing good public policy, you're not going to do well." . . . The same advice holds for the White House or anyone who has to deal with the press. You have to be able to depict your actions as good public policy.[40]

> *TerHorst*: Make sure that your governmental program is accompanied by a serious effort to explain it to the public and to the media. That requires

---

38. Speakes interview.
39. Warren interview.
40. Nessen interview.

a public relations strategy, if you will, as corporate America does, as governmental agencies do, and foreign countries. It's essential. It goes back to that biblical phrase, why put your light under a bush where no one can see it? The goal of a media strategy is not merely a good image. It is to advance the goals of the administration.

If you go too far you risk becoming known as what Michael Deaver was recognized as—a "spin doctor," a manipulator. . . . Ford did not want that. Neither did I. We were trying to treat the subject [of media relations] as a way of moving our objectives forward rather than just having a happy press, or a happy president because he had a nice image.[41]

The key for the modern White House is to know when you have gone too far—or not far enough—in trying to "manage" the news. Clearly, a public relations strategy is an integral function of the modern White House. A president who does not allow the White House to become, in part, a public relations machine will most likely end up with a bad press. To a large extent, the press is enamored with presidents who excel in the arena that journalists know best—public relations and the press. Journalists may often complain about presidential attempts at media "manipulation" but they hold in low regard presidents such as Carter who eschew public relations. President Reagan clearly ran a public relations–oriented White House and succeeded where his two predecessors did not: at managing press expectations of his leadership and, hence, press evaluations. Charles O. Jones offers the following explanation.

The trick for presidents is to make [press] expectations work for, not against, them. Reagan was masterly in this regard. Journalists' expectations of the office remained high, but their expectations of the man were consistently low. Thus even ordinary performance was rewarded with praise—without raising expectations of Reagan's performance next time around. The so-called teflon characteristic of Reagan is explained by the low standard that was being employed. Who expects a president taking his nap to be responsible for all that is happening?[42]

There is little or nothing that a White House can do to alter the idealistic press notions of presidential power, style, and policy activism. Some presi-

---

41. Author interview with Jerald F. terHorst, Washington, D.C., June 27, 1990.
42. Charles O. Jones, "The Separated Presidency—Making It Work in Contemporary Politics," in *The New American Political System*, 2d version, ed. Anthony King (Washington, D.C.: American Enterprise Institute, 1990), 24.

dents will fare better than others when measured against journalistic ideals. Ford could not fare well against journalistic ideals because he played a largely reactive role domestically, using the veto power to prevent congressional Democrats from controlling the policy agenda. He may have succeeded in that endeavor, but this leadership approach does not match journalists' calls for Rooseveltian policy activism.

Journalists also harbored generally high expectations of Ford based on their understanding of the man and of the times in which he served. Based on their understanding of the man, journalists expected Ford to work effectively with Congress to enact a far-reaching policy agenda. Journalists knew Ford as the man of Congress—someone who comprehended the legislative process and knew its players. Based on their assessment of the times, journalists expected Ford to establish himself as a complete break from his predecessors. Journalists helped to create the public's sense of euphoria that surrounded Ford's early days in office. Given the demand for new leadership and Ford's need to establish his legitimacy before the people, there was not much that Ford could have done to manage or lower the press's expectations of him.

The Ford White House learned the enormous difficulties of turning around a presidential image once created. Ford's image as a trustworthy, yet bumbling and ineffectual, leader, framed early by the press, made it difficult to use public relations to achieve substantive policy goals. The Ford White House applied a number of press relations strategies but lacked an organized, sustainable system for getting its message out to the public. The circumstances under which Ford came to the presidency made the establishment of such a system most difficult. Chief of Staff Richard Cheney offered an important lesson of the Ford White House–press relations experience.

> You've got to control what you put out. You don't let the press set the agenda. The press is going to object to that. They like to set the agenda. They like to decide what's important and what isn't important. But if you let them do that, they're going to trash your presidency.[43]

The difficulty is that the environment of press evaluations of a presidency is defined, in large part, by matters over which a White House has little or no control: the economic condition inherited by the president, international developments, the strength of the president's party in Congress, among others. Put differently, a president cannot control all of the outside events that bear upon the press assessments of his performance. As Paletz and Entman report,

---

43. Richard Cheney, quoted in John Anthony Maltese, *Spin Control: The White House Office of Communications and the Management of Presidential News* (Chapel Hill: University of North Carolina Press, 1992), 130.

"No president is master of his fate. Every president faces problems difficult to control."[44]

The situation that Ford inherited for the most part hurt White House efforts to build a good press relationship. True, Ford succeeded a disgraced president and at first benefited from the inevitable press comparisons to his predecessor. But Ford also inherited a troubled economy, a combative opposition party–led Congress, and the end of U.S. military involvement in Southeast Asia.

One factor in Ford's press relations acknowledged by scholars and journalists is the post-Watergate environment of press cynicism. William L. Rivers explains "that since the Vietnam War and the Watergate crisis, Washington correspondents are much more suspicious of the announcements of government officials."[45] Rivers based this assessment on the results of a survey questionnaire given to journalists. One question asked journalists whether their attitudes toward political leaders had changed due to the Vietnam War and Watergate. The responses are revealing of such a change toward greater press skepticism of political leaders' words and deeds.[46] Rivers cited a telling example of this phenomenon.

> Gerald Ford's press relations and the drastic change in the authority and in the demands of the post-Watergate Washington press corps can be defined by one incident: On the night of 23 January 1975, President Ford was asked by a reporter [Tom Brokaw] to comment on the belief that he was too dumb to be president. He answered that his school grades had been so good that he was in the upper third of the class. The next day, correspondents demanded that the White House produce Ford's transcripts.[47]

Rivers's assessment is corroborated by other scholars. Robert M. Entman writes that "journalists have taken a more aggressively critical stance toward the presidency since the perceived betrayals of Vietnam and Watergate."[48] Grossman and Kumar agree with this view.

> White House media relations seem to have changed between 1965 and 1974. . . . Reporters who previously exhibited a high tolerance for White House smoke screens suggested that the President and his chief

---

44. Paletz and Entman, "Presidents, Power, and the Press," 420.
45. William L. Rivers, *The Other Government: Power and the Washington Media* (New York: Universe Books, 1982), 19.
46. Rivers, *The Other Government*, 229-31.
47. Rivers, *The Other Government*, 45.
48. Entman, "Imperial Media," 156.

advisers told lies and withheld information about important events. . . . Because the Johnson and Nixon administrations succeeded for long periods in their efforts to manipulate both the press and public opinion, many later journalists pursued a more antagonistic style of reporting White House developments than was common prior to 1965. Presidents Ford and Carter were both hampered in their efforts to reap the traditional benefits accrued by the nation's chief communicator.[49]

The comments of the journalists themselves are perhaps even more telling. Haynes Johnson refers to "the poisonous aftermath of Vietnam and Watergate" in presidential press relations.[50] Because of heightened press skepticism, Johnson notes that no president can look forward to "the kind of cheering-squad support granted by much of the Washington press corps before Nixon."[51] James Deakin maintains that, after the Vietnam War and Watergate, "the public had been badly burned and was wary. The reporters, intensely so."[52] Sam Donaldson writes that "these two events left a lasting impression on reporters in my generation and convinced many of us that we should adopt a new way of looking at our responsibilities." Donaldson believes that before Ford, "the press wasn't skeptical enough" of political leaders.[53] Tom Wicker agrees that a "lack of skepticism" by the press and the willingness to ascribe virtue to public officials amounted to journalistic "neglect of duty."[54] David Broder states the following conclusions.

> Watergate changed many of the fundamentals in the White House–press relationship. . . . For the White House reporters, Watergate was a double personal humiliation. Not only were they scooped by two unknown beat reporters, but they had served as a conduit for what they gradually came to realize was a systematic set of official lies about the case. Their professional fury carried over to the presidencies of Gerald R. Ford, Jimmy Carter, and Ronald Reagan. The style of questioning at the official White House briefings became, after Watergate, almost more prosecutorial than inquisitive.[55]

U.S. News and World Report senior writer Steven V. Roberts confessed that "as a profession, we are still haunted by Watergate, petrified of missing

49. Grossman and Kumar, *Portraying*, 299, 301.
50. Haynes Johnson, *In the Absence of Power* (New York: Viking, 1980), 170.
51. Johnson, *Absence of Power*, 100.
52. Deakin, *Straight Stuff*, 295.
53. Sam Donaldson, *Hold On, Mr. President!* (New York: Ballantine, 1987), 68–69.
54. Tom Wicker, *On Press* (New York: Viking, 1978), 61.
55. Broder, *Behind*, 167.

the next Big One and tantalized by the fantasy that one day Robert Redford or Dustin Hoffman will play us in the movies."[56] Indeed, Gladys Lang and Kurt Lang put into perspective the implications of such journalistic fantasies.

> After Watergate, it sometimes seemed that every child dreamed of growing up to be an investigative reporter. What may be a harmless fantasy in children must be taken more seriously when ambitious reporters envision themselves as sleuths in constant pursuit of wrongdoing. The press can become obsessed with insignificant leads in the hope that they will develop into sensational exposes. . . . This preoccupation with exposing wrongdoing can be at the expense of reporting the more mundane but nevertheless important developments in and out of government as well as major policy options not so easily depicted as right or wrong.[57]

It is helpful to understand just how much the press-presidency relationship has changed by placing the issue in a historic context. Numerous studies make clear the significant differences in press coverage of the presidency between the Franklin D. Roosevelt years and the post-Watergate era.[58] No doubt, FDR had enormous success co-opting the White House press corps. Knowing that most newspaper editors opposed his administration's policies, FDR devoted a great deal of energy to cultivating a favorable relationship with journalists. The rules he established for the White House press corps would be dismissed today as patently absurd. For example, FDR divided presidential statements into four categories of press use: (1) information attributable to the president only in indirect quotation; (2) material for direct quotation; (3) background information; and (4) off-the-record information. Chalmers Roberts reports that "to the best of my knowledge, all of the two hundred or so reporters . . . observed FDR's off-the-record rule. Nothing appeared in the public prints or on radio newscasts."[59]

Journalistic news definitions of "newsworthy" information also differed.

---

56. Steven V. Roberts, "When Journalism Goes for the Jugular," *Washington Post Book World*, August 4, 1991, 1.

57. Gladys Engel Lang and Kurt Lang, *The Battle for Public Opinion: The President, the Press, and the Polls During Watergate* (New York: Columbia University Press, 1983), 261.

58. See, for example, Deakin, *Straight Stuff*, 296; James E. Pollard, *The Presidents and the Press* (New York: Macmillan, 1947), 773–845; Charles Press and Kenneth Verburg, *American Politicians and Journalists* (Glenview, Ill.: Scott, Foresman, 1988), 24; Chalmers Roberts, "Franklin Delano Roosevelt and the Press," in *The Media*, ed. Kenneth W. Thompson (Lanham, Md.: University Press of America, 1985), 185–93; Graham J. White, *FDR and the Press* (Chicago: University of Chicago Press, 1979); Wolfson, *Untapped Power*, 5–16; James Sterling Young, *The Puzzle of the Presidency* (Baton Rouge: Louisiana State University Press, forthcoming).

59. Roberts, "Roosevelt and the Press," 186.

A well-known story has FDR being carried into a meeting room with reporters when the president's aides lost their grip and dropped him. No pictures were taken. Over thirty-five thousand press pictures of FDR as president have been collected with just two of the photographs showing him in a wheelchair.[60] Reporters never revealed FDR's extramarital affairs.

Such journalistic deference continued through the John F. Kennedy administration.[61] Reporters with knowledge of the president's sexual indiscretions did not reveal such information to the public. JFK's back problems and adrenal insufficiency received relatively little press attention.

James Deakin correctly points out that FDR's and JFK's health problems "were more serious than a tumble on a ski slope. Why the double standard for Ford?" Deakin answers:

> The presidency had become imperial, and so had the media. Virtually everything a president said and did was to be written down, tape-recorded and photographed. Every offhand remark and gesture, every burp and blooper.[62]

Ford and his staff did work hard at trying to reverse the trend toward an increasingly cynical press corps and had some success early on. As Charles O. Jones has explained, Ford came to the presidency "very weak by all of the standard Neustadtian measures of presidential power." But Ford did have the advantage of emphasizing his ethics as compared to those of the Nixon administration. Yet "this advantage was compromised when he pardoned Nixon."[63] Many of the press officers commented that that one action brought back to the surface all of the press cynicism that existed due to the Vietnam War and Watergate. As Ford's press officers explained, the "poisonous atmosphere" already existed. The pardon brought it out even more and undermined White House efforts to restore a sense of trust and decorum to press-presidency relations.[64]

---

60. Press and Verburg, *American Politicians*, 24.

61. Broder, *Behind*, 157; Donaldson, *Hold On*, 68; Press and Verburg, *American Politicians*, 24; Rivers, *The Other Government*, 38.

62. Deakin, *Straight Stuff*, 296.

63. Charles O. Jones, "Presidents and Agendas: Who Defines What for Whom?" in *The Managerial Presidency*, ed. James P. Pfiffner (Pacific Grove, Calif.: Brooks/Cole, 1991), 204.

64. John Orman's study of "valenced reporting" in the periodical press during the period 1900 to 1982 reveals that

Gerald Ford, with his absolute pardon of Richard Nixon in September, 1974 had the shortest and the poorest honeymoon in the periodical press. Ford scored less than half support in his honeymoon period [first six months] at 30.6 percent positive support and therefore, 69.4 percent negative reporting ("Covering the American Presidency: Valenced Reporting in the Periodical Press, 1900–1982," *Presidential Studies Quarterly* 14, no. 3 (Summer, 1984): 387).

Another factor in Ford's press image that the White House could do little to change is the role that Capitol Hill plays in influencing a president's reputation. Stephen Hess notes that reporters often write White House stories based on congressional sources. Members of the legislative branch are most willing to talk with reporters, whereas executive branch personnel are less forthcoming.[65] Journalists' perceptions of a president's leadership acumen often come from Capitol Hill. As David Broder explains:

> Many reporters find that Congress is the best place to cover the executive branch. . . . To a large extent, the reputations of Presidents and their top political appointees . . . are made or broken on Capitol Hill. . . . Presidential aides may be guarded in their comments about their boss and loyally defend him, but the members of Congress have no such inhibitions. Their testimony is more plentiful, more uninhibited, and more credible than White House staff members'—and tends to define the press image of the President.[66]

President Ford suffered a disadvantage as an unelected Republican president during a time of large-scale Democratic congressional majorities. That fact alone made it difficult to establish a strong leadership reputation on Capitol Hill that would be conveyed to the public through the press corps. Members of Congress perceived Ford's leadership as not very different than the role he had played as the House Minority Leader—that of frustrating majority party initiatives. The president's veto strategy did not win plaudits from frustrated legislators who wanted to advance far-reaching economic and social policies. White House efforts to portray the president as a strong leader largely fell victim to a definition of presidential leadership as getting Congress to move positively on ambitious federal programs initiated by the administration.

White House public relations efforts also reveal the difficulties associated with the open presidency theme. All of Ford's press officers, as well as the president, emphasized the necessity of conducting an "open" administration. Their comments indicated a consensus that an administration should recognize that journalists have a legitimate job to do, that the White House should try to work constructively with journalists, but not kowtow to the press.

Ford knew what journalists wanted from the White House after Nixon: more press conferences, more access to the president, more "straight talk." He no doubt helped ease press cynicism and rancor by stressing the "open" presidency theme.

---

65. Hess, *Washington Reporters*, 100–101.
66. Broder, *Behind*, 209.

Nonetheless, a president can go too far in pursuing the admirable goal of openness, exposing all of the foibles of his administration in full view of the public. The open-to-the-public view of White House staff divisiveness hurt Ford's leadership image. The promise of an open administration creates expectations that presidents cannot live up to—for example, the belief that all internal White House deliberations and diplomatic negotiations must be conducted in full public view. Any effort to shield from public view a president who promised openness will be treated most harshly by the press. Both the Ford and Carter administrations learned that lesson the hard way. Frank Kessler cites another disadvantage that both Ford and Carter suffered from running relatively open administrations. "What incentive has a reporter to curry favor with the White House if he can get the information he wants without having to sell his soul?"[67]

There are commonsense tactics that a White House can take to shield a president from criticism. John Carlson noted that, in the Ford presidency, the president would announce good news from the White House, whereas others—cabinet secretaries or the press secretary—would issue bad news. The idea is to not have the president grilled by the press in public view on issues that could harm his image. Let the cabinet secretary in charge of the policy area take the heat.[68]

But presidents do not always follow the advice of staff to pay attention to imagery and reputation. Some White House staffers tried to convince Ford to control his public appearances to overcome the "ridicule problem." They implored him to not take skiing vacations that provided the inevitable news footage, photographs, and stories of presidential "stumbles." Ford resisted the advice and received, as predicted, press criticism not only for "stumbling," but also for vacationing during a recession.

Finally, Ford's press officers revealed the public relations importance of properly priming the press for White House actions. A White House can assure press understanding, if not necessarily agreement, by being up-front and candid with journalists about its intentions. There are, of course, exceptions. It is doubtful that such a controversial decision as the pardon of Richard M. Nixon could have generated much press understanding or acceptance, even if Ford had prepared journalists ahead of time. But on less controversial matters, the White House can influence its press coverage.

Assistant Press Secretary Larry Speakes gave one such example. Ford insisted on having a White House swimming pool built, despite the protests of staffers who worried about the symbolism of an expensive pool being built for

---

67. Frank Kessler, *The Dilemmas of Presidential Leadership: Of Caretakers and Kings* (Englewood Cliffs, N.J.: Prentice-Hall, 1982), 288.

68. Carlson interview.

the president during a recession. Speakes said that the White House diverted any potential negative commentary by emphasizing to the press that no public funds would be used to build the pool, that all private donations would be published to "show that nobody was trying to buy influence." The pool project ended up costing over $150,000 at a time when the average house cost less than $25,000. Speakes explains that the press could have portrayed the building of the pool as inappropriate and wasteful, but instead made little of the issue because the White House explained its actions up-front and then accounted for them.[69] Nonetheless, priming the press, thereby generating understanding of the White House's actions, is not the same as media manipulation, controlling the news, or turning the press corps into a group of presidential sycophants.

Ford and the Press: Conclusion

President Ford's administration represents an important transitional stage in the press-presidency relationship. In the post-Watergate environment, journalists had framed different methods for evaluating the presidency. Their reporting reflected both an increasingly judgmental and cynical view of public leaders and institutions. Journalistic cynicism toward public leaders and institutions carried well beyond the Nixon years.

As the first president to deal with the post-Watergate press corps, Ford had an important influence on the development of modern presidential press relations. Ford experienced difficulties with his press image but successfully initiated the process of moving the White House–press relationship beyond the distrustfulness and combativeness of the Nixon years.

In addition to the important changes in the methods of political reporting, journalistic assessments of the Ford White House demonstrated continuities. Despite their skepticism of the powers of the so-called imperial presidency, journalistic visions of presidential leadership had not fundamentally changed. The press still evaluated Ford against the backdrop of an idealized notion of presidential leadership: one in which the chief executive frames a leadership "vision," articulates an activist policy agenda, and successfully employs the "bully pulpit" to move the public and Congress to accept his definition of the nation's problems and his goals for the future. Journalists assessed Ford according to a standard of leadership he never presumed to achieve. He played a largely defensive role, using his powers to resist congressional Democrats in their efforts to control the policy agenda. This leadership role clearly did not conform to journalists' notions of presidential activism, and Ford's press image suffered as a result.

---

69. Speakes interview.

Many scholars write about the biases in journalism—ideological, political, economic, or structural. Regarding journalistic commentary on the presidency, this study shows a different kind of bias: one shaped by common perceptions of what it means to be a "leader." Journalists' implicit theory of leadership introduces a subtle yet very important bias into their commentaries. Presidents whose leadership traits do not conform to journalistic notions of successful leadership are portrayed as not up to the job of being president. That fate befell both Gerald Ford and Jimmy Carter. Journalistic biases do not allow for a more complex understanding of the presidency—one that would permit an assessment of whether a different mode of operation in the White House might actually suit the particular skills and goals of the president and further his objectives effectively, though not in Rooseveltian fashion.

There is little that the Ford White House could have done to overcome its general press image. Ford could not convince the press to change its basic leadership definition, and the Ford White House did about as well as possible in dealing with the increasingly cynical nature of the press corps.

This study demonstrates that journalists have basic, identifiable notions of presidential leadership over which the modern White House has little control. A central finding of my analysis is that presidents cannot script their own news coverage. Presidents, in fact, do not "control" the press. The data presented here provide a case study exception to the more common argument that the White House can deliberately control political reporting and commentary through various means of imagery, public relations packaging, and press manipulation.

That is not to conclude that the White House cannot influence press coverage. Although basic leadership notions held by journalists do not change, it is possible to influence some press perceptions and expectations of the president. It is in the interest of any White House to do as much as it properly can to encourage a positive image of a president as a means of enhancing the administration's ability to move its objectives forward. In a sense, the image of presidential leadership becomes an important part of its reality.

Bibliography

Altheide, David L. *Media Power*. Beverly Hills, Calif.: Sage, 1985.

Bayley, Edwin R. *Joe McCarthy and the Press*. Madison: University of Wisconsin Press, 1981.

Bennett, W. Lance. *News: The Politics of Illusion*. 2d ed. New York: Longman, 1988.

Bishop, George F., Robert G. Meadow, and Marilyn Jackson-Beeck, eds. *The Presidential Debates: Media, Electoral, and Public Perspectives*. New York: Praeger, 1978.

Broder, David. *Behind the Front Page: A Candid Look at How the News is Made*. New York: Simon and Schuster, 1987.

Burdick, Eugene, and Arthur J. Brodbeck, eds. *American Voting Behavior*. Glencoe, Ill.: Free Press, 1959.

Carter, Jimmy. *Keeping Faith*. New York: Bantam Books, 1982.

Casserly, John J. *The Ford White House: The Diary of a Speechwriter*. Boulder: Colorado Associated University Press, 1977.

Cater, Douglas. *The Fourth Branch of Government*. Boston: Houghton Mifflin Co., 1959.

Cohen, Bernard C. *The Press and Foreign Policy*. Princeton: Princeton University Press, 1963.

Cronin, Thomas E. "The Presidency Public Relations Script." In *The Presidency Reappraised*, ed. Rexford E. Tugwell and Thomas E. Cronin, 168–83. New York: Praeger, 1974.

Deakin, James. *Straight Stuff: The Reporters, the White House,the Truth*. New York: William Morrow, 1984.

Dean, John. *Blind Ambition: The White House Years*. New York: Simon and Schuster, 1976.

Donaldson, Sam. *Hold On, Mr. President!* New York: Ballantine Books, 1987.

Edwards, George C. *The Public Presidency: The Pursuit of Popular Support*. New York: St. Martin's Press, 1983.

Entman, Robert M. "The Imperial Media." In *Analyzing the Presidency*, 2d ed., ed. Robert E. DiClerico, 154–67. Guilford, Conn.: Dushkin Publishing Co., 1990.

Epstein, Edward Jay. *News From Nowhere*. New York: Random House, 1973.

Feerick, John D., "The Pardoning Power of Article II of the Constitution," *New York State Bar Journal* 47 (January 1975): 7–11ff.

Ford, Gerald R. *A Time to Heal*. Norwalk, Conn.: Easton Press, 1987.

Fry, Don, ed. *Believing the News*. St. Petersburg, Fla.: Poynter Institute, 1985.

Gans, Herbert J. *Deciding What's News: A Study of CBS Evening News, NBC Nightly News, Newsweek, and Time*. New York: Pantheon Books, 1979.

Graber, Doris A. *Mass Media and American Politics*. 2d ed. Washington, D.C.: Congressional Quarterly Press, 1984.

Graber, Doris A. *Processing the News: How People Tame the Information Tide*. New York: Longman, 1984.

Grossman, Michael Baruch, and Martha Joynt Kumar. *Portraying the President: The White House and the News Media*. Baltimore: Johns Hopkins University Press, 1981.

Haldeman, H. R. *The Ends of Power*. New York: New York Times Books, 1978.

Hartmann, Robert T. *Palace Politics: An Inside Account of the Ford Years*. New York: McGraw-Hill, 1980.

Hertsgaard, Mark. *On Bended Knee: The Press and the Reagan Presidency*. New York: Farrar, Strauss, Giroux, 1988.

Hess, Stephen. *The Government/Press Connection*. Washington, D.C.: Brookings Institution, 1984.

Hess, Stephen. *The Washington Reporters*. Washington, D.C.: Brookings Institution, 1981.

Hiebert, Ray Eldon, and Carol Reuss, eds. *Impact of Mass Media: Current Issues*. White Plains, N.Y.: Longman, 1985.

Iyengar, Shanto, and Donald R. Kinder. *News that Matters: Television and American Opinion*. Chicago: University of Chicago Press, 1987.

Johnson, Haynes. *In the Absence of Power*. New York: Viking Press, 1980.

Jones, Charles O. "Presidents and Agendas: Who Defines What for Whom?" In *The Managerial Presidency*, ed. James P. Pfiffner, 197–213. Pacific Grove, Calif.: Brooks/Cole, 1991.

Jones, Charles O. "The Separated Presidency—Making It Work in Contemporary Politics." In *The New American Political System*, 2d. ed., ed. Anthony King, 1–28. Washington, D.C.: American Enterprise Institute, 1990.

Kelly, Stanley. *Interpreting Elections*. Princeton: Princeton University Press, 1983.

Kerbel, Matthew. "Against the Odds: Media Access in the Administration of President Gerald Ford." *Presidential Studies Quarterly* 16, no. 1 (Winter 1986): 76–91.

Kernell, Samuel. *Going Public: New Strategies of Presidential Leadership*. Washington, D.C.: Congressional Quarterly Press, 1986.

Kessler, Frank. *The Dilemmas of Presidential Leadership: Of Caretakers and Kings*. Englewood Cliffs, N.J.: Prentice-Hall, 1982.

Kranz, Harry. "The Presidency v. The Press: Who Is Right?" In *Perspectives on the Presidency*, ed. Aaron Wildavsky, 205–20. Boston: Little-Brown and Co., 1975.

Krock, Arthur. "Mr. Kennedy's Management of the News." *Fortune*, March 1963, 199–202.

Krosnick, Jon A., and Donald R. Kinder. "Altering the Foundations of Support for the President Through Priming." *American Political Science Review* 84, no. 2 (June 1990): 497–512.

Lang, Gladys Engel, and Kurt Lang. *The Battle for Public Opinion: The President, The Press, and the Polls During Watergate*. New York: Columbia University Press, 1983.

Lee, Richard W., ed. *Politics and the Press*. Washington, D.C.: Acropolis Books, 1970.

Lichter, S. Robert, Stanley Rothman, Linda S. Lichter. *The Media Elite*. Bethesda, Md.: Adler and Adler, 1986.

Lippmann, Walter. *Public Opinion*. New York: Free Press, 1965.

McCombs, Maxwell E., and Donald L. Shaw. "The Agenda-Setting Function of the Mass Media." *Public Opinion Quarterly* 36, no. 3 (Summer 1972): 176–87.

MacKuen, Michael Bruce, and Steven Lane Coombs. *More than News: Media Power in Public Affairs*. Beverly Hills, Calif.: Sage, 1981.

Maltese, John Anthony. *Spin Control: The White House Office of Communications and the Management of Presidential News*. Chapel Hill, N.C.: University of North Carolina Press, 1992.

Miller, Arthur H., Edie N. Goldenberg, and Lute Ebring. "Type-Set Politics: The Impact of Newspapers on Public Confidence." *American Political Science Review* 73, no. 1 (March 1979): 67–84.

Nessen, Ron. *It Sure Looks Different from the Inside*. New York: Playboy Books, 1978.

Nessen, Ron. "The Ford Presidency and the Press." In *The Ford Presidency: Twenty-Two Intimate Perspectives of Gerald R. Ford*, ed. Kenneth W. Thompson, 179–208. Lanham, Md.: University Press of America, 1988.

Neustadt, Richard. *Presidential Power and the Modern Presidents: The Politics of Leadership from Roosevelt to Reagan*. New York: Free Press, 1990.

Nimmo, Dan D. *Newsgathering in Washington: A Study in Political Communication*. New York: Atherton Press, 1964.

Nimmo, Dan D., and James E. Combs. *Mediated Political Realities*, 2d. ed. New York: Longman, 1990.

Orben, Robert. "Speeches, Humor and the Public." In *The Ford Presidency: Twenty-two Intimate Perspectives of Gerald R. Ford*, ed. Kenneth W. Thompson, 231–53. Lanham, Md.: University Press of America, 1988.

Orman, John. "Covering the American Presidency: Valenced Reporting in the Periodical Press, 1900–1982." *Presidential Studies Quarterly* 14, no. 3 (Summer 1984): 381–90.

Paletz, David L., and Robert M. Entman. *Media-Power-Politics*. New York: Free Press, 1981.

Paletz, David L., and Robert M. Entman. "Presidents, Power, and the Press." *Presidential Studies Quarterly* 10, no. 3 (Summer 1980): 416–26.

Parenti, Michael. *Inventing Reality: The Politics of the Mass Media*. New York: St. Martin's Press, 1986.

Pious, Richard M. *The American Presidency*. New York: Basic Books, 1979.

Pollard, James E. *The Presidents and the Press*. New York: Macmillan, 1947.

Porter, William E. *Assault on the Media: The Nixon Years*. Ann Arbor: University of Michigan Press, 1976.

Powell, Jody. *The Other Side of the Story*. New York: William Morrow, 1984.

"The Presidency and the Press: The Press Secretaries." KPBS-TV. San Diego, Calif., April 2, 1990.

Press, Charles, and Kenneth Verburg. *American Politicians and Journalists*. Glenview, Ill.: Scott, Foresman and Co., 1988.

Rivers, William L. *The Other Government: Power and the Washington Media*. New York: Universe Books, 1982.

Roshco, Bernard. *Newsmaking*. Chicago: University of Chicago Press, 1975.

Rosten, Leo. *The Washington Correspondents*. New York: Harcourt, Brace, 1937.

Rozell, Mark J. "Local v. National Press Assessments of Virginia's 1989 Gubernatorial Campaign." *Polity* 24, no. 1 (Fall 1991): 69–89.

Rozell, Mark J. "President Carter and the Press: Perspectives from White House Communications Advisers." *Political Science Quarterly* 105, no. 3 (Fall 1990): 419–34.

Rozell, Mark J. *The Press and the Carter Presidency*. Boulder: Westview Press, 1989.

Russonella, John M., and Frank Wolf. "Newspaper Coverage of the 1976 and 1968 Presidential Campaigns." *Journalism Quarterly* 56, no. 2 (Summer 1979): 360–64, 432.

Sabato, Larry J. *Feeding Frenzy: How Attack Journalism Has Transformed American Politics*. New York: Free Press, 1991.

Schudson, Michael. *Discovering the News: A Social History of American Newspapers*. New York: Basic Books, 1978.

Smith, Hedrick. *The Power Game: How Washington Works*. New York: Ballantine Books, 1989.

Speakes, Larry. "The Ford Image." Paper presented at the Seventh Presidential Conference, Gerald Ford: Restoring the Presidency, Hofstra University, Hempstead, N.Y., April 8, 1989.

Speakes, Larry. *Speaking Out*. New York: Avon Books, 1989.

terHorst, Jerald F. *Gerald Ford and the Future of the Presidency*. New York: Joseph Okpaku Publishing Co., 1974.

terHorst, Jerald F. "President Ford and the Media." In *The Ford Presidency: Twenty-Two Intimate Perspectives of Gerald R. Ford*, ed. Kenneth W. Thompson, 209–29. Lanham, Md.: University Press of America, 1988.

Thompson, Kenneth W., ed. *The Media*. Lanham, Md.: University Press of America, 1985.

Thompson, Kenneth W., ed. *Three Press Secretaries on the Presidency and the Press*. Lanham, Md.: University Press of America, 1983.

White, Graham J. *FDR and the Press*. Chicago: University of Chicago Press, 1979.

White Burkett Miller Center. *The Ford White House*. Lanham, Md.: University Press of America, 1986.

Wicker, Tom. *On Press*. New York: Viking Press, 1978.

Wolfson, Lewis W. *The Untapped Power of the Press*. New York: Praeger, 1985.

Young, James Sterling. *The Puzzle of the Presidency*. Baton Rouge: Louisiana State University Press, forthcoming.

Zeidenstein, Harvey G. "News Media Perceptions of White House News Management." *Presidential Studies Quarterly* 14, no. 3 (Summer 1984): 391–98.

Name Index

Subject Index